The Corporation

The Corporation

WESLEY B. TRUITT

GREENWOOD GUIDES TO BUSINESS AND ECONOMICS

GREENWOOD PRESS
WESTPORT, CONNECTICUT • LONDON

Library of Congress Cataloging-in-Publication Data

Truitt, Wesley B., 1939–
   The corporation / Wesley B. Truitt.
      p. cm. — (Greenwood guides to business and economics, ISSN 1559–2367)
   Includes bibliographical references and index.
   ISBN 0–313–33606–7 (alk. paper)
   1. Corporations—History. 2. Corporations—Social aspects. 3. Business
enterprises—United States—History. 4. Corporate governance—United States.
I. Title. II. Series.
   HD2721.T78   2006
   338.7'4—dc22   2006006173

British Library Cataloguing-in-Publication Data is available.

Library of Congress Catalog Card Number: 2006006173
ISBN: 0–313–33606–7
ISSN: 1559–2367

First published in 2006

Greenwood Press, 88 Post Road West, Westport, CT 06881
An imprint of Greenwood Publishing Group, Inc.
www.greenwood.com

Printed in the United States of America

The paper used in this book complies with the
Permanent Paper Standard issued by the National
Information Standards Organization (Z39.48–1984).

10 9 8 7 6 5 4 3 2 1

Contents

Illustrations

FIGURES

Series Foreword

Scanning the pages of the newspaper on any given day, you'll find headlines like these:

"OPEC Points to Supply Chains as Cause of Price Hikes"
"Business Groups Warn of Danger of Takeover Proposals"
"U.S. Durable Goods Orders Jump 3.3%"
"Dollar Hits Two-Year High Versus Yen"
"Credibility of WTO at Stake in Trade Talks"
"U.S. GDP Growth Slows While Fed Fears Inflation Growth"

If this seems like gibberish to you, then you are in good company. To most people, the language of economics is mysterious, intimidating, impenetrable. But with economic forces profoundly influencing our daily lives, being familiar with the ideas and principles of business and economics is vital to our welfare. From fluctuating interest rates to rising gasoline prices to corporate misconduct to the vicissitudes of the stock market to the rippling effects of protests and strikes overseas or natural disasters closer to home, "the economy" is not an abstraction. As Robert Duvall, president and CEO of the National Council on Economic Education, has forcefully argued, "Young people in our country need to know that economic education is not an option. Economic literacy is a vital skill, just as vital as reading literacy."[1] Understanding economics is a skill that will help you interpret current events that are playing out on a global scale, or in your checkbook, ultimately helping you make wiser choices about how you manage your financial resources—today and tomorrow.

It is the goal of this series, Greenwood Guides to Business and Economics, to promote economic literacy and improve economic decision-making. All seven books in the series are written for the general reader, high school and college student, or the business manager, entrepreneur, or graduate student in business and economics looking for a handy refresher. They have been written by experts in their respective fields for nonexpert readers. The approach throughout is at a "basic" level to maximize understanding and demystify how our business-driven economy really works.

Each book in the series is an essential guide to the topic of that volume, providing an introduction to its respective subject area. The series as a whole constitutes a library of information, up-to-date data, definitions of terms, and resources, covering all aspects of economic activity. Volumes feature such elements as timelines, glossaries, and examples and illustrations that bring the concepts to life and present them in a historical and cultural context.

The selection of the seven titles and their authors has been the work of an Editorial Advisory Board, whose members are the following: Alan Carsrud, Florida International University; Alan Reynolds, Cato Institute; Robert Spich, University of California, Los Angeles; Wesley Truitt, Loyola Marymount University; Walter E. Williams, George Mason University; and Charles Wolf, Jr., RAND Corporation.

As series editor, I served as chairman of the Editorial Advisory Board and want to express my appreciation to each of these distinguished individuals for their dedicated service in helping to bring this important series to reality.

The seven volumes in the series are as follows:

The Corporation by Wesley B. Truitt, Loyola Marymount University

Entrepreneurship by Alan L. Carsrud, Florida International University, and Malin Brännback, Åbo Akademi University

Globalization by Robert Spich, Christopher Thornberg, and Jeany Zhao, UCLA

Income and Wealth by Alan Reynolds, Cato Institute

Money by Mark Dobeck and Euel Elliott, University of Texas at Dallas

The National Economy by Bradley A. Hansen, University of Mary Washington

The Stock Market by Rik W. Hafer, Southern Illinois University–Edwardsville, and Scott E. Hein, Texas Tech University

Special thanks to our senior editor at Greenwood, Nick Philipson, for conceiving the idea of the series and for sponsoring it within Greenwood Press.

The overriding purpose of each of these books and the series as a whole is, as Walter Williams so aptly put it, to "push back the frontiers of ignorance."

Wesley B. Truitt, Series Editor

NOTE

1. Quoted in Gary H. Stern, "Do We Know Enough about Economics?" *The Region*, Federal Reserve Bank of Minneapolis (December 1998).

Preface

Corporations, large and small, are the very heart of America's and the world's economy. More wealth is created in America and throughout the world every day by corporations than by any other type of business. Well over half of all Americans are employed by corporations and invest in them. Public or private corporations provide almost all of our food, clothing, housing, transportation, entertainment, financial services, health care, communications, and national security items.

This vital form of business organization is principally responsible for growing the American economy into the largest in the world and for transforming our and other economies into an interdependent, global economy. Corporations will continue to be the engines that generate the greatest wealth throughout the world for the foreseeable future.

Owing to the fact that corporations touch our lives so deeply and in so many ways, every citizen should be informed about what this type of business is, how it came about, what its major characteristics are, what rules and regulations govern it, how it operates, and what its future will be like. This book sheds light on these important issues, using a host of examples of familiar corporations such as Exxon Mobil, General Electric, Nike, Citigroup, and Toyota.

The first three chapters trace the development of the corporate form of business over the past thousand years, giving the reasons why this type of company came into existence in the Middle Ages, examining why it became so widely used during the Renaissance by British and Dutch traders, showing how it was the basis for the British colonies in America, and providing insights into why corporations became the dominant form of business organization by the early twentieth century with the rise of General Motors

(GM). The postmodern corporation is replacing the GM model today for a variety of reasons.

The next chapters look at the benefits gained by incorporating, how to establish a corporation, and the methods of operation of typical corporations. Their impact on our overall economy is examined in chapter 4. Two chapters address the way corporations are structured in other countries and the concept of the multinational corporation, offering Nestlé as a case-study example.

Chapter 9 focuses on corporate governance; summarizes recent front page cases of corporate fraud and greed, such as Enron and Global Crossings, and new laws intended to prevent it; and provides different views of corporate social responsibility. The final chapter takes a look at the future of this form of business organization.

My twenty-six years as an executive at one of America's major corporations, Northrop Grumman, provided insights into the inner workings of corporate America from the perspective of an operating unit to that of the office of the chairman/CEO. My PhD in public law and government from Columbia University provided the basis for my understanding of business–government relationships, the underpinning of corporations.

I want to acknowledge the technical assistance of Kathe Segall, my secretary at Loyola Marymount University, who prepared the organization charts in chapter 6. Thanks to Ira Kirschbaum, a retired U.S. Department of Justice attorney, for reviewing chapter 9. Thanks to Nick Philipson, senior editor at Greenwood Press, for his expertise and ongoing help. Special thanks to my wife, Marianne, for her encouragement and support.

The underlying purpose of this book, as with all volumes in the Greenwood Guides to Business and Economics, is to increase economic and business literacy in the United States. Our citizens need to understand better how our gigantic economy really works, and central to that understanding are insights into its fascinating and most powerful engine of wealth creation—the corporation.

Chronology

Twelfth Century

1136   Aberdeen (Scotland) Harbor Board founded as corporation; still exists.

Corporation of London founded; still exists.

Catholic Church accepts legitimacy of private property.

Thirteenth Century

"Corporate persons" emerge as legal device to organize towns, universities, guilds, and religious orders.

1279   King Edward I, England, issues Statute of Mortmain to limit corporations' rights to amass and bequeath extensive property holdings.

1288   Stora Enso, a copper mining company, begins business in Sweden; world's oldest continuously operating company.

Fourteenth Century

1347   Stora Enso issued a royal charter by the Crown of Sweden, becomes the world's first business corporation; today the company is in the lumber industry.

Sixteenth Century

"Chartered companies" emerge in England and Holland to conduct business.

1555   Muscovy Company, England, becomes first company given a royal charter and authorized as a joint-stock company with limited liability for owners; given exclusive trading rights between England and northern Russia.

1563   Church of England legitimizes private property ownership.

Seventeenth Century

1600   British East India Company granted royal charter by Queen Elizabeth I.

1602   Dutch East India Company established by royal charter and sells stock; limited liability established for stockholders.

1606   King James I granted royal charter to establish the Virginia Company of London to establish a settlement in North America (becomes Jamestown).

1611   Dutch Stock Exchange established in Amsterdam; world's first.

1613   British East India Company issued stock to finance voyages.

1629   King Charles I granted royal charter to govern Massachusetts Bay Colony.

1636   Harvard College chartered as a nonprofit corporation, first in North America.

1670   Hudson's Bay Company established; world's oldest multinational corporation.

Eighteenth Century

1776   Adam Smith publishes *The Wealth of Nations*; establishes principles of capitalism.

1784   Bank of New York founded; oldest company in continuous existence in U.S.

1791   Congress charters the First Bank of the United States as a public corporation.

1791   Society for Establishing Useful Manufacturers of New Jersey incorporated; first private corporation begun after U.S. Constitution adopted.

1798   First stock traded in New York City–the New York Insurance Co.

Nineteenth Century

1837   Connecticut enacts law permitting establishment of general purpose corporations.

1860   New York state passes similar law.

1862   British Parliament passes The Companies Act, permitting general purpose business corporations with limited liability protection and without need for royal charters or limitations on life-span; modern corporations begin.

1887   Interstate Commerce Act passed to regulate interstate commerce.

1890   Sherman Antitrust Act passed; prohibits restraints of trade and monopolies.

Twentieth Century

1908   General Motors (GM) organized as corporate holding company.

1911   U.S. Supreme Court breaks up Standard Oil Trust into 30 companies.

1914   Clayton Act and Federal Trade Commission Act passed prohibiting monopolistic practices and establishing FTC to enforce antitrust laws.

1923   Alfred P. Sloan becomes president of GM; creates the modern corporation.

1933   Securities Act passed establishing federal procedures for issuing securities.

1934   Securities Exchange Act passed establishing procedures for stock transactions and establishing Securities and Exchange Commission to regulate securities industry.

1945   Corporation Control Act passed to oversee U.S. public corporations.

1970s   Post-modern corporations emerge.

1978   Airline Deregulation Act passed; begins deregulation of key U.S. industries.

Twenty-first Century

2002   Sarbanes-Oxley Act passed; strengthened financial disclosure requirements and increased penalties for noncompliance; established Public Company Accounting Oversight Board to supervise accounting and auditing industry.

One

Development of the Corporation

Corporations have been a form of business and governmental organization for centuries. British corporations financed the settlement of the first colonies in North America and set the mold for the emergence of representative government in the American colonial experience.

In the nineteenth century business corporations became widely used, and by the twentieth century they were dominant, transforming America into the world's largest industrial economy. Today the corporation as a business structure accounts for the vast majority of the entire world's economic activity.

Four types of corporate forms have emerged over the years. This chapter identifies these forms, summarizes the reasons for the historical development of each, and presents the reasons why corporations have developed as the leading form of commercial structure in today's world.

All corporations are artificial beings. Their existence is neither tangible nor visible. Yet, before the courts, a corporation is treated as a "person," as though it were a real being. This figment is a vital feature of the corporate form, enabling corporations to engage in any activity that any natural person could undertake to accomplish the purposes for which they were created. These activities include buying and selling goods and property, entering into contracts, borrowing money, suing and being sued, hiring and firing employees, and the like. Indeed, we even speak of corporations as though they were people, such as saying "Microsoft went to court today on an antitrust matter."

There are two traditional reasons for the corporation's popularity.

1. *Financial:* Corporations can raise money (called capital) by issuing stock to finance the work of the company, and they are a mechanism for paying out to their investors the profits they make through dividends.
2. *Liability:* The corporate form protects the corporation's owners (its shareholders) and its directors and managers from *personal* liability for the actions of the corporation, thus minimizing their risk.

These two precepts rest on an even more fundamental principle: the right to own private property.

Except under very particular circumstances, no one may *pierce the corporate veil* of liability protection. For example, the corporation is the defendant in a court case, not its shareholders or its board of directors or its top managers—unless criminal activity is charged or the directors or officers failed to perform their "duty of care" to safeguard shareholders' interests. These rare exceptions are discussed in later chapters.

The next section briefly traces the history of how and why the corporation developed.

EARLY HISTORY OF CORPORATIONS

The concept of the corporation began in medieval times.[1] This legal device was used to charter towns, universities, religious orders, and some businesses—for particular purposes and for a limited time. The Corporation of London, which dates from the twelfth century, is still in existence, today owning a quarter of the land in the city of London (the financial center), three private schools, and four markets. The Aberdeen Harbour Board in Scotland dates from 1136, the same century in which the Catholic Church accepted the legitimacy of private property, a vital prerequisite for corporate ownership.[2] The oldest still-existing private company in Europe is probably Stora Enso of Sweden, a copper mine that began production in 1288 and was issued a royal corporate charter in 1347; the company is now in the pulp and paper business.

During the Middle Ages, the term *corporate person* began to be used to describe loose associations of people wishing to be treated as a collective entity. This concept was based on Roman law and canon (church) law, and jurisprudence slowly came to codify the existence of these entities. Corporate persons could be towns, religious groups, universities, and guilds, usually associations of merchants or artisans.

They represented a permanent organizational structure to preserve the customs of the group, to generate wealth, and to pass it intact to future generations. So common was this practice of preserving inherited wealth, especially land, that in 1279 King Edward I of England issued the Statute of Mortmain, which limited the amount of land that could be passed to corporate bodies, especially the church, without royal permission.

In the pre-Renaissance Italian city-states such as Venice, Florence, and Genoa, merchants and bankers formed associations to undertake projects, such as pooling funds to finance shipments of goods to distant ports. In northern Europe guilds and companies chartered by local princes copied these Italian examples, setting up businesses in a number of cities using distant family members as local representatives for shipping and receiving goods.

EMERGENCE OF CHARTERED COMPANIES

Later, during the Renaissance and the Age of Discovery, the sixteenth and seventeenth centuries, a new type of business organization emerged: the *chartered company*. These businesses were organized by wealthy merchants and members of the aristocracy who were given a charter by the Crown to undertake their business in designated parts of the world. Some famous examples are the British East India Company, which lasted for 274 years, the Virginia Company, the Massachusetts Bay Company, and the famous Hudson's Bay Company, founded in 1670 and still in existence as the world's oldest multinational corporation.

Chartered companies soon borrowed two ideas from the medieval period: joint stock companies and limited liability. The first chartered joint stock company was the Muscovy Company, chartered in 1555 by the English Crown to have exclusive trading rights between England and Russia, with ships calling at the Russian port of Archangel on the White Sea. The firm raised enough money to finance a few voyages by selling shares that could be traded; it also limited the liability of its shareholders to the amount of their investment. Because of these characteristics, this could be called the first corporation. The Moscovy Company faded seventy-five years later, but it set the mold for many imitators. In 1563 the Church of England explicitly legitimized private property.[3]

It was Dutch merchants who raised the joint stock company to a major and durable business form that became a model for others to follow. In 1602 the Dutch East India Company's 17-member board secured a monopoly charter from the Dutch Crown to trade for spices in the East Indies, now known as Indonesia. Funds to finance voyages over a period of 21 years (versus individual voyages, each with different shareholders on the English model) were raised by selling stock by which the royal charter explicitly limited the liability of the investor to the value and number of shares owned.

Dutch investors were the first to trade their shares on an open exchange founded in 1611 in Amsterdam, a block away from the Dutch East India Company's office. So aggressive were the Dutch East India traders that they drove the Portuguese and English out of the Southeast Asian spice trade, securing the spice islands for the Netherlands until 1945, when they were granted independence.

British East India Company

Contemporaneously with these events in Holland, the British East India Company was born. It began in September 1599, when a group of 80 English merchants and a few of Sir Francis Drake's crew met in London to organize the company. They elected 15 directors and the lord mayor of London, Sir Stephen Soane, as the chairman of the board. They agreed to petition Queen Elizabeth I for a royal charter to set up the company and to be granted monopoly rights to trade in Asia.

Bickering among competing groups and court politics delayed events, but eventually, on December 31, 1600, the charter was granted, giving the East India Company monopoly rights for fifteen years to trade east of the Cape of Good Hope and west of the Straits of Magellan—all lands bordering on the Indian and Pacific Oceans.

The East India Company was highly profitable, importing boatloads of high-value spices to Europe. In 1612 it began financing several voyages at once. Its first joint stock offering was in 1613, raising an unexpectedly large amount of capital. By 1620, the year the Pilgrims landed at Plymouth Rock, the company had a flotilla of 30 to 40 ships, most of them heavily armed, that traveled in convoys of 12 or more at a time for protection, mostly against the Dutch and Portuguese.

The two-tier administrative structure of this growing firm was also precedent setting. The general court was composed of all shareholders with voting rights, representing something akin to today's board of directors. The day-to-day operation of the company was handled by the court of directors, twenty-four men elected by the general court. The leader of the court of directors was called the governor, a position like today's chief executive officer. He had a deputy and a number of accountants, clerks, and other office personnel called *civil servants*, the first use of that term. Seven committees, each performing a specialized operation such as buying, shipping, finance, and accounting, reported to the governor and were the effective senior executives of the East India Company. This was a precursor of the modern corporate office.

Despite its power and growing wealth, the British East India Company was soon driven out of the spice islands by the fierce Dutch and fell back on trading mostly in India, where it then concentrated its activities. Over the next 150 years, the East India Company came to rule India in the name of the British Crown, transforming itself into an "empire within an empire," with its own army, navy, and administrative structure. The company's private army numbered 260,000 native troops, twice the size of the entire British Army. Using today's terminology, one might say that the British Crown, like the Dutch Crown, outsourced its imperial expansion to the private sector, a more effective and longer-lasting technique than that used by Spain, where the Crown sponsored and directly managed its economic imperialism.[4]

In 1774 the British parliament passed the India Act, which imposed a new government board of control over the East India Company. However, it left the directors in charge of day-to-day business. Over the years the British government tightened control over the company with each license renewal (every 20 years) and eventually abolished its monopoly of trade in 1813. In 1833, the East India Company became a government corporation, which ceased to exist in 1874 when its charter expired, 274 years after its founding. Prior to that it had turned over its Indian-based army to the Crown and disbanded its fleet of quasi-warships. Few companies have such a long, colorful, successful, and far-reaching record of achievement as the British East India Company.

CORPORATIONS IN COLONIAL AMERICA

At the time the British East India Company was getting under way, another British corporation was formed called the Virginia Company of London. By royal charter, granted by King James I in 1606, the Virginia Company was established as a trading corporation with monopoly rights to finance an exploration to North America. It provided for limited liability for its stockholders, perpetual stock, management committees, and payment of dividends.

This corporate charter not only was the basis for the first wave of settlers to Jamestown, founding that settlement in 1607, but also in 1619 became the basis for the first government in that settlement, the general assembly for the colony of Virginia. The establishment of this legislature was authorized by Sir Edwin Sandys, the treasurer of the Virginia Company, who, as a member of the British House of Commons, argued that the legitimacy of any government is founded on a mutual contract between the ruler and the ruled. The Virginia Company's procedures became the template for representative government throughout the British North American colonies—members of the corporation voted their shares, chose the company's officers, and approved company policies.

King James was so irritated by these developments, which were an affront to his rule by divine right, that he confined Sir Edwin Sandys to London and canceled the Virginia Company's royal charter seventeen years later.[5] By then, however, democratic principles and representative government had already taken root in Virginia.

The Massachusetts Bay Colony, which began in 1620 at Plymouth, had a quite different beginning, initially experimenting with a primitive form of communism. These Puritan settlers believed in the common good and therefore decided that everything in the new colony would be communal, including property. Labor was unevenly divided: young men would perform the difficult, heavy work, and old men would do easy work, while women would do housework for anyone, not just their husbands. There was no differentiation of wages based on work performed, with equal distribution of goods to all, regardless of effort.

Governor William Bradford later decried this three-year experiment with its disastrous results. The concept of private property replaced this "common wealth," and each person took ownership of his land and worked for his own family's benefit, to the benefit of all.

In 1629, King Charles I granted a royal charter to establish the Massachusetts Bay Colony formally as a trading company with the same attributes as the Virginia Company before it. Led by John Winthrop, the trading company soon morphed into a representative government called a commonwealth. All stockholders in the corporation became voters in the commonwealth, electing the twelve ruling magistrates, who then elected a governor and deputy governor. In 1634, the trading company was in effect transformed into a representative government when each town in the colony appointed two representatives to go to Boston to represent their views before the Massachusetts General Court, the name of their legislature.

Thus, the settlement of British North America was firmly based on the concepts of private property ownership and representative democracy. Political liberties were inextricably linked with private ownership of property at the beginning of the Virginia and Massachusetts colonies, both having been conceived as corporations and modeled on British corporate governance practices.[6]

BRITISH COMPANIES ACT OF 1862

In 1862 the British parliament passed a law called the Companies Act. This was a signal event in the history of capitalism. This act brought together the two strands of business organization that had been joined together before—the joint stock company and the limited liability company—with a third, new feature: government granting permission for *anyone at any time* to form a limited liability joint stock company for *any purpose*. In other words, a royal charter, that is, permission of the state, was no longer required, and a corporation could now engage in any type of business anywhere in the country by the simple act of registering itself at a government registry office.

Thus, Victorian England, the world's greatest economic power at that time,

brought together the three big ideas behind the modern company: that it could be an "artificial person," with the same ability to do business as a real person; that it could issue tradable shares to any number of investors; and that those investors could have limited liability (so they could lose only the money they had committed to the firm).[7]

It was no longer necessary to petition the monarch or parliament for a charter or to create a special-purpose company to fulfill a particular aim, such as trading with India. The new law established that the only requirements were that seven or more people had to sign a memorandum of association, register that document with the government, and have the word *limited* in the company's title to warn creditors that they would have no recourse to the company's shareholders. The company was then free to raise money by selling stock to finance its activities for any reasonable purpose anywhere in the kingdom.

The Companies Act thus permitted the establishment of the modern general-purpose business corporation. Anyone (not just friends of the monarch or peers of the realm) was able at any time to form a corporation to undertake any type of legitimate business, as long as these minimal requirements were met. Capital could be raised easily, business organizations could be formed quickly, products could be made and sold, profits could be distributed to shareholders as dividends, and the risk to investors was limited to the amount of their investments. Everyone benefited as the corporation took on a life of its own.

The British Companies Act was quickly copied by other European countries and the United States, though in 1837 Connecticut preceded it, being the first state to permit incorporation for general business purposes without special legislative permission. The state of New York enacted similar legislation in 1860.[8]

The modern corporation thus provided the organizational structure and the vast amounts of capital needed to exploit the technological progress and economic transformation then being made by the Industrial Revolution.

"The limited liability corporation is the greatest single discovery of modern times," declared Nicholas Murray Butler, the sage of the Progressive Era and president of Columbia University at the turn of the century; "even steam and electricity would be reduced to comparative impotence without it."[9] The corporation, as Butler suggested, made these scientific inventions into businesses, which harnessed them and made them available to ordinary citizens.

TYPES OF CORPORATIONS AND THEIR ORIGINS

There are four types of corporations: public, private, close, and non-profit.[10] All four types must be authorized by a governmental authority. Thus, all corporations are creatures of the state. When a corporation is created, the express and implied powers needed to accomplish its purposes come into existence. Let us briefly trace the development and describe the major characteristics of each of the four types.

PUBLIC CORPORATIONS

Public corporations are the oldest corporate form of organization, having begun in medieval Europe centuries ago under charters from the Crown. Public corporations, sometimes called government corporations, are formed by a government to meet some political or governmental purpose—a *public* purpose.

Among the earliest uses of public corporations was the incorporation of villages, towns, and cities, and this form is still widely used today for that purpose in both England and America. Incorporated municipalities are governed by a board whose members are elected by the eligible voters in the community. The board, by whatever name it is called, then hires full-time professionals to manage the town's affairs, often under the direction of a town or city manager who is the chief administrative officer. This is much like the way a business corporation is structured, with the elected board appointing full-time managers and providing oversight of their activities.

Public corporations also directly operate specific businesslike activities to benefit the public at large. Today dozens of public corporations operate major U.S. government activities, such as the Federal Deposit Insurance Corporation, the U.S. Postal Service, the Tennessee Valley Authority, Amtrak, and the Overseas Private Investment Corporation. Federal public corporations are usually chartered by Congress (though sometimes by the president on the basis of existing legislation), and their boards of directors are appointed by the president and confirmed by the U.S. Senate.

The corporate device has been used by our government since the earliest days of the United States to conduct various economic activities or commercial enterprises. The first such use under the Constitution was in 1791 when Congress passed a law that chartered the First Bank of the United States. Alexander Hamilton, the first secretary of the treasury, had proposed forming this institution for the purpose of implementing a power in the Constitution, known as the "commerce clause," that the federal government will "regulate commerce with foreign nations and among the several states" in the new country.[11] Hamilton felt a central bank was necessary to achieve this objective.

Despite this early example, little use of the public corporation was made until the twentieth century. During World Wars I and II and during the Great Depression of the 1930s, the federal government established over one hundred public corporations to meet the needs of the times. As these needs were satisfied or lapsed, many of these corporations were liquidated.

Many have remained, such as the largest of all: the Tennessee Valley Authority (TVA). This government corporation was chartered by Congress in 1933 with a three-person board to build fifty dams on the Tennessee River and its major tributaries to control flooding, generate hydroelectric power, make the river navigable, build recreational facilities, and generally boost the region's economy. TVA's initial funding came from congressional appropriations, and subsequent funding has largely come from government bonds and revenue from the sale of electric power. In fiscal year 2004 TVA's public debt was $25.7 billion.[12]

Public corporations are organized along lines similar to private business corporations. This gives these corporations greater flexibility in their structure and operations than would be the case if they were government departments or bureaus of departments. Because these corporations engage in quasi-business activities, it is believed they need flexibility to conduct their duties efficiently, largely free from congressional and executive branch micromanagement and other strict bureaucratic controls. In the famous Brownlow Commission Report in 1937, the commission stated that the advantages of the government corporation included "freedom of operation, flexibility, business efficiency, and opportunity for experimentation."[13]

This is still the case, though their freedom of activity was somewhat constrained by the enactment in 1945 of the Corporation Control Act. This act authorized Congress' General Accounting Office to conduct audits of these corporations' activities, required them to submit their budgets for congressional and presidential review, and required congressional authorization for capital expenditures.

Public corporations are given capital by congressional appropriation to launch or carry on their activities. Their boards of directors appoint managers who must conduct their affairs in a businesslike manner. Public corporations are authorized to sign contracts, borrow money, buy and sell commodities, and sue and be sued. They continue to be an important mechanism for the federal government to conduct its "business" affairs in a businesslike manner.

Private Corporations

Private corporations are formed by individuals for the purpose of conducting business to attempt to make a profit. Private corporations have to be

---

The Four Types of Corporations

Public Corporations. Public corporations, sometimes called government corporations, are formed by a government to meet some political or governmental purpose—a *public* purpose. Examples include the Federal Deposit Insurance Corporation, the U.S. Postal Service, the Tennessee Valley Authority, Amtrak, and the Overseas Private Investment Corporation.

Private Corporations. Private corporations are formed by individuals for the purpose of conducting business to attempt to make a profit. *S corporations* are a special type formed under the Internal Revenue Code, subchapter S, which exempts the corporation from paying taxes on profits. *C corporations* pay their own taxes on profits, and any dividends or other payouts they make that are passed through to their shareholders are taxed on the shareholders' individual income tax returns. Companies that are formed as private corporations can issue stock subject to federal regulatory approval.

Close Corporations. Close corporations are those whose shares are held by members of a family or by relatively few persons. These are also known as *closely held, family,* or *privately held* corporations.

Nonprofit Corporations. Also called not-for-profit corporations, these are basically private corporations that are organized to achieve a public purpose. Organizations such as charities, educational institutions, religious groups, private hospitals, and condominium homeowners' associations are often organized as *public benefit nonprofit corporations* to enable the organization to conduct its business without exposing its leaders (the members of the board of directors) to personal liability. Nonprofit corporations have no stock, generate no profits, pay no taxes, and must use any income they generate to fund and improve their operations for the public's good. Examples include the American Red Cross, the Catholic Church, and the Ford Foundation.

approved by one of the fifty state governments (or the District of Columbia) before they are legal entities, eligible to conduct business. The *purpose* of corporations differs: public corporations' purposes are to promote the public good. Private corporations' purposes are to promote the private good; that is, they operate for the benefit of their owners (their shareholders), even though they might provide a public benefit, such as an electric utility.

The vast majority of corporations are private corporations. There are two formal types of private corporations: C corporations (the typical type) and S corporations. S corporations are a special type formed under the Internal Revenue Code, subchapter S, which exempts the corporation from paying taxes on profits; profits are passed through to the corporation's individual owners who pay taxes on them on their individual tax returns.[14] C corporations pay their own taxes on profits, and any dividends or other payouts they make that are passed through to their shareholders are taxed on the shareholders' individual income tax returns. C corporations are the focus of this book and will be the sole topic of discussion.

Owing to the fact that each state has its own laws on corporations, laws governing the establishment and operations of corporations differ state by state. The Model Business Corporation Act (as revised) is a template that has been put forward to achieve some degree of standardization throughout the United States. Not all states have adopted all features of the act, and some have rejected it entirely. Therefore, because each individual state's corporation law is controlling on companies incorporated in that state, regardless of how many states in which the corporation conducts business, one has to look at each state's body of corporation law to determine regulations, procedures, and rights of companies incorporated there.

Companies that are formed as private corporations can issue stock subject to federal regulatory approval. The purchasers of such stock—the stockholders, also known as shareholders—are the owners of the corporation. Stock in C corporations, the usual type, is traded on a public stock exchange, giving these companies the name *public companies*. This does not mean, however, that they are public corporations; they are not. They are private corporations, privately owned by their stockholders.

There are numerous private non-public corporations, many of which are quite small. These are companies that are incorporated for the purpose of pursuing profit but do not issue stock, exempting them from quarterly financial reports, Sarbanes-Oxley Law requirements, and Wall Street analysts' speculations as to their next earnings report.

The largest of these companies in the United States is Koch Industries, Inc., a conglomerate based in Wichita, Kansas. In 2006 for $13 billion in cash it acquired Georgia-Pacific Corporation, maker of Brawny paper towels,

Dixie cups, and Angel Soft tissue, adding these brands to its collection of companies in petroleum refining, pipelines, pulp and paper, and fiber products. The newly combined company will have sales of about $80 billion, surpassing the previous number one closely held corporation, Cargill, Inc.[15]

When the United States gained independence from Great Britain, "American law inherited the corporation from English jurisprudence in the form in which it stood at the close of the Eighteenth Century."[16] Corporate charters thereafter were granted not by the Crown but by individual states in the Union, as the successors to the British Crown.

The first private corporation formed after the ratification of the United States Constitution was the Society for Establishing Useful Manufacturers of New Jersey, incorporated in 1791. By 1800, 335 business corporations had been established in the United States, nearly two-thirds of them in New England. The most common types were banks and transportation companies—toll bridges, turnpikes, and canals. Manufacturing and trading corporations made up only 4 percent of the total number.[17] Trading stock was quite limited; the first stock traded in New York City, the New York Insurance Company, was in 1798. Gradually Wall Street replaced Philadelphia as the main trading exchange, mostly for government bonds.

During the nineteenth century, various states modified, expanded, and redrew their corporation laws as events unfolded and as the needs of industry and commerce changed.

CLOSE CORPORATIONS

Close corporations are those whose shares are held by members of a family or by relatively few persons. These are also known as *closely held, family,* or *privately held* corporations. Because the few owners of these corporations usually know each other personally, and the number of shares of ownership is small, there is no public trading of the shares of close corporations.

The operation of this type of corporation and the transfer of ownership shares is regulated by each state. Many have rules and regulations that allow close corporations to behave much like a partnership. Once again, one has to research the rules in each state to fully understand the regulations governing this type of corporation, which is usually permitted to depart from the body of corporate law that typically governs private corporations.

For example, in Maryland and some other states a close corporation need not have a board of directors. Elsewhere, some close corporations can operate without bylaws, without annual shareholders' meetings, or even without maintaining formal records of directors' decisions. This type of corporation is regulated by very strict rules within each state, and only attorneys with corporate practices should be asked to help form or dissolve this unique business entity.

NONPROFIT CORPORATIONS

Nonprofit corporations, also called not-for-profit corporations, are another type of corporate form. These are basically private corporations that are organized to achieve a public purpose. They have a board of directors (sometimes called a board of trustees) that oversees the work of the full-time staff of officers and employees.

Organizations such as charities, educational institutions, religious groups, private hospitals, condominium homeowners' associations, and the like are often organized as *public benefit nonprofit corporations* to enable the organization to conduct its business—own property and sign contracts—without exposing its leaders (the members of the board of directors) to personal liability. Nonprofit corporations have no stock, generate no profits, pay no taxes, and must use any income they generate to fund and improve their operations for the public's good.

Among the largest nonprofit corporations in America are the American Red Cross, the Catholic Church, and the Ford Foundation. The oldest corporation in the United States is a nonprofit, Harvard University, chartered in 1636. Columbia University, which was granted a royal charter in 1754 by King Charles II of England, was originally called King's College; today, Columbia University is a nonprofit corporation chartered under the laws of the state of New York. Its purpose, like Harvard's, is, of course, to provide education.

RAND Corporation, one of the nation's largest and most famous "think tanks," is headquartered in Santa Monica, California, with offices in numerous cities around the world. It is a nonprofit corporation incorporated under the laws of the state of California to conduct research on public policy issues, such as national security and defense, civil justice, education, public health, and so forth. RAND's annual income of roughly $250 million is all spent on performing its research and on improving its ability to conduct research for its government and private clients, who pay for its research reports and other services it provides.

SUMMARY

These, then, are the four major types or classifications of corporations: public, private, close, and nonprofit. The principal bases for determining the classification of a corporation are its purpose and ownership characteristics.

Hereinafter, the focus of the discussion will be on the private corporation, specifically the C corporation, because its purpose is to engage in business with the aim of making money for its shareholder owners. Whenever the word *corporation* is used hereafter, it refers to the C corporation.

EMERGENCE OF THE CORPORATION AS THE DOMINANT FORM

The private corporation form of business organization became popular in the second half of the nineteenth century and emerged as the dominant form by the early twentieth century for a number of reasons. The underlying reasons, examined in the next chapter, can be summarized here: the corporation was the most useful business form because it could raise the enormous amounts of capital needed for business expansion in our rapidly industrializing economy, it provided a structure to organize and manage large-scale business activities, and it provided legal protection for its owners and directors against liability.

Pre–Civil War Era

From the beginning of the United States under the Constitution in 1789, America's "business" remained largely unchanged until the time of the Civil War, 1861–1865.[18] The United States was largely an agrarian country whose population lived mostly in rural areas—80 percent as late as 1860—and its economy was based on the family-owned farm, the chief source of livelihood for most people. Though farms were small and inefficient, they were largely self-sufficient and provided the largest source of national income, greater than trade and shipping.

Manufacturing, such as it was, was based on handicrafts, and the firms that produced manufactured goods were small, inefficient, and technologically primitive. In the early 1800s no single firm controlled as much as 10 percent of the output in any manufacturing industry.[19] Indeed, in 1810, the largest manufacturing plant in the country had a value less than $250,000.

The ten companies today that have been in continuous existence the longest are listed in Table 1.1. All of these were founded as sole proprietorships or partnerships, none initially as corporations, but later all became corporations.[20]

At the beginning of the nineteenth century, when the U.S. population was barely 5.5 million people, only a few hundred corporations existed in the entire nation. These were mostly in the major commercial centers of the

TABLE 1.1
The Ten Oldest Companies in Continuous Existence in the United States

Current Company Name	Year Founded	Earliest Company Name
Bank of New York Co.	1784	The Bank of New York
Cigna	1792	Insurance Co. of North America
State Street Corp.	1792	Union Bank
Dominion Resources	1795	Upper Appomattox Co.
JP Morgan Chase Co.	1799	The Manhattan Co.
DuPont	1802	E. I. DuPont de Nemours & Co.
Colgate-Palmolive	1806	The Colgate Co.
Hartford Financial Services	1810	Hartford Fire Insurance Co.
Constellation Energy	1816	Gas Light Co. of Baltimore
PPL	1822	Lehigh Coal & Navigation Co.

Northeast (Philadelphia, New York, and Boston), where "merchant princes" in shipping and trading were based.

The principal forms for the businesses there were sole proprietorships and partnerships, with corporations being rare. Even tycoons such as John Jacob Astor and Stephen Girard and early industrialists such as Eli Whitney ran their businesses as sole proprietorships or partnerships, not corporations.[21] The typical businessperson was a man who was a shopkeeper, peddler, or blacksmith. The first million-dollar corporation did not emerge until 1853.

POST–CIVIL WAR INDUSTRIALIZATION

Big business began after the Civil War with the full advent of the Industrial Revolution in the northern states. The preconditions for this vast economic expansion and industrialization were a growing population; major improvements in technology (a myriad of inventions), communications (first the telegraph and later the telephone), and transportation (railroads); an open and fluid social system with no defined class structures to inhibit upward mobility (except of course for slavery, which had only recently been abolished); abundant natural resources (especially land); and ample capital (especially foreign investment) to finance business expansion. As much as anything, Americans were blessed with an entrepreneurial spirit: a willingness of inventers, investors, and ordinary people to take risks as they strove to improve their lot in life.

After the Civil War, which itself was a major stimulus to industrialization, America rapidly industrialized, and business enterprises in railroads, steel, oil, and textiles quickly emerged in these large-scale, complex industries. All of these gigantic companies were organized as corporations, and they played the leading role in the rapid transformation of the American economy.

The same transforming power of industrial enterprises was occurring also in Great Britain and Germany, which, together with the United States, were the three largest economies in the world by 1870, accounting for just over two-thirds of the world's industrial output. The populations of these three countries were nearly the same: the United States and Germany each had 39 million, and Britain had 31 million. Their GDPs were also quite close: $39 billion each for the United States and Prussia/Germany, and $31 billion for Britain.[22] These countries, wrote Alfred Chandler, "had been rural, agrarian, and commercial; they became industrial and urban. That transformation, in turn, brought the most rapid economic growth in the history of mankind."[23]

Railroads

A major part of that growth was tied to railroads, which were a transforming force in all industrial economies. Railroad construction began in earnest in the United States in the 1850s and went hand in hand with the telegraph, which used railway rights-of-way for stringing lines. By 1860, on the eve of the Civil War, the United States had more than 30,000 miles of railroad, and 93,000 miles had been built by 1880. In 1910, when the infrastructure was largely complete, the United States had 240,000 miles of track.[24]

The 1880s and 1890s was the era of freewheeling *laissez-faire capitalism*, characterized by the so-called *robber barons*, railroad corporation leaders such as Cornelius Vanderbilt, Jay Gould, and James J. Hill. Their excesses, giving rise to the term *Gilded Age*, stimulated the rise of the populist movement, representing farmers and the rapidly expanding class of blue-collar workers, that pressed the federal government to rein in the tycoons. Congress responded by enacting the Interstate Commerce Act of 1887, to set railroad rates among other things, and the Sherman Antitrust Act of 1890, to enforce competition among major companies in the same industry.[25]

By the 1890s, the U.S. railroad industry had become the largest business in the world. The Pennsylvania Railroad, founded in 1871, alone employed 110,000 workers. By contrast, the entire civilian workforce of the federal government was 20,000 people at that time, and the armed forces totaled 40,000. The New York Central Railroad and the Pennsylvania Railroad were initially the largest, but with the westward expansion of the railroads, fueled by free land grants from the federal government, soon the Union Pacific, the Great Northern, and the Southern Pacific surpassed those eastern lines. Each of these companies was organized as a corporation. The New York Central, initially the largest, was under the control of its largest shareholder, Commodore Cornelius Vanderbilt, who had initially made his fortune operating clipper ships carrying freight and passengers to the West Coast.[26]

At the time of the Spanish-American War in 1898, the United States had in a mere quarter century become the largest economy in the world, an industrial giant that was larger than Great Britain, the home of the Industrial Revolution that had earlier had the largest gross domestic product (GDP). The other great powers of the world began to adjust their foreign policies to the fact of America's new status. By 1920, the United States' GDP equaled the next three largest GDPs combined. In 1929, the United States accounted for 42 percent of the world's industrial production; the next two largest economies, Germany and Britain, accounted for 12 percent and 9 percent, respectively.[27] This rapid and enormous growth of America's industrial economy was almost entirely organized around and driven by corporations.

CONSOLIDATION OF AMERICAN INDUSTRY

Consolidation was a key to efficiency and expansion.[28] Efficient mass production on the magnitude American industry now experienced required economies of scale, achieved first by *horizontal integration*, that is, competing companies acquiring each other to gain efficiencies and market share. Later, *vertical integration* occurred in two respects: backward and forward integration of productive assets, meaning that producers acquired their suppliers below them in the supply chain, and in some instances they also acquired companies after them (or above them) in the production and distribution process. Today, this is called vertical supply chain integration.

Corporate Consolidation

A massive wave of merger activity between 1897 and 1904 reduced the number of corporations dramatically, with the result that few enormous companies now dominated production, having the size and resources to expand at an ever faster pace. During this seven-year period, 4,227 companies were merged into 257 corporations.[29] By 1904, when Theodore Roosevelt was elected for a full term as president, a mere 318 giant corporations controlled 40 percent of the nation's manufacturing assets. This was the period of the largest consolidation of business in the country's history.

United States Steel Corporation

Carnegie Steel Corporation is the leading example of horizontal and vertical integration. On the horizontal level, Andrew Carnegie's steel mills initially put smaller, less efficient steel mills out of business by ruthlessly exploiting his company's economies of scale or by acquiring these firms. Next, Carnegie vertically integrated backward in the supply chain into mining, shipping, and processing iron ore, acquiring companies performing those tasks. Then he vertically integrated forward by expanding his activities into the fabrication of finished steel products from the raw steel produced in his mills, selling those end products, such as rails, directly to railroads, for example.

In the 1880s, he adopted the latest technology in the steelmaking process, the open hearth furnace, gaining efficiencies and quality superior to his remaining competitors. Finally, in 1901, in the largest merger in history, Carnegie sold his company to form the United States Steel Corporation, a consolidation of two-thirds of the nation's expanding steelmaking capacity. This mammoth transaction was financed by J. P. Morgan's bank. When the deal closed, Morgan said to Carnegie, "Congratulations, Mr. Carnegie, you are now the richest man in the world."

At the turn of the twentieth century, the economy of the United States had fully taken off into a mature, industrial, technologically driven modern economy, and by the "roaring 20s" it had become a high mass-consumption economy.[30] In the early twentieth century, in sharp contrast to the early nineteenth century, America now had a remarkably complex, large-scale, business-driven industrial economy.

Business enterprises had replaced agriculture as the major source of livelihood for most people. The typical person no longer was an independent property owner (farmer, shopkeeper, merchant) deriving his income from that property, but had become an employee of someone else, a wage or salary earner working for a corporation.[31] In the decade of the 1920s, agriculture had shrunk to represent only 11.2 percent of the U.S. GDP; industry had grown to 41.3 percent; and service had grown to 47.5 percent.[32]

Major shifts in population accompanied industrialization. In 1920, for the first time, the urban population outnumbered the rural population. This shift to urban centers is a hallmark of industrialization that happened first in England, the home of the Industrial Revolution, and is today, in the early twenty-first century, occurring in China and India, the last major nations to modernize their economies—largely by sprinting past the Industrial Revolution stage of growth into the knowledge revolution. Today's rural-to-urban migration in China is on a scale unprecedented in all of human history, with possibly as many as 300 million people leaving the land and immigrating to cities; this is a population as large as that of the United States.[33]

With rapid industrialization immediately following the Civil War, it did not take long for major corporations, the engines of this mighty transformation of the American economy, to discover that they were engaged in intense competition with one another for markets, sales, and profits. This was the era of laissez-faire capitalism, a time when virtually no restraints or regulations inhibited companies to do whatever they desired to gain customers, to hire workers and treat them as they liked, and to make money— which they did, hand over fist.

Great fortunes were being made for the corporations and for the individuals who ran them: Rockefeller, Gould, Vanderbilt, Harriman, Hill, Carnegie, Flagler, and the like. Control over many industries and whole sectors of the economy became concentrated under the control of only a few major businesses. During the 1870s and 1880s, companies ran roughshod, engaging in practices that within a decade or two became illegal or sharply regulated. Between 1890 and 1904 the consolidation wave peaked; about fifty holding companies controlled most of the nation's industrial base. The largest were United States Steel, National Biscuit, American Tobacco Company, International Harvester, AT&T, United Fruit, American Cotton, and General Electric.

Purpose of Trusts

Seeking ways to lessen the cutthroat competition and to further improve efficiencies, businessmen sought ways to protect themselves from mutual destruction and many were found. Monopolistic agreements were forged between major competitors to fix prices, limit production, carve out geographic territories to allocate markets, and share profits. Independent companies were joined together through acquisition, merger, alliances, or other means to form monopolistic combinations, generically known as cartels, or, as they were called then, *trusts*.

Trusts were business combinations created by large corporations to lessen the impact of competitive forces on themselves and to improve efficiency. This was a device for combining independent companies under the control of a single entity. It permitted a centralized management to direct the entire productive process of an industry to achieve the lowest possible production costs, which in turn vastly improved profits because prices did not have to be reduced, there being no competition.

A trust was formed by persuading the majority stockholders of a number of independent firms to give control of their shares, and voting rights, to a single group of "trustees." The trustees could then run the previously independent companies as a single enterprise. The stockholders in turn received for their shares "trust certificates," which entitled them to receive dividends from the trust's profits.[34]

Thus, trusts became a sort of "super corporation," a company of companies that controlled most of the firms doing business in a particular industry.

The industries that trusts came to dominate by the 1880s included coal, fruit, gunpowder, lead, matches, meatpacking, nickel, oil, steel, sugar, tobacco, and whiskey.

Standard Oil Trust

A classic example of a trust at work is the oil industry. Well before 1890, the year the Sherman Antitrust Act was passed, the oil industry had been consolidated into John D. Rockefeller's Standard Oil Trust. This trust held a vertically integrated monopoly of the oil industry in the United States—from wells, to refineries, to distribution systems, to retail outlets. It controlled supply, and it controlled prices.[35]

The trust rationalized oil and kerosene production to improve its efficiency, shutting down inefficient refineries, building new ones, improving distribution, and better coordinating the flow of materials from the oil fields to the customer. In doing so, the trust reduced the cost of production per gallon from 2.5 cents to 1.5 cents from 1880 to 1885, with the resulting savings going into profit. This one-cent-per-gallon profit was the core of four of the world's greatest fortunes: Rockefeller, Harkness, Payne, and Flagler.[36]

Using the power of the Sherman Act for the first time, President Theodore Roosevelt prosecuted the Standard Oil Trust, and in 1911 the U.S. Supreme Court found in the government's favor and broke up the trust into thirty separate companies that then competed with each other.[37] Some of the larger companies that emerged after the breakup were the Standard Oil Company of New Jersey (later renamed Exxon), Standard Oil Company of California (later Chevron), Standard Oil Company of Indiana (later Amoco), Standard Oil Company of Ohio (later Sohio), and Standard Oil Company of New York (later Mobil). Ninety years later the two largest, Exxon and Mobil, were allowed to remerge.

REGULATION OF BIG BUSINESS

The emergence of the trust form of monopoly may have been good for big business, but not for its workers or for small and medium-sized companies that were helpless in the face of monopolies' control over whole industries. And it was not beneficial for society because capitalism requires free markets and open competition to work properly. Hence, the injured groups—small and medium-sized businesses, workers, farmers, and "progressive" groups—began to press for a mechanism to control these behemoths.

The mechanisms centered on federal legislation: first the Interstate Commerce Act of 1887 and then the Sherman Antitrust Act of 1890, which stated that every "combination in the form of trust or otherwise, or conspiracy, in restraint of trade or commerce among the several states . . . is hereby declared to be illegal."[38] With these two powerful tools, the federal government began its now familiar role of regulating the size and operation of big business.

Soon, the Progressive Era produced a plethora of additional laws, and with them regulatory agencies to establish and enforce the principles of free and open competition and to set high standards for products within our increasingly industrial economy. The next two most important acts were the following:

- The Clayton Act of 1914, which made it unlawful to undertake certain business practices that are conducive to restraining competition
- The Federal Trade Commission Act of 1914, which made it illegal to engage in "unfair methods of competition" or deceptive business practices, also established the Federal Trade Commission to enforce anticompetition law

Later, the Robinson-Pattman Act of 1930 made it illegal to engage in price discrimination, that also being an anticompetitive practice.

Along with these statutes that established America's antitrust legal system, a host of laws passed during the early 1900s established regulations for pure food and drugs, hours of service establishing the eight-hour day, prohibitions against child labor, and so forth.

ANTITRUST ENFORCEMENT: 1920s AND 1930s

The Progressive Era produced legislation empowering the federal government to police corporate America to ensure that there was sufficient competition among the country's big businesses, almost all of which were corporations. Yet, laws do not enforce themselves.

During the Theodore Roosevelt/William Howard Taft administrations, 1901–1913, these Republican presidents did use the newly minted laws to break up many of the major trusts. President Woodrow Wilson, a Democrat, who followed them, 1913–1921, also enforced the anticompetition regulations as well as introduced new legislation that further deepened the federal government's role in the nation's economy: the personal income tax in 1913 (by constitutional amendment), the Federal Reserve System in 1914, and additional regulatory agencies, such as the Federal Trade Commission and the Federal Power Commission (to regulate rates on interstate electric power).

New Business Combinations

It was during the roaring 20s, however, that the three Republican administrations that governed back-to-back not only did not prosecute monopolistic practices of big business but also encouraged business combinations. Herbert Hoover, who was secretary of commerce for both Presidents Harding and Coolidge, and later as president, argued that business "associations" were legitimate and appropriate, adding to efficiency. Therefore, during the 1920s, businesses recombined, this time not as trusts, but in more direct and sometimes sophisticated ways—through mergers and acquisitions, interlocking directorates, and other business relationships.

The decade of the 1920s was the high-water mark of concentration of American industry and finance.[39] In manufacturing and mining during that decade, there were 1,268 business combinations involving the merger of four thousand firms and the disappearance of six thousand firms. Some 3,744 public utility companies disappeared through merger, and almost half of the banks disappeared through merger or failures—from 30,139 to 16,053 by 1935.

When President Hoover left office in 1933, a mere 594 corporations owned 53 percent of all corporate wealth in the United States. The other 387,970 corporations owned 47 percent. The J. P. Morgan Bank alone controlled directly or indirectly about one-fourth of the nation's total corporate assets, according to the Senate Banking Committee. These same concentrations were present in virtually every important industry: railroads, electric power, and natural resources.[40] Looking just at natural resources, the concentrations were quite dramatic in percent of total American production:

- Copper—four companies owned over half.
- Iron ore—U.S. Steel Corporation owned up to 66 percent.
- Nickel—International Nickel Company owned 90 percent.

- Bauxite—Alcoa held a monopoly on aluminum.
- Coal—eight companies owned 75 percent.
- Oil—five companies produced 33 percent.
- Hydroelectric power—six companies controlled 100 percent.

Regulations may be on the books, but they have to be enforced to be effective. This is especially true of antitrust regulations, because businesses react to these lapses. The 1920s therefore came to resemble the 1880s with respect to concentrations of industry and monopoly practices—as though the Sherman Antitrust and Clayton Acts had never been passed.

Franklin Roosevelt

When Franklin Roosevelt came into the presidency in 1933, during the nadir of the Great Depression, the federal government began the large-scale intervention into the economy that became associated with the label he gave his administration, the New Deal. His administration introduced a host of legislative initiatives to reinvigorate the economy, put people back to work by hiring them if necessary in public works programs, and introduced social legislation, such as the Social Security program and the Wagner Act, allowing labor unions to organize and operate without hindrance.

Roosevelt also introduced legislation to regulate the securities industry, which had taken some of the blame for the Depression. The Securities Act of 1933 and the Securities Exchange Act of 1934 established regulations for the issuance of stocks and bonds and established the Securities and Exchange Commission to enforce those regulations. None of this, however, had much to do with antitrust enforcement against big business, which was a secondary policy issue at the time. The primary issue was economic recovery, and businesses of all sizes were encouraged to participate.

MODERN CORPORATE ACTIVITIES

During the 1930s and subsequently, did the concentration of corporate power increase or diminish—that is, did the number of companies operating in an industry grow or shrink? Fewer companies means greater concentration; more companies means less. Studies indicate that the degree of concentration remained about the same. A Federal Trade Commission report stated that "in 1935 the 200 largest manufacturing corporations accounted for 37.7 per cent of the total value of products of all manufacturing enterprises; by 1950 the proportion had risen to 40.5 per cent."[41]

Between 1935 and 1958, the degree of concentration went from 28.0 percent to 29.8 percent of total corporate assets held by the one hundred largest firms in manufacturing, mining, and distribution. The concentrations in some industries increased slightly, and in some other industries they diminished. The top four companies' share of total industry output increased in autos, steel, and brewing, but diminished in petroleum refining, tobacco, and meatpacking. At midcentury, there was no clear trend across the entire economy in either direction of industry concentration.

By the midtwentieth century, the corporation had consolidated its position as the dominant form of business organization, notwithstanding the continued existence of millions of sole proprietorships, partnerships, and private farm units. In 1953, industry accounted for 48.4 percent of the U.S. GDP, services 45.7 percent, and agriculture 5.9 percent. Over the previous hundred plus years, 1839–1953, industry had grown in percentage terms by 39.1 percent, services by 8.4 percent, and agriculture had declined by 47.5 percent.[42] The growth in industry and much of services (such as banking, retailing, insurance, shipping, etc.) was fueled by corporations.

In 1960, corporations accounted for 95 percent of the net income of all manufacturing enterprises, and they predominated in public utilities, transportation, communications, mining, and finance. Over half of all wholesale and retail businesses were corporations.[43] In 1961, a mere 2,632 corporations out of a total of 1,190,282 corporations in America owned 63 percent of all corporate assets; this represented 0.2 percent of total corporations, a clear quantification of the "bigness" of America's big businesses.[44]

CORPORATIONS AT THE BEGINNING OF THE TWENTY-FIRST CENTURY

At the beginning of the twenty-first century, corporations continued as the dominant form of America's business organization. In 2004 they ranged in size from $288 billion in revenues for the largest, Wal-Mart Stores, Inc., to $3.6 billion for the smallest of the *Fortune* 500 companies, Cincinnati Financial Corporation.

The *Fortune* magazine list of the nation's 500 largest companies began publication in 1956, reporting on the largest companies in 1955. In 1955 total revenue for these 500 companies was $1.2 trillion (adjusted for inflation); 49 years later, in 2004, their total revenue was $8.2 trillion. Over those 49 years, the list changed from *million*-dollar companies to *all billion*-dollar companies. And the geography had a tectonic shift: from a concentration of companies in the Northeast and the upper Midwest to a wider distribution, so that Texas and California now have 21 percent of the companies' headquarters, whereas they were barely represented on the first list. The largest company of all is headquartered in Arkansas!

The type and size of these largest of America's corporations changed dramatically over the past half century, as Table 1.2 from the *Fortune* 500 list illustrates in billions of current dollars.[45]

Standard Oil Company of New Jersey later took the name Exxon. Throughout the history of the *Fortune* 500 list, General Motors and Exxon were number one or number two (reversing roles from time to time) until 2002, when Wal-Mart captured the number-one position and has held it since.

Nothing illustrates more dramatically the transformation of American industry than the seven companies that were on the 1955 list but disappeared from the 2004 list:

- U.S. Steel—all American-based steel companies (except for Nucor) suffered.
- Mobil—acquired by Exxon.
- Esmark—a general manufacturer that was later acquired.
- Chrysler—acquired by Daimler-Benz of Germany to form DaimlerChrysler AG
- Armour—a meatpacker later acquired.
- Gulf Oil—later acquired by Chevron, which also acquired Texaco.
- DuPont—chemicals have declined in importance and Dow has passed DuPont in sales.

Thus, traditional industries such as steel and meatpacking declined, and the smallest of the major American auto manufacturers and two oil companies disappeared through acquisition by larger firms.

TABLE 1.2
The Ten Largest Corporations in the United States

1955		2004	
Company	Revenue ($ in billions)	Company	Revenue ($ in billions)
General Motors	9.823	Wal-Mart	288.1
Standard Oil N.J.	5.661	Exxon Mobil	270.7
United States Steel	3.250	General Motors	193.5
General Electric Co.	2.959	Ford Motor Co.	172.2
Esmark	2.510	General Electric Co.	152.3
Chrysler	2.071	ChevronTexaco	147.9
Armour	2.056	ConocoPhilips	121.6
Gulf Oil	1.705	Citigroup	108.2
Mobil Oil	1.703	American Intern'l. Group	98.6
DuPont	1.687	IBM	96.2

The giants that are on the 2004 list but not the 1955 list also illustrate the sea change that occurred in America's industry over the past five decades, each one of them being a global company:

- Wal-Mart—a global discount retailer becoming the largest firm in the world
- General Motors and General Electric—holding their own on the list
- Citigroup—a financial services company created by the merger of Travelers Insurance and Citibank of New York to become the largest financial services firm in the world
- IBM—just missed the 1955 list but has been a major player for over fifty years in high technology; transformed itself in the 1990s into a high-tech services firm as well as a computer manufacturing company
- American International Group—the largest insurance company in the world
- Exxon Mobil, ChevronTexaco, and ConocoPhilips—oil companies that qualify to be on the list as a result of having merged, as their names clearly indicate

Companies listed on the 1955 list were all *industrials*. In the 1990s, *Fortune* decided to change the rules for listing companies and integrated industrials with *service* and *financial* companies to form a composite list, which the 2004 list illustrates. If the same ground rules for listing had been present in 1955, the number-three company would have been AT&T; number four the Great Atlantic and Pacific Tea Company (A&P markets); number six Sears, Roebuck;

TABLE 1.3
Manufacturing Corporations' Selected Financial Performance, 1980–2001 ($ in billions)

Year	Sales	Profits after Taxes	Stockholders' Equity
1980	$1,913	$93	$668
1985	2,331	88	866
1990	2,811	110	1,044
1991	2,761	66	1,064
1992	2,890	22	1,035
1993	3,015	83	1,040
1994	3,256	175	1,241
1995	3,528	198	1,241
1996	3,758	225	1,348
1997	3,992	244	1,464
1998	3,949	234	1,487
1999	4,149	258	1,637
2000	4,548	275	1,892
2001	4,308	36	1,827

and number nine Metropolitan Life Insurance Company. Companies on the original list would have been pushed down or off the list accordingly.

This discussion focused on the type and nature of the changes in American corporations over the past half century. Let us now look at the size of America's corporations from a strictly financial perspective, focusing on manufacturing corporations. Table 1.3 reports manufacturing firms' revenue (sales), after tax profits, and stockholders' equity over a twenty-one-year period, 1980–2001:[46]

In the recession year of 2001, corporations' after tax profits ($36 billion) were the lowest since 1992, which was also a recession year. The heady profits of the second half of the 1990s were not duplicated again until 2004, when the *Fortune* 500 companies' profits were $513.5 billion, nearly three times what they had been a decade before.[47] Of key significance to an investor is stockholders' equity, which is calculated by multiplying the number of shares outstanding by the price per share of stock; it nearly tripled in twenty years, during which time sales only doubled. This tells you that the market valued companies more than their sales by themselves would warrant.

CONCLUSION

The historical development of the corporate form of business organization began in the Middle Ages, developed in the Age of Discovery, was the organizing mechanism for the founding of the British colonies in North America, and became dominant beginning in midnineteenth-century England and America.

The corporation was the principal organizing mechanism for the companies that developed and managed the Industrial Revolution throughout the Western world. It went through several changes and perturbations, including cartels, trusts, and holding companies, but finally emerged in the 1920s in its modern form. The chapter summarizes the development of each of the four types of corporations—public, private, close, and nonprofit—and explains their purposes.

Writing in 1932, two of the most insightful analysts of the corporation, Adolf Berle and Gardiner Means, made the following profound observation that is as true in the twenty-first century as it was then:

The corporate system has done more than evolve a norm by which business is carried on. Within it there exists a centripetal attraction which draws wealth together into aggregations of constantly increasing size, at the same time throwing control into the hands of fewer and fewer men. The trend is apparent; and no limit is as yet in sight.[48]

NOTES

1. This discussion is largely based on John Micklethwait and Adrian Wooldridge, *The Company: A Short History of a Revolutionary Idea* (New York: Modern Library, 2003), Chapter 1.

2. Stephen Innes, "From Corporation to Commonwealth," in Jack Beatty, ed., *Colossus: How the Corporation Changed America* (New York: Broadway Books, 2001), 21.

3. Ibid.

4. John Micklethwait and Adrian Wooldridge, *The Company*, 34–35.

5. Jack Beatty, ed., *Colossus*, 17–18.

6. This discussion of colonial America is based on Stephen Innes, "From Corporation to Commonwealth," in Jack Beatty, ed., *Colossus*, 18–22.

7. John Micklethwait and Adrian Wooldridge, *The Company*, xvii.

8. George David Smith and Davis Dyer, "The Rise and Transformation of the American Corporation," in Carl Kaysen, ed., *The American Corporation Today* (New York: Oxford University Press, 1966), 38.

9. John Micklethwait and Adrian Wooldridge, *The Company*, xxi.

10. This discussion is based on Frank B. Cross and Roger Leroy Miller, *West's Legal Environment of Business,* 5th ed. (Mason, OH: Thomson South-Western, 2004), 413–416.

11. Article I, Section 8 of the Constitution. See Alexander Hamilton, "No. 36," in Alexander Hamilton, James Madison, and John Jay, *The Federalist Papers* (New York: New American Library, 1961).

12. For a discussion of TVA, see Wesley B. Truitt, *What Entrepreneurs Need to Know about Government: A Guide to Rules and Regulations* (Westport, CT: Praeger, 2004), 59–60.

13. President's Committee on Administrative Management, *Report with Special Studies* (Washington, D.C.: U.S. Government Printing Office, 1937), 44.

14. For a discussion of S corporations, see Wesley B. Truitt, *What Entrepreneurs Need to Know about Government*, 93–94.

15. *Wall Street Journal*, November 14, 2005, A3; *Los Angeles Times*, Nov. 14, 2005, C2.

16. Adolph A. Berle, Jr. and Gardiner C. Means, *The Modern Corporation and Private Property* (New York: Macmillan, 1948), 128. See pp. 128–152 for this state-by-state discussion.

17. William Roy, *Socializing Capital: The Rise of the Large Industrial Corporation in America* (Princeton, NJ: Princeton University Press, 1997), 49, cited in John Micklethwait and Adrian Wooldridge, *The Company*, 44.

18. This discussion is based on John E. Anderson, *Politics and the Economy* (Boston: Little, Brown, 1966), 2–5.

19. Robert S. Heilbroner, *The Making of Economic Society* (Englewood Cliffs, NJ: Prentice-Hall, 1962), 118.

20. www.Fortune.com/500/archive.

21. John Micklethwait and Adrian Wooldridge, *The Company*, 45.

22. Angus Madison, *Phases of Capitalist Development* (New York: Oxford University Press, 1982), Tables 1.4, A3, B2, B3, and B4, cited in Alfred D. Chandler, Jr., *Scale and Scope: The Dynamics of Industrial Capitalism* (Cambridge, MA: Harvard University Press, 1990), 52.

23. Alfred D. Chandler, Jr., *Scale and Scope*, 3.

24. Ibid., 53.

25. For a discussion of the Progressive Era, the Interstate Commerce Commission Act, and the Sherman Antitrust Act, see Wesley B. Truitt, *What Entrepreneurs Need to Know about Government*, Chapter 1.

26. For railroads, see Alfred D. Chandler, Jr., ed., *The Railroads: The Nation's First Big Business* (New York: Harcourt, Brace and World, 1965).

27. Walt W. Rostow, *The World Economy: History and Prospect* (Austin, TX: University of Texas Press, 1978), 52–53.

28. This discussion is based on George David Smith and Davis Dyer, "The Rise and Transformation of the American Corporation," in Carl Kaysen, ed., *The American Corporation Today*, 40–41.

29. Roland Marchand states that 1,800 companies consolidated into 157 between 1898 and 1904; see his *Creating the Corporate Soul* (Berkeley, CA: University of California Press, 1998), 7.

30. Walt W. Rostow, *The Stages of Economic Growth* (London: Cambridge University Press, 1960).

31. John E. Anderson, *Politics and the Economy*, 2–3.

32. Simon Kuznets, *Economic Growth of Nations: Total Output and Production Structure* (Cambridge, MA: Harvard University Press, 1971), 144–147, cited in Alfred D. Chandler, Jr., *Scale and Scope*, 5.

33. Michel C. Oksenberg, Michael D. Swaine, and Daniel C. Lynch, *The Chinese Future* (Los Angeles: Pacific Council on International Policy, University of Southern California, and the Center for Asia-Pacific Policy, RAND Corporation, 1999). The author participated in this study.

34. John E. Anderson, *Politics and the Economy*, 162.

35. Samuel Eliot Morison and Henry Steele Commager, *The Growth of the American Republic* (New York: Oxford University Press, 1958), Vol. II, 137–138.

36. Alfred D. Chandler, Jr., *Scale and Scope*, 25.

37. For the classic discussion of Standard Oil of New Jersey after the breakup, see Alfred D. Chandler, Jr., *Strategy and Structure: Chapters in the History of Industrial Enterprise* (Cambridge, MA: MIT Press, 1962), Chapter 4.

38. 15 U.S.C. Section 1.

39. Data in this and the next paragraph are from Samuel Eliot Morison and Henry Steele Commager, *The Growth of the American Republic*, 534–537.

40. For a discussion of concentration of economic power, see Adolf A. Berle, Jr. and Gardiner C. Means, *The Modern Corporation and Private Property*, Chapter 3.

41. Federal Trade Commission, *Changes in Manufacturing 1935 to 1947 and 1950* (Washington, D.C.: U.S. Government Printing Office, 1954), 17, quoted in

John E. Anderson, *Politics and the Economy*, 6. Data in the next sentence are from Anderson, 6.

42. Simon Kuznets, *Economic Growth of Nations*, 144–147, cited in Alfred D. Chandler, Jr., *Scale and Scope*, 5.

43. Edward S. Mason, ed., *The Corporation in Modern Society* (Cambridge, MA: Harvard University Press, 1960), 87.

44. U.S. Department of Commerce, *Statistical Abstract of the United States, 1964* (Washington, D.C.: U.S. Government Printing Office, 1965), 489–490.

45. *Fortune*, April 14, 2003, F32 insert; April 18, 2005, F1; www.Fortune.com/500/archive.

46. U.S. Department of Commerce, *Statistical Abstract of the United States, 2002* (Washington, D.C.: U.S. Government Printing Office, 2002), 496.

47. *Fortune*, April 18, 2005, 232.

48. Adolf A. Berle, Jr. and Gardiner C. Means, *The Modern Corporation and Private Property*, 18.

RECOMMENDED READINGS

Berle, Adolph A., Jr., and Gardiner C. Means, *The Modern Corporation and Private Property* (New York: Macmillan, 1948).

Chandler, Alfred D., Jr., *The Visible Hand: The Managerial Revolution in American Business* (Cambridge, MA: Harvard University Press, 1977).

Kindleberger, Charles, *A Financial History of Western Europe* (Oxford, England: Oxford University Press, 1993).

Means, Howard, *Money and Power: The History of Business* (New York: Wiley, 2001).

Perrow, Charles, *Organizing America: Wealth, Power and the Origins of Corporate Capitalism* (Princeton, NJ: Princeton University Press, 2002).

Two

Transformation of the Corporation

The modern business corporation has deep roots going back to the Middle Ages. It has been revised, updated, and transformed over the centuries to meet the needs of the times. As we have seen, the basic structure of the business corporation was fashioned in the late nineteenth century.

In the early twentieth century it had undergone significant adaptations as a result of government regulatory intervention and the expanded size and scope of companies' activities, becoming the modern corporation. This is the topic of chapter 2. In the 1970s the corporation embarked on its second modern transformation, which continues today with the emerging postmodern corporation, the subject of chapter 3.

No changes were more important to shape and transform the corporation and enable it to take its place as the most important social institution of modern times than those that occurred during the decade following the end of World War I. During this time the corporation took on its modern form, the multidivisional structure, and its modern core feature, the professionalization of management. An explanation of how this occurred, the reasons why it occurred, the model that was used, and the consequences of it on America's and the world's economy for the next half century follows.

Along with the corporation's transformation, a new type of company leader emerged. If the Gilded Age of the 1880s–1890s was characterized by the swaggering robber baron, the roaring 20s were characterized by the professional manager. The latter was a far less colorful figure that eventually gave rise to the stereotypically gray flannel suited "organization man" of the

1950s and 1960s. The archetype of this new breed of management capitalist was Alfred P. Sloan, president of General Motors and the father of the modern corporation.

CORPORATE EXPANSION

Corporations had become the dominant business form by the beginning of the twentieth century. Although under attack by the federal government for their concentrations of power and monopolistic abuses, corporations grew, adapted, and transformed themselves with remarkable skill and agility during the 1910s and 1920s.

The usefulness of the corporate form of business organization had become well understood. In addition to its other attributes (ability to raise money and provide liability protection for its owners), the corporation as a business structure was more flexible and practical than any other type of organization for meeting the needs of the large-scale businesses that had developed in the United States by the time of World War I, 1914–1918.

Growth and expansion were the hallmarks of that era, and businesses that were already large needed to grow even larger to achieve the economies of scale needed to justify the enormous capital investments they required. Between 1919 and 1929, capital investment rose by an average annual rate of 6.4 percent, yielding a phenomenally large productivity increase per manufacturing worker of 43 percent over that decade.[1]

The corporation provided both a fund-raising mechanism through the sale of stock and an organizational structure that enabled its managers to grow organically (internally) as well as by merger and acquisition (externally).

Organic Growth

Internal or organic growth was accomplished by corporations in the latter part of the nineteenth century in a number of ways.

Expanding the Geographic Territory

An example of expanding the geographic territory served by the corporation was the penetration of the American railroad industry into virtually every area of the country. Major cities across the entire nation had already been linked by 1910 when railroads largely completed their track systems. They then extended their reach to smaller cities and towns to expand their

Corporate Growth

Corporations had become the dominant business form by the beginning of the twentieth century, and their growth quickly accelerated. Expansion was achieved organically and externally.

Organic Growth

- Expanding the geographic territory served
- Reaching more customers through mass merchandizing
- Research and development to create new products
- Process and technology improvements to increase productivity and reduce costs

External Growth

By acquiring or merging with other companies, big businesses instantly grew larger, instantly gained market share, and in some cases instantly diversified into industries other than the one(s) in which they were already dominant. Companies that merged with and acquired other companies in the same industry (called rivals) reduced competition, increased market share, expanded and improved production and distribution capabilities to quickly achieve greater efficiencies, and ultimately their objective was to achieve dominance in that industry to be able to control prices.

business base by providing passenger and freight service to virtually every community in the country.

Mass Merchandising

A similar expansion strategy was pursued by department stores, a new form of mass merchandising that had begun in the 1850s and 1860s. Companies such as R. H. Macy and Lord & Taylor in New York City, Jordan Marsh in Boston, John Wanamaker in Philadelphia, Marshall Field in Chicago, and a little later the Emporium in San Francisco began during this period. In later decades they began building stores in other locations within the cities where their flagship stores were located, and still later they expanded to other nearby cities. These became known as chain stores. Penetration into the suburbs waited until the suburbs were developed, a phenomenon that mostly followed World War II and the second explosion of automobile ownership.[2]

Research and Development Activities

Another technique for organic growth was through product development. Some major high-technology corporations, mostly in electricity and chemistry, not only pursued product innovation strategies but also undertook expensive basic scientific research that would lead to the development of new and different products, in addition to the single product on which most of them had been founded.

By 1920, 350 corporations had research and development (R&D) activities ongoing within their own corporate structures. Because this type of research usually was conducted by universities, these large companies developed close links with those universities. Dominant players within their industries, such as AT&T in circuitry, General Electric in electronics, and DuPont in chemicals, had world-class research laboratories as well as product development centers within their companies.

AT&T. AT&T's Bell Laboratories, named for Alexander Graham Bell, the inventor of the telephone in 1876, was among the most famous for its far-reaching research activities into the nature of matter (mostly examining the structure of electrons) and was among the most prolific at developing advancements in the communications industry based on that research. Bell Labs invented the vacuum tube, the transistor, and the laser. Alcoa, which held a monopoly in the aluminum industry, conducted basic research into the nature of metal—its structure and composition—which benefited itself and the entire society.[3]

Process and Technology Improvements

Not only did large corporations grow through internally produced *product* development, they also grew through what we call today *process* improvement. Andrew Carnegie, as we have seen, introduced the latest steelmaking technology, the open hearth furnace, replacing the less efficient Bessemer converter, to maintain technological leadership over his industry rivals.

Ford Motor Company. A classic example of innovative process improvement is Henry Ford's moving assembly line. In 1913 Ford introduced this process improvement into his auto assembly factories in Dearborn, Michigan, revolutionizing the manufacturing process used throughout the world as others copied his technique. Ford fundamentally changed manufacturing as much as Eli Whitney had when, a century earlier, he invented the process of using standardized interchangeable parts that he had developed for manufacturing his cotton gin.[4]

Through improved productivity by using the moving assembly line, Ford was able to produce his cars faster and at significantly lower cost than any of his rivals. Production time was cut more than 75 percent, and production costs were reduced so much that the price of the car could be cut from $850 to $260, making it affordable even for his own workers when he introduced the $5-per-hour, 8-hour workday in 1914. This more than doubled wages and reduced the workday by 90 minutes, cutting employee turnover, which had been running at 370 percent per year. In one magnificent stroke, Henry Ford elevated his blue-collar workers to the threshold of the middle class and at the same time expanded the customer base for his product.[5]

Over the next 20 years, Ford sold 17 million cars, about half of all the cars produced in the world. In 1929 alone, all U.S. auto manufacturers produced more than 4.5 million autos, about nine times as many as Britain, France, and Germany combined. With the explosion in automobile ownership, the entire fabric of our society began to be revolutionized—suburbs were created, new industries were developed by and for the increasingly mobile middle class (massive road building, travel and tourism, auto dealerships, motels, drive-ins, gas stations, etc.). The auto changed where and how people worked and lived more than any other invention.

At the midpoint of the twentieth century, one-sixth of the U.S. economy was dependent on the automobile, making autos "the industry of industries."[6] In 2000, Henry Ford was named by *Fortune* magazine as the most important industrialist of the entire twentieth century because of the far-reaching consequences of his process improvement and his early industrial policies.

IBM. Today, process improvements usually involve technology, especially information technology (IT). The basis of the Information Age was itself a technology breakthrough: the IBM System/360. In 1966 Thomas Watson, Jr., the son of IBM's founder and CEO of the company that had commercialized the computer, was in a quandary. No common computer language existed to enable various computer companies' products to talk with other computer companies' products, and, worse of all, IBM's own systems had no common computer language, creating an incompatibility between its own products.

Determined to overcome this, Thomas Watson embarked on a $5-billion three-year gamble to create a system with a universal language to perform virtually every business task. He named it the System/360 because it had all-round compatibility—with all present and future systems. For the first time computers had a common language.[7]

Citibank. Using this technology, in 1975 Citibank (now part of Citigroup) sought ways to increase its share of the consumer banking business in New York City, which had been flat for a decade. John Reed, the brash young president of the bank, convinced his boss, the legendary CEO Walter Wriston, to invest $100 million in a new technology-based system called the automatic teller machine (ATM).

When the plan was rolled out two years later, 400 ATMs were installed throughout New York City. At first they did not catch on, but the next winter a heavy snowstorm closed most of New York's banks for days. Soon a TV commercial appeared showing people sloshing through the snow to Citibank's ATMs for cash, with the catch phrase: The Citi Never Sleeps! The machines caught on, and by 1981 Citibank's share of deposits doubled.[8]

Microsoft. Bill Gates and Paul Allen, of course, revolutionized computer language again in the late 1970s and 1980s with their Microsoft software, which became the operating system for the personal computer (PC) that IBM invented in 1981.[9] This early software was the precursor to the company's Windows operating systems, the baseline computer language used throughout the world. The success of Microsoft made Bill Gates the world's richest man within twenty years of his founding the Microsoft Corporation.

Wal-Mart Stores. Another technology application that improved internal processes resulted from a $24-million decision in 1983 by Sam Walton, the founder of Wal-Mart, to invest in a private satellite system to transmit data of all types from all its stores to headquarters and to be able to communicate from headquarters with his associates at the growing number of stores, which then numbered about 1,000.

When the system went online in 1987, Wal-Mart's sales were growing rapidly and had reached $9 billion; a decade later they had increased tenfold to $93.6 billion. In 2005, nearly 20 years later, they were at $288 billion, making Wal-Mart the largest company in the world and the largest private employer with over 1.5 million employees worldwide.[10] Wal-Mart continues to invest heavily in technology, giving it a major competitive advantage.[11]

MERGER AND ACQUISITION GROWTH

Growth from within was an important way for big businesses to grow, but it paled in comparison with growth from without—namely through mergers and acquisitions.[12] By acquiring or merging with other companies, big businesses instantly grew larger, instantly gained market share, and in some cases instantly diversified into industries other than the one(s) in which they were already dominant. As Alfred Chandler has written, "The merger movement was the most important single episode in the evolution of the modern industrial enterprise in the United States from the 1880s to the 1940s."[13]

The cost of mergers and acquisitions (M&A) was often less than the cost of organic growth, given the high cost of establishing and operating R&D facilities, the high salaries of scientists and engineers, and the heavy fixed costs of laboratory facilities and equipment needed to develop products that often failed, and the time it took from initial invention to delivery of a marketable product.

Companies merged with and acquired other companies in the same industry (called rivals) to reduce competition, increase market share, expand and improve production and distribution capabilities to quickly achieve greater efficiencies, and ultimately achieve dominance in that industry to be able to control prices. These monopolistic motives and tendencies of large firms were the reasons for the enactment of antitrust legislation and its aggressive enforcement in the first two decades of the twentieth century. With the lapse in enforcement in the 1920s, big businesses restarted their M&A strategies in an attempt to achieve these same business goals.

Two examples provide insights into the M&A process, and later we will look at General Motors as the classic example of growth by acquisition.

United States Steel

First, we have already seen how Andrew Carnegie's steel company acquired or merged with its rivals in the 1880s and 1890s to become the single largest maker of steel in the country. Later, through the trust mechanism, financed by J. P. Morgan & Company, Carnegie Steel morphed into the United States Steel Corporation, not only the world's largest maker of raw steel but also a vertically integrated corporation from the mining of iron ore, through smelting, to production of steel end items, and their distribution to end users, such as rails to railroad companies.

AT&T

Second, the precursor of the American Telephone and Telegraph Company (AT&T) was launched by Alexander Graham Bell and his business partners shortly after he invented the telephone in 1876. The firm was then called the Bell Telephone Company. Initially it had limited resources and therefore limited geographic reach, given the heavy capital requirements of stringing wires and laying in other needed equipment. Over time, the company did expand by establishing phone service into areas adjacent to its existing locations. But it soon faced newly emerging rivals that used Bell's technology.

Theodore N. Vail, as general manager of the Bell Telephone Company in the late 1890s, proposed expanding the firm into a big business to compete better. He was fired by the Boston bankers who then controlled the firm for being too ambitious. A decade later, at age sixty, he was rehired as chief executive officer because the company was going under and needed to be rescued.

Vail had a vision of providing a nationwide network of telephone service exclusively operated by what he called the Bell System. To achieve that end, he embarked on an acquisition strategy—buying or merging with one after another of the company's rivals. During the 1910s, Vail cobbled together the Bell System, a nascent nationwide telephone company, together with the Western Electric Company, the maker of Bell's telephones and wire, to form what would later become the world's largest privately held corporation.[14]

Because the Bell System was a monopoly and the need for telephone service was no longer viewed as anything other than a necessity, the federal and state governments began to regulate the company, particularly its prices. Eventually the company changed its corporate name to the American Telephone & Telegraph Company (AT&T) and continued as a regulated monopoly until its breakup in 1984 into seven "baby bells," each of the new companies handling local telephone service on a regional basis, with AT&T providing only long-distance service on a national basis. AT&T spun off two of its key parts, Bell Labs and Western Electric, to form a new company called Lucent Technologies. AT&T's long-distance revenues steadily declined as price competition intensified and customers switched to alternative technologies, e-mail and wireless.

With the enactment of the Telecommunications Act of 1996, the entire industry was deregulated. That year there were 10,000 mergers in the United States with $660 billion changing hands; four of the five largest mergers in 1996 were telephone companies.[15] The baby bells were swallowing each other up, and by 2005, only three were still standing: Bell South, the smallest, SBC Communications, and Verizon.

In 2000, AT&T was split into four companies, all of which were acquired one by one by other corporations, and AT&T itself ceased to exist as a separate company, having been acquired for $16.5 billion by one of its previous "babies," SBC Communications, which changed its name to

AT&T, Inc.[16] The demise of this venerable company thus occurred in the reverse process of the way the Bell System had been assembled a hundred years earlier by its great visionary Theodore Vail.

THE MULTIDIVISION CORPORATION

Large firms used the vehicle of the corporation during this era to grow and expand. As they grew organically from within and through merger and acquisition from without, they became so large that their existing highly centralized structures were inadequate to direct and control their expanded activities effectively.

Mere size was not the only problem they faced; diversification was another.[17] All these corporations had begun as single-product companies, such as steel and telephone communications, and their management structures were focused and organized around that product—how best to produce it, market it, and support it. With growth often came a diverse product line, and single-product management structures were inadequate to cope with the complexity of having several products, each in a different market (or different segments of the same market), having different customers.

Another reason for diversification was the fear that the single product the company had been producing might not have a robust future, and the company, to continue in business, needed other, additional products to ensure its future. The corporation thus took on a life of its own, preparing for its own perpetuation.

DUPONT'S MULTIDIVISIONAL STRUCTURE

No finer example of this diversification process exists than the DuPont chemical company.[18] Before and during World War I, E. I. du Pont de Nemours & Company was as it had been since its founding during Thomas Jefferson's presidency, primarily a maker of gunpowder and explosives. With the end of World War I, DuPont's leaders feared there would be an erosion of the market for their major product, which, of course, did happen. DuPont's leaders sought new products that could utilize the company's skills, technologies, and facilities in the peacetime era. Today, this would be called diversification utilizing core competencies. They focused on celluloid products, plastics, dyes, paints, and other coatings.

Initially this strategy had little success. The new products were being produced and marketed by the same company organization that had produced and sold explosives, despite the fact they had quite different customers and required different distribution channels. Pierre S. du Pont, the company's chief executive officer (CEO), quickly appreciated the problem and moved to correct it.

In the 1920s he crafted a new type of management structure that provided each major product line with its own general management, its own functional capabilities (such as production and marketing organizations), and its own R&D laboratories. The essence of this new concept was decentralization within the larger corporation—separate companies within the company. He called the separate operating units divisions, each with its own management structure reporting to him, the corporation's CEO. The corporate office, no longer concerned with operational issues, then became a staff function, providing overall strategic direction, coordination between divisions, auditing and tracking of the divisions' performance, and support for each operating division, which actually ran its own business.[19]

The multidivisional corporate structure created limitless opportunities for companies to grow into as many diverse industries as they chose or to operate a number of businesses within different segments of the same industry. Manufacturing corporations with diverse product lines, such as General Electric and Westinghouse, quickly adopted the multidivisional format to operate more efficiently in their various industries, such as power generators, electrical appliances, and industrial equipment. A clear example of the application of the multidivisional model to the same industry was General Motors, in which the concept was further developed and perfected.

GENERAL MOTORS INVENTS THE MODERN CORPORATION

The economic boom of the roaring 20s was largely based on the automobile. After the country recovered from World War I and the recession of 1920, it became the challenge of the automakers to fill the country's near-fanatical demand for cars. The two leading American auto manufacturers at that time, Ford and General Motors (GM), each took a different path in the race to meet that demand. They and their domestic rivals produced plenty of cars: 5,358,000 in 1929, almost as many as total U.S. production in 1953—5,700,000.

GM won this race, for reasons that will become clear, and as a result GM's was *the* growth stock to own during the 1920s. Anyone who had bought $25,000 of GM common stock in 1921 was a millionaire by 1929, when GM earned a then-staggering $200 million in profit.[20]

GENERAL MOTORS CORPORATION VERSUS FORD MOTOR COMPANY

Initially, GM was organized much like the Ford Motor Company, with the founder running the show. GM began as a corporation, but Ford did not; it was privately held, first by Henry Ford and his partners, but Ford soon bought them out, taking over total ownership to have total control. GM had a highly personalized, centralized management structure under its founder, William C. Durant, but, unlike Ford, it soon changed leaders and then divided itself into five operating divisions, each labeled with the brand name of its automobile. GM was responsible to its shareholders; Ford Motor Company was responsible to Henry Ford.

Another critical difference between the two companies was the heritage of their founders' major focus.[21] Henry Ford began in Dearborn, Michigan, as a mechanic. So when he organized his company in 1903, his focus was on production, a decade later inventing the moving assembly line, automating the factory floor as much as possible, and developing the most vertically integrated company of all time—from his own steel mills, through the fabrication of parts, their assembly, and the delivery of cars to dealers.

William Durant was a salesman who began as co-owner of a carriage-making company in Flint, Michigan. His focus was on selling the carriages through a network of dealers and agents; he let others build the carriages and put his brand name on them, Blue Ribbon. When he saw the auto threatening his carriage business, he bought the just-failed Buick Motor Company in 1904 and quickly turned it into profitability by redesigning the car, tapping into the supply chain of companies he had used in his carriage business, and using some of the same distributors and dealers. Durant hired Walter P. Chrysler to be his chief of production; Chrysler built the cars while Durant zeroed in on the company's growing organizational needs, its dealer network, and the ultimate customer, who demanded service, spare parts, and support.

In 1908 Durant's Buick Motor Company built 8,487 cars, the most of any American manufacturer; Ford, which introduced the Model T that year, produced 6,181 cars; and independently owned Cadillac, the third largest producer, made 2,380 cars. The fact that Durant's Buick had such spectacular success in just four years was largely due to his excellent sales organization. That same year, Durant forecast that the auto industry would soon explode to a half-million cars per year, and he laid plans to build the factories and the organization needed to meet that demand.

That same year he formed the General Motors Company as a holding company, which by the end of the year owned the stock in Buick, Olds, and a body maker. Soon Durant had a controlling interest in Cadillac, six other auto companies, three truck firms, and ten parts and accessory producers. In 1915, after he acquired Chevrolet, Durant turned GM into an operating company. Meanwhile, Ford focused on making the product.

The adoption in the early 1920s of the multidivisional model by General Motors was no accident. GM's chairman of the board at the time was none other than Pierre S. du Pont, the CEO of DuPont chemical company, which had recently bought 37 percent, a controlling interest, of the then-struggling car company. DuPont, fearing that there was not much growth potential in its company's own industry, decided to invest the bulk of its profits from World War I in GM.[22] And having experimented with the multidivisional model at his own company, Pierre du Pont brought that organizational structure to the attention of GM's board, which by this time was controlled by the Du Pont family.

In 1921 Ford Motor Company was the dominant producer of autos in the world with 55.6 percent of U.S. market share. GM had just 22.8 percent.[23] Ford had highly centralized management in the hands of Henry Ford. GM, having been organized by William Durant during the preceding two decades through a series of acquisitions of each car brand beginning with Buick, lacked internal coordination and production efficiency, and the recession of 1920 hit it hard. Durant had speculated wildly in the stock market in 1920, and GM's sales badly slumped.

GM's board fired Durant in November 1920, and Pierre du Pont reluctantly took over as president. He and the board approved a multidivisional organizational plan developed by Alfred P. Sloan, and in 1923 Sloan was elevated to president of GM.

SLOAN'S MANAGEMENT REVOLUTION

Under Alfred P. Sloan, General Motors Corporation not only organized itself into a multidivisional corporation, with each division having its own general management and product responsibilities; it also provided differentiation for each of its five division product lines, each brand representing a different rung on the ladder of success to the average American.[24] Even though these divisions' products overlapped somewhat, they nevertheless competed fiercely with one another. In time, Chevrolet's major competitor was not Ford but Buick.

GM developed a pricing pyramid to provide cars throughout a customer's lifetime. The Chevrolet division provided entry-level cars, and the Pontiac division gave the up-and-coming young adult a step up in prestige. The Oldsmobile division offered early middle-age managers a more prestigious family car. The Buick division provided a prestige car for the executive or professional who wanted luxury without flaunting it. Finally, the Cadillac division offered the ultimate grande luxe car for those who had arrived at the pinnacle of wealth and power.[25] Today this is called market segmentation. Each car division targeted a different market segment based on socio-economic status and assigned the product an appropriate price tag to meet the target customer's profile. As Alfred Sloan said at the time, GM offered a car "for every purse and purpose."[26]

Sloan, like Baskin-Robbins a half century later, understood that the American consumer wants choices, and he offered lots of them. The basic choice was selecting a brand that represented a buyer's socioeconomic status. The second choice was in color; Sloan offered several colors and eventually two-tone paint for GM's cars in each price category. Later, he provided a choice of options such as radios, heaters, white side-wall tires, air conditioning, and so on, each carrying an extra price. And finally Sloan offered styling—a sharp-looking car that was not only a transportation vehicle but also a symbol of what its owner wanted to project to the world about himself.

Against all this, the Ford Motor Company continued to offer a single product, the Model T and later the Model A, with no optional features and in basic black only. The Model T was reliable transportation, period. GM offered status and fun, plus transportation. Moreover, Henry Ford, stubborn to the end, refused to relinquish total control, to decentralize management, to organize his huge company like the big business it was, and to offer his customers choices.

Needless to say, GM overwhelmed Ford in the marketplace; in 1929 GM passed Ford in market share with 32.3 percent versus 31 percent.[27] Even the brand-new Chrysler Motor Company quickly passed Ford in market share, partly because Walter P. Chrysler organized his new company along Sloan's lines, on Sloan's own recommendation.[28] Within another decade Ford was reduced to an also-ran, driven within two decades from market dominance to near bankruptcy. Ford never again regained the number-one position in U.S. market share. In 2004, Toyota surpassed it, reducing it to third place.

GM'S MODEL GOES GLOBAL

Sloan turned GM's corporate office into a powerful centralized control structure that most multidivisional companies eventually copied, improving on DuPont's initially weak central office. GM's corporate staff tracked market information and consumer tastes, provided forecasts of market and economic trends, allocated resources among the divisions, and provided general corporate support in the form of legal, financial, and other administrative services.

More importantly, headquarters also closely monitored the performance of the divisions from a sales and efficiency standpoint, even inventing financial measures to perform that tracking, enabling top management to control and direct what became the world's largest corporation. Return on investment (ROI) and other financial metrics, invented at GM, became the common denominator for management to gauge the performance of disparate types of activities—from an assembly plant, to a spark plug plant, to a paint shop. How efficiently and productively each "cost center" used capital became the key measure.[29] The work of designing and building cars was being done at the five automobile divisions; how well they did it showed up in the numbers at corporate headquarters.

Under Alfred P. Sloan, General Motors Corporation developed the prototype for the modern corporation. As Peter Drucker put it in his seminal study of GM, *The Concept of the Corporation*, Sloan sought "to combine the greatest corporate unity with the greatest divisional autonomy and responsibility; and like every true federation, it aims at realizing unity through local self-government and vice versa. This is the aim of General Motors' policy of decentralization."[30] The *federation* or multidivisional model worked very well and was replicated in a host of companies throughout the world.

Procter & Gamble

The basic federative principle was applicable to other situations, such as multiproduct companies. For example, at Procter & Gamble (P&G), at which during the Great Depression advertising budgets were typically fat ($15 million per year) but sales were flat, the concept of *brand management* was invented by Neil McElroy, who later became P&G's CEO and in the 1950s was named secretary of defense by President Eisenhower.

Multibrand companies, such as P&G, had always had a problem assigning responsibility and accountability for the sales of individual brands, such as Ivory for soap and later Pepto-Bismol for upset stomachs, Crest for toothpaste, Olay for skin cream, Folgers for coffee, Tide for detergent, Iams for pet food, and so forth. But by appointing a specific team, with a single leader called the brand manager, to focus and manage all the activities associated with a particular brand, the responsibility and accountability were clear. Sales began to soar.[31]

Global Applicability

The multidivisional corporation, invented by DuPont and perfected by General Motors, at first was copied by only a few other major corporations, such as Westinghouse, General Electric, Sears, Roebuck, and Standard Oil of New Jersey. It was partially accepted by some others: General Mills, U.S. Rubber, B. F. Goodrich, and Swift & Company.

Only after World War II (1941–1945), did American industry widely adopt the multidivisional model, partly because the Great Depression (when industrial output fell by one-third) and the refocus of industry to a wartime footing for World War II interrupted organizational innovation. In the late 1940s and 1950s, it became widely accepted by such iconic firms as IBM, Alcoa, RCA, and even Ford Motor Company, which by then was incorporated and led by Henry Ford's grandson, Henry Ford II.[32] It transformed the way business was managed even over vast geographic distances, being adopted by large corporations headquartered throughout the globe.[33]

This structure allowed for the almost infinite expansion of a company into multiple products and multiple brands that target multiple customer groups. So flexible, useful, and effective was this model that it became the core idea of the conglomerate (a corporation that controlled a number of unrelated businesses) as well as the multinational corporation (a corporation based in one country and doing business in many).

American industry, and later world industry, for the half century following the 1920s, organized itself on the multidivisional model with a powerful corporate office. Practically every major corporation borrowed generously from Alfred P. Sloan's playbook.

CONCLUSION

In the early part of the twentieth century America's big businesses grew even bigger. This expansion was fueled both by internal (organic) growth and especially through mergers and acquisitions. With increased size, some of these vast corporate empires came to realize they needed new and better ways to manage themselves than the highly centralized control of their inventor-founders, such as Henry Ford.

The first major company to face this challenge was DuPont, whose chief executive officer was also the chairman of the board of General Motors. In 1923, GM made Alfred P. Sloan its president, and he introduced to the automaker a multidivisional, decentralized structure with a powerful corporate office. GM was then struggling to keep pace with the Ford Motor Company. Along with his other management innovations, Sloan quickly outstripped Ford in the marketplace, while transforming GM into the first thoroughly efficient corporation. Sloan has since been known as the father of the modern corporation.

Following World War II, the multidivisional corporate organization structure was widely adopted by other corporations in the United States and throughout the world as the appropriate model to effectively manage these firms as they grew still larger and expanded with their multiple products into multiple national markets.

NOTES

1. John Kenneth Galbraith, *The Great Crash, 1929* (Boston: Houghton Mifflin, 1979), 180.

2. Alfred D. Chandler, Jr., *Scale and Scope: The Dynamics of Industrial Capitalism* (Cambridge, MA: Harvard University Press, 1990), 59.

3. Leonard S. Reich, *The Making of American Industrial Research: Science and Business at GE and Bell, 1876–1926* (New York: Cambridge University Press, 1985); cited in George David Smith and Davis Dyer, "The Rise and Transformation of the American Corporation," in Carl Kaysen, ed., *The American Corporation Today* (New York: Oxford University Press, 1996), 41–42.

4. For a discussion of Henry Ford and Eli Whitney, see Wesley B. Truitt, *Business Planning: A Comprehensive Framework and Process* (Westport, CT: Quorum Books, 2002), 82–83, 87.

5. *Fortune*, June 27, 2005, 65.

6. For a discussion of the auto industry, see James P. Womack, Daniel T. Jones, and Daniel Roos, *The Machine That Changed the World* (New York: Rawson Associates, 1990).

7. *Fortune*, June 27, 2005, 74.

8. Ibid., 80.

9. Hale C. Bartlett, *Cases in Strategic Management for Business* (New York: Dryden Press, 1988), 89–127.

10. Ibid., 82; *Fortune,* April 18, 2005, F1; www.Wal-Mart.com/facts.

11. Anthony Bianco and Wendy Zellner, "Is Wal-Mart Too Powerful?" *Business Week,* October 6, 2003, 100–110.

12. This discussion is based on George David Smith and Davis Dyer, "The Rise and Transformation of the American Corporation," in Carl Kaysen, ed., *The American Corporation Today,* 40–43.

13. Alfred D. Chandler, Jr., *Scale and Scope,* 79.

14. Peter F. Drucker, *Management: Tasks, Responsibilities, Practices* (New York: Harper & Row, 1974), 769.

15. Shaifali Puri, "Deals of the Year," *Fortune,* February 17, 1997, 102.

16. *Wall Street Journal,* October 26, 2000, A1; December 21, 2000, A3; *Los Angeles Times,* July 21, 2005, B5.

17. Alfred D. Chandler, Jr., *Strategy and Structure: Chapters in the History of Industrial Enterprise* (Cambridge, MA: MIT Press, 1962).

18. For a discussion of DuPont's diversification, see Alfred D. Chandler, Jr., *Scale and Scope*, 181–193.

19. Alfred D. Chandler, Jr., *Strategy and Structure*, Chapter 2.

20. Paul Johnson, *Modern Times* (New York: Harper & Row, 1983), 237–238.

21. Alfred D. Chandler, Jr., *Strategy and Structure*, 114–120.

22. Peter F. Drucker, *Management*, 771.

23. Richard S. Tedlow, "Ford vs. GM," in Jack Beatty, ed., *Colossus: How the Corporation Changed America* (New York: Broadway Books, 2001), 237.

24. Alfred D. Chandler, Jr., *Strategy and Structure*, 128–144.

25. Before World War II, GM had three major groups of divisions: (1) auto and truck group, composed of the five car divisions plus GM Truck and Fisher Body, which made all the auto bodies; (2) auto parts and accessories, later spun off as Delphi Automotive; and (3) diesel engine group, making diesel engines for trucks, boats, and locomotives. See Peter F. Drucker, *The Concept of the Corporation* (New Brunswick, NJ: Transaction Publishers, 1993), 41–43.

26. Alfred P. Sloan, *My Years with General Motors* (Garden City, NY: Doubleday, 1963).

27. John Micklethwait and Adrian Wooldridge, *The Company: A Short History of a Revolutionary Idea* (New York: Modern Library, 2003), 107.

28. Peter F. Drucker, *Management*, 769.

29. Joan Magretta, *What Management Is* (New York: Free Press, 2002), 136.

30. Peter F. Drucker, *Concept of the Corporation,* 46.

31. Thomas McCraw, *American Business 1920–2000: How It Worked* (Wheeling, IL: Harlan Davidson, 2000), 48.

32. Alfred D. Chandler, Jr., *Strategy and Structure*, 342–378.

33. Richard P. Rumelt, *Strategy, Structure and Economic Performance* (Boston: Harvard University Press, 1974).

RECOMMENDED READINGS

Chandler, Alfred D., Jr., *Strategy and Structure: Chapters in the History of Industrial Enterprise* (Cambridge, MA: MIT Press, 1962).

Drucker, Peter F., *The Concept of the Corporation* (New Brunswick, NJ: Transaction Publishers, 1993).

Farber, David R., *Sloan Rules: Alfred P. Sloan and the Triumph of General Motors* (Chicago: University of Chicago Press, 2002).

Micklethwait, John, and Adrian Wooldridge, *The Company: A Short History of a Revolutionary Idea* (New York: Modern Library, 2003).

Sloan, Alfred P., *My Years with General Motors* (Garden City, NY: Doubleday, 1963).

Three

The Postmodern Corporation

The problem for many American corporations beginning in the 1970s was that they now needed a new type of structure. Why? Some companies based in other countries played the game better than they did, technology was changing rapidly, and the competition got rougher. This is the period when the modern corporation morphed into the postmodern corporation, the subject of this chapter.

BIG BUSINESSES SHAKEOUT

In 1974, the one hundred largest industrial corporations accounted for 35.8 percent of the gross domestic product of the United States. Within fifteen years that figure dropped by half to 17.3 percent. The one hundred largest companies' workforces and their corporate assets were also reduced by roughly half. What happened?

Big businesses continued to grow, but they grew more slowly than small companies, which then generated the majority of new jobs throughout the industrial world. Big businesses remained big; the average revenue of the 50 largest U.S. companies was $51 billion in 1999. But big companies in large numbers went out of business during this era through acquisition or bankruptcy; half of the *Fortune* 100 firms listed in 1974 disappeared from the *Fortune* 100 list in 2000.[1]

Airlines

Look at just one industry, the airlines.[2] During this period, 1975–2000, the following airline companies disappeared through acquisition or entered the business boneyard: Braniff, Eastern, Western, Piedmont, Pan American, PSA, Republic, and TWA. The government's airline deregulation in 1978 and the resulting industry consolidation had a Darwinian effect—only the fittest survived, and 135,000 workers lost their jobs.

The airline shakeout continues. From 2000 to 2005 the remaining "legacy" airlines (old-line carriers such as United, American, Northwest, and Delta) lost $35 billion before taxes and added $30 billion in long-term debt. Low-cost, newer airlines (such as Southwest and JetBlue) had a collective pretax profit of $2.3 billion. In 2005 half of the seats flying in the United States were owned by airlines in bankruptcy. The same year Southwest carried more passengers in the United States than any other airline—and made the highest profit.[3]

Table 3.1 is a sample of American corporations that disappeared as independent corporations through either merger, acquisition, or bankruptcy after 1955, the year Bill Gates (Microsoft) and Steve Jobs (Apple Computer) were born.[4]

During this period of time, rapid technological advancements obsolesced old industries and generated a host of new businesses; and entirely new corporations were founded, most of them based on the computer, its operating systems, and the Internet. Some of the new corporations founded after 1975 were Apple Computer, Microsoft, Dell, Sun Microsystems, Oracle, Netscape, AOL, Amazon.com, Google, Yahoo!, and so many others.

TABLE 3.1
Sample of U.S. Corporations that Disappeared, 1955–2000

Aerospace	*Autos*	*Meatpacking*	*Metals*
Curtiss-Wright	American Motors	Cudahay	Jones & Laughlin
Douglas	Nash	Iowa Meat	LTV Steel
McDonnell	Packard	Oscar Mayer	Republic Steel
Republic	Studebaker	Ralston Purina	Reynolds Metals
Consumer Products	*Oil*	*Electronics*	*Manufacturing*
General Foods	Ashland	Admiral	Champion International
Nabisco	Atlantic	Burroughs	Dresser Industries
Schlitz Brewing	Gulf	Philco	Litton Industries
Shoe Corp. of America	Richfield	RCA	Otis Elevator
Singer	Sinclair	Sperry	Union Carbide

Department Stores

One old industry that saw many of its famous companies die or consolidate was mass merchandizing retail. B. Altman, Montgomery Ward, I. Magnin, Jordan Marsh, Bullock's, E. J. Korvette, May Company, Marshall Field, Bonwit Teller, Lord & Taylor, Foley's, and Robinson's all vanished.[5] In 2005 Federated Department Stores (Macy's) acquired May Company and Kmart acquired Sears, Roebuck. Faced with hypercompetition from Wal-Mart, Target, Mervyn's, and regional discount retailers such as Kohl's on the low end of the price range and from high-end, upscale retailers such as Saks Fifth Avenue, Nordstrom, and Neiman-Marcus, these old-line companies in the middle were simply squeezed out. Only JC Penney and Macy's survived through acquisition of a host of weaker rivals.

Supermarkets

A similar pattern emerged in the retail food industry. Traditional supermarket groceries have been squeezed from below by discounters, especially Wal-Mart Stores Inc., since 2002 the nation's largest food seller, and from above by high-price stores, such as Whole Foods Market Inc., that specialize in natural foods, premium meats, and organic produce. Unable to compete particularly against Wal-Mart, Albertson's supermarket chain, the nation's second largest, put itself up for sale in 2005.

The plight of the traditional supermarket is exemplified by A&P, the company that invented the industry. The Great Atlantic & Pacific Tea Company was founded in New York City in 1859 as a tea, coffee, and spice emporium. It expanded into a full-line market and at its peak in the 1930s operated a chain of 16,000 stores, the largest in the nation. By 2005 it had been reduced to 325 stores in the mid-Atlantic region, plus 235 in Canada and a few in New Orleans. A&P is a chronic money loser, and its parent company, Tengelmann Group of Germany, announced it would shed nearly half its remaining stores in a major restructuring.[6]

New Industries

Some of the companies that emerged in the latter two decades of the twentieth century founded entirely new industries, such as personal computers, represented by Dell; software, represented by Microsoft; Internet communications, represented by Netscape,[7] AOL, and Oracle; online auctions represented by eBay; online retailing represented by Amazon.com.; and online stock trading, represented by E*Trade and Ameritrade. These new companies generated wealth for Bill Gates, Michael Dell, and Larry Ellison as great or greater than that which the first Industrial Revolution made for its leaders—Rockefeller, Carnegie, and Vanderbilt.

FIVE CHANGES IN THE ENVIRONMENT

Beginning in the 1970s the world changed in at least five dramatic ways, fundamentally altering the external business environment companies faced.

1. The international financial system that was erected following World War II based on the Bretton Woods Agreement was dismantled in 1971; individual national currencies were no longer tied either to gold or to the U.S. dollar. That system had provided global stability and was one of the key reasons for the spectacular growth in world trade and national incomes during the preceding quarter century.

Since 1971 currencies have "floated" against one another without external controls. Currencies became something like commodities, having a market value. Central banks, such as the U.S. Federal Reserve, occasionally intervene to prevent major instabilities, but there are times, such as the massive Asian financial crisis of 1998, when currencies do collapse.

2. Also in 1970–1971, President Nixon instituted a wage/price freeze to stabilize the U.S. economy in the face of the first oil shocks, and he devalued the dollar, making U.S. goods temporarily more competitive on world markets. These moves signaled the fact that the United States was no longer economically dominant and now, for the first time in more than a quarter century, was in a truly competitive worldwide marketplace.

3. Europe was beginning to gain competitiveness with U.S. companies as the European Common Market (today called the European Union) institutions took hold and Western Europe became a single integrated market able to compete with the immense American domestic market. The European Union continued to expand its membership and in 2005 grew to include twenty-five countries, having a GDP similar in size to that of the United States.

4. Japan emerged again as a major player on the world stage. Its companies, backed by their large banks and the government, took the worldwide lead in a number of key industries: consumer electronics, steel, shipbuilding, and increasingly autos. By 2000, Japan's steel and shipbuilding industries were passed by those of other countries, but its dominance in consumer electronics and its rising dominance in autos were clearly apparent.

5. Technology changes began to alter fundamentally the way business was done, the value of assets changed (brains became more valuable than factories), real-time global communications and competition had become

a reality, and the speed by which decisions had to be made to remain competitive in this new, hypercompetitive global business environment accelerated.

Eastman Kodak Company

An example of the devastating impacts Japanese competition and changing technology had on a company is Eastman Kodak. This industry leader, whose core business for 125 years was making and processing cameras and film, was overtaken by new technologies—first video cameras, then digital cameras, and later camera phones. Its chief rivals were based in Japan: Fuji Film undercut Kodak's film sales. Film-camera sales declined faster than the company had expected, even sales of single-use cameras: 20 percent projected versus 31 percent actual decline in 2004 alone. Kodak's losses mounted, its debt sunk to *junk* status, and its dividend was slashed. Reflecting its decline, Kodak had previously been removed as one of the thirty components of the Dow Jones Industrial Average.

Hoping developing countries would still be a strong market for film cameras, Kodak built a $500-million factory in China. The Chinese however quickly moved past even digital cameras, most of which were made by Japanese companies, to camera phones, and Kodak's strategy failed there in just six years. As a result, Kodak wrote off the Chinese investment, shuttered about two-thirds of its worldwide manufacturing assets, and laid off about one-third of its 64,000 workers worldwide. Within one year its 2004 major restructuring plan had already failed.[8] In 2005, when the company lost $1.3 billion, Kodak's chairman/CEO retired amid the painful shift to digital.[9]

Summary

Corporations have had to adjust to all five of these fundamental changes in their external environments by altering their internal management structures, as well as their products and business relationships with other companies. Alfred Sloan's multidivisional model became increasingly irrelevant because it was too slow paced, too bureaucratic, too expensive with its multiple hierarchical layers of management, and not entrepreneurial enough to develop new products and processes quickly enough to keep pace with leaner competitors. Drastic changes in structure and management were needed to enable companies to compete in this fundamentally new, hypercompetitive, global environment.

These five factors underlay changes in the external environment, demanding equally fundamental changes in the ways companies faced the world. Some companies adapted, such as GE and IBM, yet others did not adapt quickly enough, such as Kodak and its previous archrival Polaroid, which went bankrupt.

FOUR CHANGE AGENTS

Between 1975 and 2000 four specific factors powerfully motivated changes in ways companies did business: Wall Street, Japanese management, Silicon Valley, and the government.[10]

WALL STREET

The cozy relationships that large investment bankers, stock brokerage houses, and money center bankers on Wall Street had with corporate America began to change in unexpected ways.

Over the years these financial firms had supported and financed decisions made by corporations' management, and the owners of the corporations, the shareholders, were mostly ignored. The key link was Wall Street to the executive suite. Main Street was hardly even considered.

How did this happen? Over the previous century, stock ownership in American corporations expanded from the wealthy few to the point where, by the 1970s, a large percentage of U.S. households began to own stock, either directly as investors in particular companies or most often as members of mutual funds or, later, as employees investing in their companies' savings plans, especially 401(k) stock savings plans.

Wide-scale stock ownership left the decision-making firmly in the hands of the corporations' management, not the shareholders, because ownership was so widely dispersed. Control cannot be concentrated in many hands, only a few; and corporate executives were free to make decisions about their companies without much concern about stockholders, who were largely submissive to corporate management anyway.

This state of affairs began to change after the 1970s for four main reasons.

First, by 1980 big institutional investment organizations owned at least one-third of all the shares on the major stock exchanges, and by 2000 they owned more than 60 percent. Who were these institutions? The largest were pension funds for state and county employees, such as the largest of all: the California Public Employees Retirement System (CalPERS), which in 2006 had a $194 billion global portfolio.[11] These public (county and state) pension fund managers controlled 30 percent of all shares actually traded on the New York Stock Exchange by the year 2000.

Their influence was so great that they began to threaten CEOs with "perform or die." Owing to the fact that these institutions controlled such large blocks of stock in blue-chip corporations, they could not easily sell their investment stakes. So their managers decided to force corporate executives to improve their companies' financial performances or face the consequences.

For example, CalPERS owned 7.2 million shares of General Motors in the early 1990s when GM began losing billions. After repeatedly urging GM to improve performance, the manager of CalPERS finally gave GM's board an ultimatum: fire the CEO, Roger Stempel, and replace him with a faster-moving executive, or CalPERS would dump its GM stock. GM's board fired the CEO, the first coup at GM since Pierre du Pont fired William Durant in 1920. Other poor performing companies' CEOs soon followed Stempel out the door: those at IBM, Westinghouse, Kodak, and American Express.[12]

The second largest institution was mutual funds, whose fund managers invest the savings of their members to get the highest possible growth and return. Fidelity, Vanguard, T. Rowe Price, and other mutual funds' managers developed such clout on the stock exchanges that they became TV celebrities, such as Peter Lynch of Fidelity, offering their sage advice as to which stocks to buy and which to dump. One of the largest institutional mutual funds is TIAA-CREF, which has $350 billion in assets under its management.[13] Fund managers bought and sold stock so quickly, based on companies' performance, that the daily volume on the New York Stock Exchange grew from 27 billion shares traded in 1985 to 262 billion in 2000, and growing. Corporations turning in poor quarterly profit reports would see their stock trashed the next day.

A third factor also emerged that brought terror into the hearts of those in elegant executive suites: corporate raiders. Wealthy individuals such as T. Boone Pickens, Carl Icahn, and Kirk Kerkorian placed huge bets on poor performing stock, buying low hoping to sell high, after they took over the management of companies and improved performance, usually through massive layoffs.

These were usually *hostile takeovers*, prompting corporate managers to erect defenses against the raiders (for example, incorporating in Delaware, which offered a phalanx of protections for management), while they tried to improve performance. Soon 90 percent of the largest American companies were incorporated in Delaware as a defensive move. If raiders improve shareholder value, it is usually only for the short run; they are certainly not good for the economy as a whole, according to Peter Drucker, the father of modern management.[14]

A fourth factor was another scary form of raider that emerged, the private-equity leverage buyout firm, known as an LBO. Companies such as Kohlberg Kravis Roberts (KKR), formed in 1976 by three bankers from

Bear Stearns, bought stock in companies, borrowing heavily to do so; took over the management of the firms once they gained control; and later sold the stock at a higher price. KKR's first ventures were taking over Beatrice Foods for $8.7 billion and Safeway for $4.8 billion. After takeover it would reduce payrolls (at Safeway it cut 63,000 jobs) and realign management to improve overall company financial performance.

KKR's legendary deal was RJR Nabisco.[15] The R. J. Reynolds tobacco company had merged with Nabisco, the large food company, to form this new, diversified company. In 1988, KKR in the largest private-equity deal ever invested only $1.5 billion of its own money and borrowed the rest to pay $25 billion for control of RJR Nabisco. It then installed Louis Gerstner as CEO, who quickly cut costs, streamlined management, and turned the company around. His performance was so stellar, RJR Nabisco's stock price rose dramatically, as did Gerstner's own star. Within a few years he was asked to perform the same turnaround feat at IBM.

These four Wall Street techniques were somewhat successful in stimulating America's corporate behemoths to reform, to streamline to become more competitive, and to pay attention to their owners, the shareholders. For the most part, however, only a few companies with energetic management paid attention, such as General Electric and eventually IBM. Many others built a protective moat around their corporate fortresses, using every antitakeover device the state of Delaware permitted.

JAPANESE MANAGEMENT

Companies that ignored pressures to change stemming from Wall Street could scarcely ignore the invasion of Japanese firms and their products. The latest management techniques were embraced by Japanese firms, such as quality circles, shared decision-making with suppliers and employees, integrated product development teams, and a laser-like focus on customer tastes and desires.

Within a decade or two, these high-performance companies decimated American companies in consumer electronics, steel, autos, and other high-profit industries, gaining the commanding heights of industrial leadership. By the early 1990s they appeared to threaten the very existence of many of America's major industries. Japan had become the world's second largest economy with a gross domestic product of $5 trillion.

At the end of the twentieth century, the country that a half century before had been pulverized during World War II and had lost its overseas empire, discovered its own new, more durable form of empire—global industrial leadership and the profits it brought home to Tokyo. Japanese firms had become world leaders in consumer electronics (Matsushita's brand, Panasonic, was number one), autos (in 2004 Toyota was number two in the United States and number three in world), communications (Nippon Telegraph and Telephone was the largest in the world), and computer chips and applications (Hitachi was the largest in the world).[16]

Taking the automobile as an example, this had become a global industry. Toyota emerged as a titan, based on its styling, high quality standards, lean manufacturing systems, and aggressive marketing, and it now challenges General Motors for the number-one position in the world marketplace. Meanwhile, GM was still foundering; its share of the U.S. auto market dropped from 35.8 percent in 1989 to 26.2 percent in 2005, and it reported the loss of $8.6 billion in 2005.[17] Toyota had already passed Ford as number two in the United States in 2004. Chrysler had had to seek a federal government bailout in 1980 to remain in business; it recovered with new designs and reduced overhead costs, only to be bought out by Daimler-Benz in 1998 for $42 billion to form DaimlerChrysler.[18]

Despite these successes, for Japan as a whole and for many Japanese companies the dozen or so years following 1991 were a time of trouble. The country entered a period of deflation, the reverse of inflation, in which there is a decline in the general level of prices for goods and services in the domestic economy. This corrosive condition eroded property values, corporate profits, employment levels, consumer confidence, and produced a general malaise that hung over the country. As late as 2005, consumer prices fell by 0.1 percent, and the Bank of Japan predicted at least one more year of this hobbling effect on the Japanese economy.[19]

What had happened? Japanese corporate boards and management had been used to ignoring their shareholders, favoring instead other company stakeholders: their own managers, their suppliers, their banks, and their distribution channels. Except for some leading companies, many others had lost their competitive edge; their investors put no pressure on company management to produce financial benefits for them. Without this external discipline, many companies were mired in inaction.

SILICON VALLEY

This nongeographic term characterizes the area south of San Francisco that is centered on Stanford University and the city of Santa Clara. A local technology writer gave the area its name, using the substructure of memory chips as the basis for the name.

Since the late 1930s this area had been a breeding ground for technology, the place where Bill Hewlett and Dave Packard, two Stanford engineering students, set up shop in Hewlett's rented garage in Palo Alto to make their first invention in 1938. After that time, it remained a fertile field for new start-ups. Steve Jobs and Steve Wozniak, in 1976, started Apple Computer in the Jobs's family garage, mirroring the start of Hewlett-Packard (H-P) four decades earlier.

The unique thing about Silicon Valley was and is that it is the home of a large number of high-technology businesses, both big and small, that has spun off innovations, products, other companies, and whole new industries at a faster rate than ever before in history. The ideas and inventions that stemmed from this beehive of activity is legendary—memory chips, microprocessors, the Internet, and all types of electronic devices that were increasingly miniaturized. This was and remains "the most dynamic industry cluster in the world."[20]

Silicon Valley also created a new mind-set that has spread to all high-tech industries throughout much of the world. It could be called hyperentrepreneurship. This new corporate culture eagerly tried out new ideas, hoped for success but accepted failure, and then went on to try again. Every day was casual day, suits and neckties were not worn, and a relaxed attitude toward invention and exploitation was evident everywhere.

An example is how the semiconductor industry was formed. The "traitorous eight" left Shockley Laboratories in 1957 (William Shockley had invented the transistor and won the Nobel Prize for it) to form Fairchild Semiconductor, Inc., which later spawned Intel and an additional thirty-six companies over the next few years. These eight people were the archetypes of the independent thinkers who knew no bounds—they looked for no corporate security and gave no loyalty to their present employer. They had ideas, were determined to exploit them, and wanted to make money and enjoy themselves while doing it. This whole picture would have been unimaginable to Alfred P. Sloan.

According to the Silicon Valley mind-set, age, education, nationality, and family ties were not factors. What counted were ability, ideas, drive, follow-through, and success. (One-third of the valley's residents were foreign born in 2001.) This true meritocracy rewarded entrepreneurship. The walls of multidivision, professionally managed corporate behemoths were destined to crumble in the face of this relentless pursuit of creativity and drive by the best and brightest.

THE GOVERNMENT

Adding to the unsettled atmosphere in corporate America sparked by these three change factors were actions emanating from another quarter—

government. Government produced two opposite and competing trends: one stimulated entrepreneurship by loosening the bonds of governmental control over business through a series of deregulations of key industries with the intent to increase competitiveness and reduce prices for consumers. The other trend went in the reverse direction; it was a major increase in government regulation of how companies operated, making the job of managing even small firms more difficult and greatly adding to their operating costs.

Deregulation

Let us look first at deregulation. It began in the United States during the presidency of Gerald Ford, when, in 1975, he began to deregulate the energy industry with the enactment of the Energy Policy and Conservation Act. This act mandated the decontrol of petroleum products within six years.

Every administration after Ford's continued deregulation on an industry-by-industry basis. In 1978 Carter began deregulation of the airline industry and in 1980 trucking and railroads. Reagan completed deregulation in these industries and in 1985 abolished the airlines' regulatory agency, the Civil Aeronautics Board. George H. W. Bush continued the policy, laying the groundwork for Clinton's legislation that completed deregulation in telecommunications in 1996 and banking in 1999.[21]

Thus, for twenty-five years, deregulation was a bipartisan policy of the U.S. government. It not only reduced companies' operating costs but also vastly increased competition, forcing poor performers to reform or exit the business.

Regulation

The second trend, in the opposite direction, increased government regulation of how companies operated. This was essentially *social* regulation at both the federal and state level. Oddly, a Republican administration initiated this new wave of regulation with a host of new social legislation.

Beginning with Richard Nixon, the federal government penetrated deeper into the inner workings of private business than it had since Franklin Roosevelt's New Deal in the 1930s. This vast increase in regulatory oversight began in 1969 with a piece of landmark legislation, the National Environmental Policy Act, and the following year Congress established the Environmental Protection Agency (EPA). These were the first of more than a dozen acts of Congress tightening controls on the ways companies produced their products with respect to putting emissions into the air, lakes, rivers, and groundwater and regulating the impacts of companies' processes and products on forests, endangered species, drinking water, coastal zones, and the like.

In 1970 President Nixon signed laws establishing the National Highway Traffic Safety Administration, to establish and enforce highway safety standards, and the Occupational Safety and Health Administration (OSHA), which established regulations to ensure that workplaces are healthy and not hazardous to employees. In 1972 Nixon signed the Consumer Product Safety Commission Act to protect consumers from hazardous products. In 1977 President Carter signed the Mine Safety and Health Administration Act to establish and enforce mine safety regulations.

The five agencies created over this seven-year period came to employ 19,000 federal workers, all devoted to monitoring private industry to enforce the regulations they imposed on it. By the late 1990s, when the wave of new regulations and their enforcement agencies was completed, there were 53 major federal agencies and commissions with 126,000 employees writing regulations and enforcing them; the cost of these agencies was $17 billion per year.[22]

The cost of compliance for America's businesses with this growing list of regulations is staggering. A government study in 1995 concluded the cost of compliance with all federal and state regulations was $395 billion that year. This included equipment needed to comply with clean air standards, water pollution control, and the like, plus the salaries of workers needed to file reports to government agencies (e.g., EPA and OSHA), tax preparation, and related paperwork. The average cost for smaller companies (fewer than 500 employees) was $5,000 per employee and for larger companies (over 500 workers) was $3,400 per employee.[23]

Governmental intrusion into the private sector was not finished with the establishment of these new regulatory agencies. When corporate scandals began to surface in 1999–2000, the public was enraged and demanded that government tighten regulations against future Enrons, WorldComs, and the like. This set of issues is the subject of corporate governance, chapter 9.

SUMMARY

These four change agents—Wall Street, Japanese management, Silicon Valley, and government—together with the five longer-term changes in the external business environment, confronted corporations in the United States and in Europe with a startling new set of challenges. Some large corporations ignored these pressures to change at their peril, such as Kodak and General Motors, and others faced up to the new realities and promptly

---

The Four Agents of Change

Beginning in the 1970s, four major factors affected the fundamental ways in which corporations were managed.

Wall Street. The cozy relationships that large investment bankers, stock brokerage houses, and money center bankers on Wall Street had with corporate America began to change in unexpected ways. Institutional investors, mutual funds, and corporate raiders were among the new players whose ownership of large amounts of corporations' stock exerted greater pressure on corporate leaders and managers.

Japanese Management. Only thirty years after World War II, Japanese businesses emerged on the global scene, employing the latest management techniques, such as quality circles, shared decision-making with suppliers and employees, integrated product development teams, and a laser-like focus on customer tastes and desires. Within two decades, these high-performance companies had decimated American companies in consumer electronics, steel, autos, and other high-profit industries.

Silicon Valley. A region south of San Francisco became home to a large number of high-technology businesses, both big and small, that spun off innovations, products, other companies, and whole new industries at a faster rate than ever before in history.

Government Deregulation and Regulation. Government produced two opposite and competing trends: one stimulated entrepreneurship by loosening the bonds of governmental control over business through a series of deregulations; meanwhile, there was an increase in government regulation of how companies operated, making the job of managing even small firms more difficult and greatly adding to their operating costs.

---

began to deal with them.[24] Outstanding examples of the latter are General Electric and Nike.

THE RESTRUCTURED CORPORATION

Faced with these external environmental and change agent pressures, how did corporations respond? They restructured the way they were organized and emphasized internal entrepreneurship. The old Alfred Sloan model was scrapped. Two new models emerged: one put authority and accountability into the hands of autonomous operating units that were highly focused on specific customers, and the other emerged as the networked corporation. There were two complimentary motivations behind both approaches: adopt a strategy that put decision-making closer to the customer and reduce operating costs.

Autonomous Operating Units

Beginning in the 1980s, large Sloan-like corporations began to "unbundle" specific activities into semiautonomous units that focus on particular products for particular customers. These units go by different names at different companies: strategic business units, operating units, sectors, or lines of business. They are bound to the corporate headquarters but also make their own decisions and are held accountable for them.

Operating units were given many of the roles and authorities formerly played by the corporate headquarters: planning, marketing, financing, hiring/firing, product development, and so forth. Corporate headquarters performed a more strategic role, as well as the overall financial role. Thus, operating units were given power and accountability for their own profit and loss. These are also known as *P&L centers*.

Companies everywhere fragmented their operations. Aetna set up 15 separate operations, AT&T 22, and Johnson & Johnson carved out 150. ABB Ltd., a multinational electrical engineering firm based in Switzerland with 240,000 employees worldwide, set up 4,500 profit/loss centers, averaging only 50 employees in each.[25] In 2005 ABB announced another reorganization, breaking up its two main divisions into five in an attempt to tap growth markets in Asia and the United States; two of the divisions will be based in Connecticut and Shanghai.[26]

The breakup of formerly centralized structures resulted in reduced staff size at corporate headquarters. IBM is an example: its corporate staff shrunk from 5,100 to 3,900 during the 1990s. It even considered selling its headquarters building. As one IBM senior vice president stated, "Our view of corporate headquarters is that there should be as little of it as possible."[27]

The philosophy behind this new model was that decision-making should be made at the lowest possible level of the company by the people who know the customer's needs and wants the best. Compressing and flattening the corporation from that level of decision-maker to the CEO was the goal; that is, from bottom to top. The old Sloan model had layers and layers of management between the customer-connected manager at the bottom and the top executives, who held the decision authority in their own hands. (Henry Ford never let it go.) Full decentralization of authority was the motto, with accountability at the end of each quarter.

Companies were broken up to make decision-making faster, to gain greater focus on particular market segments, and generally to make their core activities more competitive. To concentrate on its core auto and truck business, GM sold off its locomotive unit (Electro-Motive), its data processing company (EDS), its aerospace company (Hughes Aircraft), and its

Delphi parts division to form a new $28 billion corporation, Delphi Automotive, Inc. Ford did the same thing with its parts operation, Visteon Corporation. AT&T broke up into four companies, too late to save the parent company.

Marriott broke itself into two separate companies: Marriott International (the hotel management company that operates 2,700 hotels) and Host Marriott (the real estate trust that owns 107 hotels).[28] In its restructure, Starwood Hotels sold a large number of its 140 owned hotels (operated under the Sheraton, Westin, St. Regis, and W brands) to Host Marriott.[29] Microsoft stayed together as a company but split into three operating divisions, each headed by a president: platform products and services, business, and entertainment and devices.[30] Divestiture and restructure became the order of the day.

GTE

GTE is a good example. This old-line telephone company, now part of Verizon, had 230,000 workers at its peak in the early 1970s. Through divestitures, plant closings, and layoffs, it consolidated to one-third that size 20 years later. During that time it restructured its work processes, giving lowest-level managers the power to perform in the new and more competitive environment.[31] Getting costs out meant getting people out. Layers of middle management were eliminated throughout American industry.

Empowerment was also extended to the factory floor. Borrowing from Japanese quality circles and other management practices, American companies extended to foremen and other line supervisors the power to manage the production process within clear-cut guidelines. Once again, the idea was to push decision-making to the lowest possible level of the company, and the factory floor was just that.

As a result the number of people employed by the largest corporations diminished for the first time in a hundred years—by half. In the 1970s the *Fortune* 100 companies employed 20 percent of all nonagricultural workers; just twenty years later they employed only 10 percent. Employment growth in the American economy occurred at smaller firms and start-ups, more than making up for the losses at the giant corporations.

General Electric Company

Among the first American corporations to see the emerging threats in the world environment and to recognize that draconian changes were needed to meet them was General Electric.[32] It chose the autonomous operating unit strategy.

In 1980 Reginald Jones, GE's chairman and CEO, faced the most difficult decision of his long tenure in that position: choosing a successor to face up to the new challenges he foresaw. Following an almost legendary evaluation and selection process, Jones chose Jack Welch to succeed him. Why? Welch saw the need, as did Jones and few others, for fundamental changes at GE. Jones also saw that Welch was a change-agent leader.

Welch was hardly anyone's favorite to take over GE. He was relatively young, brash, edgy, passionate, and fiercely determined. These were not the suave, statesman-like qualities GE's CEOs typically had. But what the courtly Englishman Jones saw in fiery Boston Irishman Welch was that these were exactly the personal qualities needed to pull GE through the dark days ahead.

When Welch took over as GE's CEO in 1981, its sales were $25 billion, and its profits were about $1.5 billion. GE had always been recognized as one of the icons of American industry, having been founded by Thomas A. Edison nearly a century before. Indeed, GE was the only company listed on the Dow Jones Industrial Average that had been there from the beginning. What could possibly disturb the success of such a powerful, almost legendary company? Plenty, said Jones and Welch.

The challenges Welch identified made a long list. He saw the changes in the world and realized GE was not meeting the challenge. Many of the hundreds of operating units within GE were poor performers in their industry segments, overall costs were too high, there was a bloated bureaucracy, some products were increasingly irrelevant, and there was little spirit of entrepreneurship anywhere in the company. He also saw the rise of Asian manufacturing that was eating the lunch of company after company in America. In 1981 GE was viewed as an icon of industry, but it was an icon covered with dust with little life in it.

Welch set out to change all that. He put sparks of energy into the firm, reorganized its businesses by scrapping the Alfred Sloan model, weeded out poor performers, both individuals and businesses, restructured the company into thirteen business groups, and remade the company into a global powerhouse able to compete with anyone, anywhere. He initiated simple strategies any of his operating units could grasp: be number one in your industry or number two (having a chance to become number one), or "fix it, sell it, or close it." Welch's philosophy was simplicity itself: if you can't compete, don't.

In the twenty years under Welch, GE went from an internal atmosphere of a funeral parlor to that of an electric oven, sparks flying everywhere. Under him sales increased to $125 billion, profits soared to $10 billion, and GE's market capitalization became the largest of any company in the world.

Welch saved GE and transformed it into an even mightier powerhouse, a restructured postmodern corporation.

NETWORKED COMPANIES: NIKE

Philip Knight, cofounder of Nike, originated the idea for a new type of business model in the 1960s called a *networked* company. The idea was later picked up by many others; the largest user of the concept today is Dell, Inc., which adopted this model at its founding in the early 1980s.

The basic idea of a networked company is that it owns little or nothing of its own processes. It buys virtually everything from other companies and forms a network of those companies' activities that it manages.[33] Networking is exactly the opposite of a vertically integrated company, such as Ford Motor Company in the 1920s—owning *everything* from the raw iron ore, through the entire production process, to the delivery of the completed auto to dealerships.

Phil Knight wanted to own *nothing*. Nike's business is designing and marketing sports apparel, beginning with athletic shoes, inventing the use of celebrity sports figures to endorse its products, such as Michael Jordan and Tiger Woods who wear the ubiquitous swoosh logo. Nike developed an expertise in supplier management that allows it to keep focused on its core activities and produce its products at the lowest possible cost, allowing it to generate fat margins.

Here's how it works. At its leased headquarters in Beaverton, Oregon, Nike managers and creative people design athletic footwear and other sports apparel. They then transmit the designs electronically to mills, cutters, and assemblers in low-cost locations mostly in East and Southeast Asia, where the work is outsourced at over forty factories, mostly owned by Korean and Taiwanese companies. United Parcel Service delivers the piece parts from one supplier to another in the work process and then delivers the finished products to retailers' warehouses and distribution centers around the globe. Payments are made electronically using VISA International. The entire process is managed from Oregon, where none of the work is performed except design and management oversight.

The supplier companies throughout the entire process are networked with one another electronically, with management control from the top in Oregon. *All* manufacturing, distribution, and financial transactions are outsourced to others. Nike owns nothing but manages everything. There is nothing traditional in the way Philip Knight designed and operates this breakthrough business model that supports his cutting-edge marketing and hip fashion designs.

Is it successful? From its founding through the late 1990s, Nike experienced an astonishing 49 percent growth per year. In 2004 Nike had sales of $14 billion and 36 percent of market share of the U.S. athletic-footwear market, which accounts for half of the $33 billion spent worldwide each year on athletic shoes. It biggest rivals, Adidas and Reebok, had 8.9 percent and 12.2 percent of the U.S. market, respectively. Total sales in 2004 at Adidas, based in Germany, were $8.1 billion and at Reebok, based in Massachusetts, were about $4.0 billion. Adidas announced its intention to acquire Reebok to strengthen its hand against Nike.[34]

CONCLUSION

By the 1970s, the prevailing multidivisional corporate organizational structure of the modern corporation was becoming obsolete. This bureaucracy-heavy, slow-paced structure was not capable of facing the fundamental changes that had emerged by the last quarter of the twentieth century. Firms that failed to address these long-term trends and some shorter-term challenges were acquired or disappeared into the corporate graveyard.

Others that did face them reorganized, grew, and thrived, becoming restructured postmodern corporations, GE being one of these. A new business model also emerged, the networked company, invented by Nike. This fundamentally new type of company was based on a whole new structure—managing a global supply chain of activities that supported its core purpose, in Nike's case sports apparel design and marketing. GE and Nike moved to the top of their game and became dominant world-class players.

NOTES

1. Nitin Nohria, Davis Dyer, and Frederick Dalzell, *Changing Fortunes: Remaking the Industrial Corporation* (New York: Wiley, 2002), 4, 24; cited in John Micklethwait and Adrian Wooldridge, *The Company: A Short History of a Revolutionary Idea* (New York: Modern Library, 2003), 129–130.

2. *New York Times*, September 15, 2005, C1; *Wall Street Journal*, September 19, 2005, A1, A8.

3. *Wall Street Journal*, September 19, 2005, A1.

4. www.Fortune.com/500/archive.

5. *Wall Street Journal*, September 21, 2005, A15.

6. Ibid., May 11, 2005, B3.

7. *Fortune*, July 25, 2005, 144–170.

8. *Wall Street Journal*, July 21, 2005, A3.

9. Ibid., May 12, 2005, A3; *Los Angeles Times*, January 31, 2006, C3.

10. This section is largely based on John Micklethwait and Adrian Wooldridge, *The Company*, 132–151.

11. *Wall Street Journal*, February 6, 2006, A9.

12. Ibid., 138.

13. *Wall Street Journal*, September 1, 2005, C13.

14. Peter F. Drucker, "The Hostile Takeover and Its Discontents," in Jack Beatty, ed., *Colossus: How the Corporation Changed America* (New York: Broadway Books, 2001), 396–402.

15. *Wall Street Journal*, January 9, 2006, C1.

16. *Fortune*, July 25, 2005, 119.

17. *Business Week*, May 9, 2005, 93; *Wall Street Journal*, January 7, 2006, A1; January 27, 2006, A3.

18. *Los Angeles Times*, January 2, 1999, C1.

19. *Wall Street Journal*, April 29, 2005, A15; November 19, 2005, A8.

20. John Micklethwait and Adrian Wooldridge, *The Company*, 144.

21. For a discussion of U.S. deregulation, see Wesley B. Truitt, *What Entrepreneurs Need to Know about Government* (Westport, CT: Praeger, 2004), 29–32.

22. Murray L. Weidenbaum, *Business and Government in the Global Marketplace,* 7th ed. (Upper Saddle River, NJ: Pearson Prentice Hall, 2004), 32–35.

23. U.S. Small Business Administration, "The Changing Burden of Regulation, Paperwork, and Tax Compliance on Small Business: A Report to Congress," October 1995.

24. Regarding General Motors, see "Why GM's Plan Won't Work," *Business Week*, May 9, 2005, 85–93.

25. Michael Useem, "Corporate Education and Training," in Carl Kaysen, ed., *The American Corporation Today* (New York: Oxford University Press, 1996), 297.

26. *Wall Street Journal*, September 7, 2005, A12.

27. *New York Times*, January 13, 1993, A1, cited in Michael Useem, "Corporate Education and Training," in Carl Kaysen, ed., *The American Corporation Today*, 298.

28. *Business Week*, September 26, 2005, 70.

29. *Wall Street Journal*, September 1, 2005, A12.

30. Ibid., September 21, 2005, A3.

31. Michael Useem, "Corporate Education and Training," in Carl Kaysen, ed., *The American Corporation Today,* 299.

32. This account of General Electric is largely taken from Jack Welch, *Jack: Straight from the Gut* (New York: Warner Books, 2001).

33. This discussion is based on Kenichi Ohmae, lecture to faculty at Anderson Graduate School of Management, UCLA, February 11, 1997. See also Kenneth Labich, "Nike vs. Reebok, a Battle for Hearts, Minds & Feet," *Fortune*, September 18, 1965, 90.

34. *Wall Street Journal*, August 3, 2005, A1, A6; August 4, 2005, A1.

RECOMMENDED READINGS

Baker, George P., and George David Smith, *The New Financial Capitalists: Kohlberg Kravis Roberts & Co. and the Creation of Corporate Value* (New York: Cambridge University Press, 1998).

Nohria, Nitin, Davis Dyer, and Frederick Dalzell, *Changing Fortunes: Remaking the Industrial Corporation* (New York: Wiley, 2002).

Four

Benefits of the Corporation

Corporations provide numerous benefits not offered by other business entities. This chapter compares and contrasts these attributes with those of the other major business forms. Moreover, corporations provide economic benefits to our economy and to society, and this chapter summarizes them, along with offering a discussion of corporate profits. Also summarized are the benefits corporations provide to their employees to attract and retain good quality workers, along with executive compensation. A discussion of two key employee benefits, health care and pensions, is also included because their costs have become critical issues for companies and for our society.

TYPES OF LEGAL ENTITIES

There are six major types of legal entities that can be chosen as the way to organize a business:

- sole proprietorship
- partnership
- limited partnership (LP)
- limited liability partnership (LLP)
- limited liability company (LLC)
- corporation (Inc.)

The entity you choose is a critical decision because significant legal, business, regulatory, and tax consequences result from your selection. The pros and cons of each type are addressed next.[1]

FACTORS THAT DRIVE THE CHOICE

The inherent nature of the business you intend to operate will help drive your decision. Some businesses have large capital requirements, thus arguing for a corporation because of its ability to raise money. Other businesses carry high liability risks to their owners, arguing for either a corporation, a limited liability partnership, or a limited liability company. Others are low-risk/low-capital types of companies, arguing for sole proprietorship or partnership. Some business types have large marketing requirements, which may best be addressed by a franchise; yet the franchise company needs to have a business form itself, which will likely be best as a limited liability company or corporation because of its liability protection features.

The differences between these six types center on the speed, convenience, and cost to establish the company; liability exposure; financing requirements; the tax consequences of each type; and the operating requirements for each (such as financial reporting, government regulatory approvals, keeping minutes of meetings, etc.).

Only one of these six entities has federal government regulatory requirements and consequences: a corporation that issues stock. All the others, including the corporation, are governed by state law and state regulators. Franchises, incidentally, are also regulated by federal law through the Federal Trade Commission; because franchising is not a business entity per se, it will not be addressed here.[2]

SOLE PROPRIETORSHIP AND PARTNERSHIP

The most popular and prevalent business form in the United States is the sole proprietorship, followed by the partnership. They are the quickest, easiest, and least expensive to establish and require little government involvement to initiate. For these reasons start-up firms usually begin as sole proprietorships or partnerships.

They each have two major drawbacks: they provide no mechanism for raising capital and no liability protection for their owners. The owner(s) is entirely responsible for the business' debts, and that liability includes all the personal assets of the owner(s)—your car, house, boat, and so forth. Once sole proprietorships and partnerships are up and running, their owners frequently convert them into limited liability companies or corporations to gain the liability protection these forms provide. If significant capital will be need for expansion, the most useful mechanism is a corporation to issue stock, assuming the firm has chosen not to undertake debt financing.

To form a sole proprietorship or a partnership, all you need do is this: choose a business name, file a certificate of trade name (your own name) or fictitious business name with the appropriate municipal authority, print a notice of your existence in the newspaper, apply to your city for a business license and pay a license fee (if any), and hang out your sign. Fictitious business names are "doing business as" (dba) names, such as John Jones dba John's Plumbing Service.

Partnerships are created when two or more persons voluntarily form a business relationship and become co-owners of the firm, personally sharing in its management, costs, liabilities, and profits. The partners are *jointly liable* for the debts and contracts of the partnership, and they are *jointly and severally liable* for breaches of trust or of fiduciary duty (such as fraud) or other illegal acts. This means that all partners are liable, even the ones who did not commit the illegal act.

Advantages of these forms are that you own the business completely, you manage it, you gain all the profits and bear all the losses, you can easily sell or liquidate the business, and in most municipalities there are no separate business taxes (except for the business license). Your profits and losses are reported on your individual income tax return, by which you also pay your self-employment tax (FICA).

LIMITED LIABILITY PARTNERSHIP (LLP)

Limited partnerships (LPs) are a special type, involving a general partner, who invests in and runs the business, and at least one limited partner, who is a passive investor and does not participate in management. The liability to the general partner is unlimited; the limited partners' liability is limited to the amount invested. One-time business ventures, such as making a movie, often use this form.

Limited liability partnerships (LLPs) are different in that all partners' liabilities are limited to the amount they invest; that is, there is no personal liability. All partners are equal in that all share in the management of the firm and its profits. This is a popular form for professionals who wish to work together, such a physicians, dentists, lawyers, accountants, and so forth. LLPs are formed by filing articles of partnership with the office of the secretary of state in your state. LLPs pay no taxes because, just as the case with limited partnerships, the firm's profits flow through to the partners, who pay tax on them on their individual income tax returns.

Limited Liability Company (LLC)

This form, called a limited liability company (LLC), is a fairly recent invention and works much like an LLP, except that any type of business can be organized as an LLC. The owners of the business, those who contribute capital, are called the members. They have no personal liability beyond their capital contribution. The LLC pays no taxes because profits flow through to the individual members, who pay tax on them on their individual income tax returns. An LLC must meet certain key criteria: it has a limitation on its life span, and there are restrictions on transferring interests in the LLC to others.

LLCs are formed when two or more "persons" (individuals, corporations, LLPs, etc.) agree to form an LLC, select a company name not already in use, and file articles of organization with the secretary of state's office. The company name must include the words *limited liability company, LLC,* or *LC.* LLCs are quicker, easier, and much less expensive to form than corporations and carry the same liability protections and no separate LLC taxes.

Corporation (Inc.)

A corporation is a legal person having the ability to hold and transfer property, raise money through stock issuances, borrow money, sign contracts, sue and be sued, and conduct business, being liable for its contracts and debts. American corporation law limits the liability of directors, officers, and shareholders—the owners of the corporation—to the extent of their investment, permits the transferability of ownership by selling shares, centralizes management in its directors and officers, and has perpetual existence unless voluntarily dissolved by its shareholders or involuntarily dissolved by its creditors through a bankruptcy proceeding.

A document called the articles of incorporation, also known as the corporate charter, is the main governing document of the company and must be approved by the state in which the business will be incorporated. Once approved, the charter is filed with the secretary of state, establishing the corporation. The approving and filing process is complex and must precisely follow procedures required by the state. To assure proper compliance, attorneys specializing in corporation law should perform these services; their fees and registration costs can be considerable.

A corporation that is incorporated in one state can do business in any state but must obtain a certificate from each state's secretary of state in which it wishes to do business. The name of the corporation must not already be registered or trademarked by another company and must contain one of the following words or its abbreviation: *corporation*, *incorporated*, *company*, or *limited*. Corporations pay tax on their profits.

Summary of Major Benefits

As this discussion has shown, the corporation as a business entity has three principal benefits over other types: it can raise capital by issuing stock and by issuing bonds or debentures (debt financing); it offers liability protection for its owners (shareholders), directors, and officers; and it provides a flexible structure for organizing large-scale multidivisional and multiproduct activities, even on a global basis.

The corporation has these major advantages:

- It provides a structure to organize and conduct business (to buy and sell property, sign contracts, borrow money, etc.) that centralizes management in its directors and officers and has the capacity to expand to include multiple activities and products.
- It is a mechanism for raising capital through the issuance of stock and bonds.
- It provides protection for its owners, directors, and managers from personal liability for the actions of the corporation by limiting the exposure to risk of its owners to the extent of their investment in the stock of the company.
- It provides easy transfer of ownership by selling shares on the open market.
- It has perpetual existence, unless dissolved voluntarily by its shareholders or involuntarily by its creditors through bankruptcy.

The major reason the corporation has come to be so widely used is that it is so *useful*. It is a powerful mechanism for raising money, it provides flexibility for its managers to organize and grow the business either organically or by merger and acquisition, and it provides a way to distribute profits (through dividends) to its shareholders without exposing them to personal liability for the firm's actions. No other business entity has so many useful features.

CORPORATIONS' CONTRIBUTIONS TO THE ECONOMY

One of the major benefits of corporations is the immense contributions they make to the overall economy of the United States and the world. Since before the 1980s, according to U.S. Department of Commerce data, "private industry" has contributed between 86 percent and 88 percent of the value added to the U.S. economy each year.[3] Although not all of the companies in private industry are corporations, the vast majority of the contributions represented in this category is from corporations, large and small. For example, this means that in 2004, when the U.S. GDP was $11.728 trillion,[4] the private sector contributed $10.203 trillion to the U.S. GDP, again not all of which was from corporations.

The immense contribution of nonfinancial corporate business to the U.S. economy over the past four decades, as recorded by the U.S. Department of Commerce, is summarized in Table 4.1.[5]

Thus, corporations have steadily added value to the American economy over the years, both gross and net value (after taxes). Nonfinancial corporations, which in 2003 added $5.6 trillion gross value and nearly $5 trillion net value to the economy, made an after tax profit of $386 billion, which represented 6.8 percent of gross. Looking only at the last four-year period, 2000–2003, shown in Table 4.1, nonfinancial corporations made an after tax profit that averaged 5.8 percent.

PROFITABILITY

One of the major benefits of the corporate form of business organization is its profitability, and its ability to distribute that profit to its shareholders through dividends. There is no magic feature in the corporate form compared with any other type of business entity that makes it profitable, but, largely because of their size and scope of operations, corporations generate more profit in absolute numbers than any other type of business.

TABLE 4.1
Gross Value Added of Nonfinancial Corporate Business, 1960–2003
($ in billions)

Year	Gross Value Added of Nonfinancial Corporate Business	Net Value Added Total	After Tax Profits
1960	$ 276.4	$ 253.8	$ 23.1
1970	558.3	511.5	33.6
1980	1,537.1	1,368.9	65.0
1990	3,041.5	2,722.3	175.8
1995	3,879.5	3,464.5	311.4
2000	5,272.2	4,704.3	306.2
2001	5,293.5	4,646.7	245.5
2002	5,377.7	4,722.0	329.4
2003	5,606.8	4,930.5	386.4

TABLE 4.2
U.S. Corporate Profits and Dividends, 1959–2003 ($ in billions)

Year	Corporate Profits (with inventory valuations and capital consumption adjustments)	After Tax Net Dividends
1959	$ 55.7	$ 12.6
1964	76.5	18.2
1974	115.8	33.2
1984	318.6	90.8
1994	600.3	234.7
2003	1,021.1	395.3
2004*	1,181.6	443.9

*Data for 2004 are from U.S. Department of Commerce, www.bea.gov/bea/newsarchive/2005/gdp.

All companies, whatever their form, must work hard to attain and maintain profitability. If they are profitable, they can pay dividends to their shareholders, if their boards decide to do so. Table 4.2 summarizes corporate profits and dividends in the United States over the past four decades for all types of corporations, financial and nonfinancial, large and small.[6]

For the years shown in Table 4.2, the average after tax net dividend was roughly 3.1 percent. This represents the profit to shareholders for having made their investments in America's corporations. Incidentally, dividends have increased in the post-2001 period owing to reduced federal tax on corporations' profits.

In 2004, total profits of all the *Fortune* 500 companies was $513.5 billion on revenues of $8.2 trillion. The corporation in the United States that had the largest profit that year was Exxon Mobil with $25.3 billion, though it was number two in sales to Wal-Mart, whose profit was $10.2 billion. The smallest corporation in terms of sales in the *Fortune* 500 in the same year was Cincinnati Financial, making a profit of $584 million. The company on the *Fortune* 500 list with the largest *loss* in 2004 was Viacom, parent of CBS and Paramount Pictures, with a staggering loss of $17.4 billion.[7]

Profitability by Industry Segment

An important way to look at profits is to analyze which industries are the most and least profitable. For investors, this is a vitally important exercise. The Standard & Poor's 500 index, the 500 largest companies in America, provides profit information. In 2003 the total group of S&P 500 companies recorded approximately 17.2 percent profit, and in 2004 their profitability grew to approximately 22.5 percent. For all four quarters of 2005 they were projected to record 15.9 percent.

The S&P 500 index also provides a breakdown by industry categories. The index has ten major industry sectors, all of which recorded or projected profits in 2005 and into 2006 and five of which recorded outstanding, double-digit profits. Table 4.3 provides the data.[8]

These robust earnings generated record levels of cash. For all the S&P 500 companies, their cash holdings totaled $634 billion as of June 30, 2005. The 376 industrial companies on the S&P 500 index recorded extraordinary amounts of cash. On June 30, 2005, their cash holdings (cash and short-term securities) stood at $634 billion, up from $352 billion at the end of 2001.[9] Strong cash positions mean that companies have greater financial flexibility to make acquisitions, invest in their own business operations, pay off debt, pay out higher dividends to their shareholders, and buy back their own stock. Cash is still king.

EMPLOYEE BENEFITS

Traditional manufacturing corporations have two categories of workers: white collar and blue collar. White-collar employees are the salaried managers and professionals who are usually college educated and who form the ranks of the company's management/professional cadre and perform skilled work, such as scientists and engineers. Blue-collar workers are noncollege wage

TABLE 4.3
Earnings by Industry Sector of S&P 500 Companies, 2005–2006 (estimated year over year change in operating earnings)

	Q2 2005	Q3 2005p	Q4 2005p	Q1 2006p
Basic materials	+26%	+4%	+4%	0%
Consumer discretionary	−1	+4	+10	+22
Consumer staples	+6	+7	+9	+11
Energy	+42	+38	+18	+22
Financial services	+3	+25	+15	+1
Health care	+10	+5	+8	+8
Industrials	+20	+20	+21	+14
Technology	+14	+11	+16	+18
Telecom	+17	+4	+3	+11
Utilities	+11	+16	+14	+9
Total S&P 500	+12	+16	+14	+11

The sector called "consumer discretionary" includes such industries as automobiles and hotels.

earners; these hourly employees punch the time clock and perform the physical tasks needed to get the company's products made and shipped out the door.

The analogy with the military is not accidental. White-collar people are the junior and senior officers of the firm who give the orders and set the strategy. Blue-collar workers are the enlisted personnel, the foot soldiers who staff the trenches of the company and are directed at the first level by noncommissioned officers (foremen and first-line supervisors), who, like sergeants in the army, are closest to the enlisted personnel and transform the officers' orders into action. White-collar workers hope to rise up the chain of command to achieve lofty ranks at which the power and compensation are the greatest. Blue-collar workers hope to rise to line supervisors because they rarely rise to the management ranks today.

MANAGEMENT TRAINING

Teaching white-collar employees how to "manage" became important as corporations consolidated their hold on the American economy and became increasingly more complex. Gaining this training was a major benefit to the rising young stars of the company's future management. Once managers learned their skills within a company, the task of that firm's top management was to keep them—not lose skilled managers to other firms. The same problem arose with respect to skilled blue-collar workers. *Retention* is the term used for this issue today.

Business Schools

At the beginning of the Industrial Revolution there was no equivalent of West Point or Annapolis to teach junior officers their management skills, and

---

White-Collar versus Blue-Collar Employees

White-collar employees are the salaried managers and professionals who are usually college educated and who form the ranks of the company's management/ professional cadre and perform skilled work, such as scientists and engineers.

Blue-collar workers are hourly employees who punch the time clock and perform the physical tasks needed to get the company's products made and shipped out the door.

Traditional lore holds that the white collar refers to the white, buttoned-down shirts worn by the professionals (who don't get their hands dirty), and distinguishes them from manual laborers, whose durable blue uniforms can withstand more physical damage in the workplace.

so this was done within the firm, and loyalty to the firm became paramount. The first professional school of business administration soon arrived; in 1881 the Wharton School of Finance and Commerce was established at the University of Pennsylvania by Joseph Wharton, founder of the Bethlehem Steel Company. Harvard's Business School was begun a quarter century later in 1908. Others soon followed. Graduates of business schools were snapped up by corporations to fill their ever-expanding junior officer ranks.

By the time of World War I, 1914–1918, the profession of management had arrived. It was beginning to be recognized as a separate and legitimate skill set, such as being an attorney, physician, dentist, or physicist. In 1923 the establishment of the American Management Association signaled the arrival of management as a "profession."[10] Indeed, Alfred P. Sloan at General Motors was the first chief executive officer of a major company to declare that his profession was "management."[11] Before Sloan, most CEOs would have said they were finance experts, engineers, salesmen, or inventors.

Today, of course, many colleges and universities offer a business major for undergraduates and masters of business administration (MBA) programs for college graduates who have some work experience. These schools produce thousands of well-trained business professionals each year to add to the "officer corps" of the world's major corporations.

Increasingly these graduates either start their own businesses or join smaller firms, seeing more opportunities in these options than those in the large corporate setting. It is an increasing rarity for corporations to pay for an MBA education, and they never pay for an undergraduate business education. The employee is expected to come to work at the company on the first day armed with the needed business skills.

Corporate In-house Training

Today, many large corporations have their own in-house management training centers, such as Motorola University, at which midlevel and senior managers have an opportunity to upgrade their skills and gain critical insights into how the CEO and other top company leaders want them to run the company. Other companies send their future leaders to university business schools for specially designed management development programs.

The country's one hundred largest companies (*Fortune* 100) spend approximately $2,600 per person per year on training. Looking across all industries and all size companies, they spend approximately $2,100 per person per year for training. These totals for corporate training expenditures are roughly equal to the tuitions paid at the top 3,500 universities and colleges in the country.[12]

Why do companies train their employees? There are five major reasons:

1. To learn how to grow the business—usually involves gaining marketing skills
2. To recruit and retain talent—constantly upgrading management and technical skills
3. To foster innovative thinking—challenging managers and professionals to think creatively outside the box
4. To create a global mind-set—expanding managers' horizons to include today's global, hypercompetitive world
5. To remake the internal dynamics of the company—instituting and perpetuating a change in management style

General Electric

The archetype for in-house training is General Electric Company, whose training center at Crotonville, New York, is world famous. Former GE chairman Ralph Cordiner built this fifty-two-acre center (near Ossining) in the 1950s to remake GE's management style. In 1981, Jack Welch, GE's new CEO, used the center to remake GE's internal dynamics—the management structure and style—and to give its managers a permanent sense of entrepreneurial fervor.

The CEO and other top GE executives regularly visit the center to address the classes on the GE way of doing things and to lead open discussions on real-time management problems, using them as case studies for improving decision-making. The center also brings in top professors and leaders from other industries to impart the latest management principles. Welch considers the Crotonville center to have played a vital role in his massive restructuring of GE's businesses and its future leaders' mind-sets.[13]

Northrop Grumman

Another example of in-house training on a smaller scale is Northrop Grumman Corporation, the nation's third largest defense company (B-2 bomber, F-14 Tom Cat, spy satellites), which is also the world's largest builder of military ships (nuclear aircraft carriers, destroyers, and submarines).

Northrop Grumman estimated in 2005 that within three years over 27 percent of its current management staff would arrive at an age at which they could begin to take retirement. To strengthen its management ranks and prepare for succession, the company began its own Space University on the California campus of its Space Technology Sector operation, where mid- and upper-level managers from the Space Technology Sector are selected to attend classes to update their management skills and retool to compete better in today's hypercompetitive environment.

The breakdown of the company's learning content at its Space University is typical of many in-house operations: 10 percent devoted to leadership development, 25 percent to professional development, and 65 percent to critical skills development.[14]

For its senior executives, Northrop Grumman sends them to UCLA's Anderson Graduate School of Management for advanced courses in marketing and management. Many other companies have tie-in programs with business schools at local universities to help their executives keep abreast of the latest management techniques.

EMPLOYEE FRINGE BENEFITS

How to retain skilled people, whether white collar or blue collar, is a perennial problem. What incentives to offer employees has become the touchstone of this issue. Should the firm do more than merely pay a salary or wage? Training has already been discussed as a retention incentive.

The concept of employee benefits emerged as a technique to attract and retain good workers. Benefits came to mean compensation over and beyond base salary or wages. Sears, Roebuck and Company was the first corporation to establish an employee pension fund. International Harvester (now Navistar) was the first to have a profit-sharing plan for its senior salaried workers. And Procter & Gamble was the first company to offer its employees disability and retirement pensions, the eight-hour workday, and the guarantee of work for at least forty-eight weeks a year.[15]

Later, companies introduced additional benefits for their employees to attract and retain them: paid vacations, paid sick days, salaried savings plans such as 401(k)s, dental plans, and on-the-job day care for toddlers (when mothers of preschoolers joined the workforce in vast numbers). These benefits, known generically as *fringe benefits*, added cost to the company and therefore added to the price of the company's goods. In companies that had unionized employees, these additional benefits were negotiated between management and union leaders in addition to base salary and became part of the management–union contract.

For some companies these fringe benefit packages represent as little as 10 percent to 15 percent of base and for others as much as 50 percent of the base salary of the employee. Thus, if an employee hypothetically makes $1.00 per hour, the fringe benefit package adds another $.10 to $.50 to the company's wage bill for that employee.

THE PROBLEM OF PENSIONS

A major fringe benefit cost to companies is retiree pension benefits.[16] For firms with traditional pension plans, formally known as *defined benefit pensions*, these expenses have to be paid either out of a company trust fund or out of the company's current earnings.

Traditional defined benefit plans were once popular with employees because they paid nothing into the plan; only the employer paid. They were also popular with employers because the amount they paid into the plans represented a tax deduction. This system worked well as long as the company's sales were strong, and there were large numbers of workers near the bottom of the age pyramid and few near the top, ready to retire or already retired. In recent times for many companies these fundamentals have changed for the worse: the country's aging workforce means there are fewer workers at the bottom of the age pyramid and more at the top, either retired or close to doing so, for whom the company will have to pay pensions.

These traditional pension plans have also lost their popularity with employers because of the onerous paperwork, reporting, and other federal compliance requirements imposed by ERISA—the Employee Retirement Income Security Act, which regulates these pension plans and is administered by the U.S. Department of Labor.[17] Federal regulations make traditional pension plans difficult and expensive to administer.

Pension Benefit Guaranty Corporation

Over the years, employers have promised employees $1.5 trillion in traditional pension benefits, and yet they have funded their plans to only $1.2 trillion, leaving an unfunded deficit of $300 billion, which is growing. In the event of a pension plan default, the federal government's agency can take over the plan: the Pension Benefit Guaranty Corporation (PBGC). Its mission is to guarantee defined pension plans—up to a point. Current law limits the PBGC to pay a maximum of $45,614 annually for employees who retire at age 65. In reality this translates to about 50 cents on each dollar of promised monthly pension payments for those who retire at any age, which means the retiree may take it on the chin.

Congress created the PBGC in 1974 after some high-profile auto industry bankruptcies (Studebaker-Packard Corp.) left their retirees without pensions. It is currently the trustee of 3,500 pension plans with about 1 million participants. Some industries are more likely to default on their pension obligations than others. See Table 4.4 for a list of the most and least exposed industries to default on defined benefit pension plans.[18]

TABLE 4.4
Weakest and Strongest Industries' Defined Benefit Pension Plans

Five Weakest	Five Strongest
Auto components	Computers and software
Automakers	Real estate
Airlines	Biotech
Aerospace and defense	Hotels, restaurants, leisure
Construction and engineering	Thrifts, mortgage, finance

The industries with by far the largest underfunded defined benefit plans are autos and auto component makers. These companies' plans are $45 billion to $50 billion short of the promises they made to their workers. Delphi Automotive, Inc., the largest American auto parts supplier, alone has a pension liability of $4.3 billion, plus $9.6 billion in retiree health care liabilities. As of mid-2005, PBGC had taken over the pension plans of 12 airlines, including United, which had underfunded plans totaling $11.6 billion; and 141 bankrupt steel companies, whose underfunded total was $10.2 billion.[19]

Defined Benefit versus Defined Contribution Plans

Traditional pension plans have lost much of their appeal not only to employers but also to employees, especially younger workers. These plans require the employees to remain at the company for much of their working lives if they expect to collect much of a pension at retirement. This lifelong employment model is outmoded today, with most employees changing jobs every few years, whether voluntarily or through layoffs. Owing to the fact that these defined benefit pensions are not portable and *defined contribution plans* are, the latter are presently preferred by workers. Employees of all ages now see great risk to their future by having these traditional plans because of the large number of defaults in recent years.

Thus, in 2000, only 48 percent of companies even offered traditional pension plans and many had begun to terminate them. Only 12 percent of private companies still had the traditional defined benefit plans at all, and an additional 7 percent had both a defined benefit plan and a defined contribution plan.[20]

By 2005, it had become clear that traditional defined benefit pensions were being phased out by the few corporations that still had them. This was one important way companies had to reduce current costs and future financial risks. Companies in a variety of industries announced substantial alterations in their pension programs for current employees: a freeze on benefit participation, discontinuation of participation for new hires and younger workers, and a cap on the number of years that go into the base for calculating payments after retirement. At the same time companies were enhancing their defined contribution plans.

Two trends emerged making these changes desirable for companies.[21] Financially weak companies, such as autos and airlines, jettisoned badly underfunded pension liabilities as one way to try to stay afloat. Second, rising interest rates offered employers the possibility of a large income boost if they froze their pensions, effectively wiping out part of a debt owed to future retirees. Assets in a plan would still be paid out when workers retire, but benefits would no longer grow with additional years on the job.

General Motors announced it would "substantially alter pension benefits" for salaried workers, and IBM told 117,000 salaried employees that they will stop earning additional benefits after 2007, saving IBM $2.5 billion over five years. Verizon Communications, Inc., Sears Holdings Corporation, and Circuit City Stores, Inc. all announced a similar move; their salaried workers will get pensions upon retirement, but they will not accrue additional benefits with additional years on the job.[22]

An even larger number of companies are closing defined benefit plans altogether to new hires and younger workers. These include Motorola, Lockheed Martin, Hewlett-Packard, Anon Corporation, and NCR Corporation.

There is no legal barrier to freezing a pension plan for current employees unless it is prohibited by a union contract. For example, in December 2005, Verizon unilaterally froze the pensions of its 50,500 managers, saving an estimated $3 billion over the next decade, but changes to pensions for its union employees are subject to negotiations.[23]

Instead of traditional pension plans, companies now prefer to offer defined contribution plans, such as 401(k) type plans. As of 2000, 29 percent of private companies had such plans. They are popular with employers because they pay in at maximum only half of the amount as a match to what the employee pays. The employee decides what percent of his or her salary to contribute (usually up to 10 percent of gross salary), and the employer typically makes a matching contribution. Unlike traditional pensions, these plans are portable, meaning you can take your nest egg with you when you leave the company, providing you put it into a similar plan within a specified time period. In 2005, both Ford Motor Company and General Motors, facing weakened sales in their core auto businesses, announced discontinuation of paying the company match portion of 401(k)s for their salaried employees.[24]

Employees also like these plans because the employees, not the company, decide where to invest the money. Younger workers usually make more aggressive investments than older workers in hopes of generating a larger future payout. Older employees like 401(k)s because, at retirement, they can be rolled over into an individual retirement account (IRA); traditional pensions cannot be moved.[25]

Other Companies' Pension Problems

All sorts of companies face pension plan problems, mostly underfunded shortfalls. The largest group of these is in manufacturing, in which in 2005 there was a $48 billion possible termination liability. This means that if a

---

United Airlines: Pension Problems

The largest pension problem in the country occurred at United Airlines, which faced a host of other problems, too. The airline industry had changed fundamentally, beginning with its deregulation mandated by the Airline Deregulation Act of 1978. Airline companies now face competition from other established carriers, plus a number of new carriers (Southwest and JetBlue) that joined the industry with cost structures far lower than the old heritage companies, such as United, American, and US Airways.[26] United Airlines and US Airways' fixed cost expenses were more than 11.0 cents per seat mile versus 7.4 cents for Southwest and 6.3 cents for JetBlue, the lowest.[27]

Already in financial trouble, the established air carriers hit a "perfect storm" in 2001: the recession, a dramatic increase in fuel cost, the terrorist attack on 9/11, and war. For the 18 months following September 11, 2001, discretionary air travel died, and U.S. domestic airlines lost $12.4 billion, half for heightened security. United and US Airways filed for bankruptcy in 2002, and Northwest and Delta filed in 2005. American Airlines threatened bankruptcy in an attempt to wring cost savings from its unions, lenders, and suppliers.

United Airlines had $6.6 billion in unfunded pension obligations when it went into chapter 11 bankruptcy in December 2002. Unable to fund these pension obligations and unable to obtain a government loan guarantee, United had no choice but to go under. During its period of protection under chapter 11, the company succeeded in shifting its pension obligations to the government. In 2005, the Pension Benefit Guaranty Corporation agreed to take over United Airlines' pension liability; this was the largest single pension plan the PBGC had ever taken on.[28] United emerged from chapter 11 in early 2006.[29]

company were to terminate its pension plan, it still would have a long-term obligation to those employees who have already retired; if the company were to remain in business and had reasonable prospects for future profitability, it could conceivably pay its promised pensions. If a company were to go into bankruptcy, it could terminate its pension liability to its current employees and, if the government agreed, it could shift that liability and the liability to those already retired to the government's Pension Benefit Guaranty Corporation.

Look at three traditional manufacturers: Bethlehem Steel, AK Steel Holding Corporation, and Maytag Corporation. Bethlehem, the larger steel company, claimed its pension was 84 percent funded, but on a "termination" basis it was only 45 percent funded when it declared bankruptcy and handed its plan over to the PBGC. AK Steel had a $1.3 billion underfunded liability, which was larger than its stock market value, when it defaulted. Maytag Corporation had an underfunded liability of $554 million, or about 46 percent of its total market capitalization; it was acquired by Whirlpool Corporation.

In 2005 companies in the wholesale/retail trade sector of the economy had $5.8 billion in termination liability, and companies in the services sector had $7.9 billion in liability, not counting airlines. The airlines had nearly $60 billion in underfunded liabilities, not counting United Airlines' $6.6 billion.[30]

THE PROBLEM OF HEALTH CARE PLANS

Retiree health insurance premiums are paid out of current company earnings. This is of course a major issue for many of today's largest corporations, especially those in the airline, auto, and communications industries. These industries are being restructured, and airline and communications companies face fierce competition following deregulation.

To reduce cost, many companies are reducing or simply canceling their retiree health plans and other benefits, such as dental plans, death benefits, and spouse insurance. (Federal law prohibits companies from reducing pension payments from defined benefit plans once the employee retires and begins to collect.) The cumulative effect of these changes in several major industries is the virtual collapse of the half-century-old employer-based social welfare system. Lifetime employment combined with a worry-free comfortable retirement with pension and health benefits is vanishing as corporations face hyper-competition and try to restructure outmoded business models.

General Motors

General Motors is the classic case, once again. In the years when GM was selling cars in vast numbers (1950s–1970s) and had to hire and retain an army of skilled workers, it offered very generous pension and health benefits. As its sales sagged in the 1980s and in the 2000s in the face of fierce foreign competition, it laid off or retired many of these surplus workers. But the company's commitment to them as retirees remained, and GM's labor contracts with the United Auto Workers covering its current workers were also fixed for a number of years.

GM's health benefit costs are huge: $5.2 billion in 2004 for 1.1 million employees, retirees, and dependents. These costs add $1,500 to the price of each vehicle GM produces.[31] Toyota and GM's other Japanese rivals do not have these overhead costs because the Japanese government pays for retiree health costs through a national tax.

Ford Motor Company

In early 2006 the number three U.S. automaker announced its cost-cutting moves over the next few years: closing 14 plants, laying off 28 percent of its North American workforce, and reducing retiree health benefits and raising retirees' fees for them. "We cannot play the game the old way," stated William Clay Ford, Jr., the Chairman and CEO. On the positive side, Ford offered an astonishingly candid new management strategy: "Our product plans for too long were defined by our capacity. From now on, our vehicles will be designed to satisfy the customer, not just fill a factory."[32] This had been Toyota's strategy for years.

Communications Industry

Western Electric, once part of AT&T and now part of Lucent Technologies, is an example of the trend in the telephone/communications industry. This was once a stable and growing industry, and to attract employees companies offered generous pension plans and retiree health benefits, knowing these would not have to be paid for many years.

That industry underwent a sea change in the 1980s and 1990s with deregulation and consolidation, plus technological changes that reduced the need for large numbers of workers. Also the new accounting rules ("cash balance" plans) that went into effect in the 1990s enabled companies to calculate benefits for future retirees in a different way, enabling them to reduce current obligations as well as future costs and thus to boost income. After 2000, the industry needed to shed even more costs and began to cut benefits being paid to current retirees, such as death benefits, retiree and spouse health insurance, and life insurance.

Some companies eliminated life insurance for certain retirees in recent years: Quest Communications, NCR Corporation, Lucent Technologies, CNA Financial Corporation, Phelps Dodge, Pathmark Stores, and St. Paul Travelers Companies. These corporations thus save millions of dollars of current and future costs, and their retirees, many of whom are on small pensions to begin with, bear that cost.[33]

EXECUTIVE COMPENSATION

The compensation package for senior executives of large corporations is usually very substantial. In addition to base salary, senior executives typically also receive a bonus, which is usually calculated as a percentage of base salary, shares of stock in the company, and *perquisites* (commonly called *perks*).

The median CEO base salary for the 500 largest companies in the United States (the S&P 500) in 2003 was $950,000. For the same year, the median bonus was $1,064,000. Total median cash compensation therefore was $2.029 million. (See chapter 9 for a discussion.)

BONUS

The bonus could be as low as 20 percent of base salary or as high as 50 percent of base salary for mid- to upper-level executives. For example, say an executive has a salary of $100,000 per year; using that as a base the bonus might range from $20,000 to $50,000.

In the financial industry, senior Wall Street executives receive modest salaries ranging from $100,000 to $250,000 per year, but their bonuses are perhaps ten times base—in very good years. Thus, a $100,000 salary could swell to a $1 million bonus. Another factor in the calculation is the overall financial performance of the corporation and of the particular business unit in which the employee works; these criteria are weighted along with the base salary of the executive. In 2005, a very good year on Wall Street, the average pay package was between $2.2 million and $3.3 million for an investment banker at the managing director level.[34]

For many CEOs bonuses are often far larger than the median, which is slightly above 100 percent of base. CEOs in the 100 largest companies can earn bonuses that are several times their base salary, sometimes as much as 500 percent. Thus a CEO earning $1 million in base might get as much as $5 million in bonus, plus the base amount.

For non-top-level executives, managers, and key professionals, in 2005 salaries rose 3.6 percent, keeping them ahead of inflation, which ran at 3.1 percent that year. Bonuses for this level of salaried employees, factored from this higher base salary, also rose. Based on survey results across very wide samples, employers are increasingly using one-time compensation payments, like bonuses, as a big part of the total compensation package for these employees. In 2005 86 percent of companies responding to surveys reported they used performance bonuses, and 55 percent of respondents paid signing bonuses. These were used especially in information technology, finance, engineering, and accounting firms.[35]

PERQUISITES

Perquisites could include such items as free use of a company-owned car, membership in an exclusive country club, free use of the company's executive lunch room, use of a company jet, company-paid life insurance, moving expenses, and so forth. The dollar value of perquisites could total to a large sum of money. Top executives in smaller companies typically rely on a base salary plus bonus; perquisites are generally not provided.

STOCK

The stock portion of the compensation package could be one of two types:

1. It could be a straight gift, based on, say, a five-year commitment with 20 percent of the stock being granted annually over those five years. These are called *restricted stock rights* because the employee is restricted from obtaining the stock all at once and from selling the stock until after a waiting period has passed, typically one to three years.
2. Alternatively, the stock could be a *stock option*, which is a grant of stock that the employee must keep for a set number of years, say three years, before he or she is permitted to "exercise the option" of buying the stock for the price stated on the face of the option. For a number of reasons stock options are declining in use, with the percentage of employers using options dropping from 37 percent in 2002 to 31 percent in 2005.[36]

Take a typical example. The stock option could be for 100 shares of the company's stock with a face value at a recent closing price of the stock, say $25 per share. The employee is required to hold the stock for a minimum of three years before exercising the option of buying the stock at that price. In three years, the employee hopes, partly through his or her good efforts, the share price will rise to a dollar figure much higher, say triple to $75 per share. Thus the employee in the third year could buy one hundred shares at $75 and have to pay only $25 per share, the "option" price. The employee would thus gain a $50 per share benefit, or $5,000.

The underlying purpose of these stock grants and options is, of course, to reward the employee for good performance and to keep the employee at the company, as long as he or she is performing well. In the event the employee voluntarily leaves the company before the exercise date on the stock grant or option, he or she forfeits the stock.

The average CEO's salary in the United States is 475 times greater than the average worker's salary. In Japan, it is 11 times greater; in France, 15 times; in Canada, 20; in South Africa, 21; and in Britain, 22. The highest paid U.S. CEO in 2004 was Terry Semel of Yahoo, with $230 million; the highest paid athlete was Tiger Woods, who made about $80 million.[37]

TREASURY SHARES

Where does the company get the shares of its own stock it gives to its executives? Corporations usually retain a certain number of their own shares for corporate purposes when they make their initial public offering (IPO) of stock to investors. These are called *treasury shares* because they remain in the corporation's own treasury. Later, if more stock is needed, corporations can increase the number of shares by a decision of the board of directors, retaining a certain number of shares at that time for corporate purposes.

Finally, from time to time corporations simply buy back some of their own company's stock on the open market, usually discretely at major stock

---

Sample of Pay Packages for 2006[37]

- Mellon Financial Corporation: New Chairman and CEO Robert Kelly was eligible for compensation up to $10 million each year: $975,000 salary, bonus up to $3.9 million, and stock valued up to $5.1 million.

- Ingersoll-Rand Company: CEO H. L. Henkel earned $8.5 million through two bonus programs in 2005, payable in February 2006.

- Toys "R" Us Inc.: New Chairman and CEO Gerald Storch will earn $1 million a year and a bonus that could exceed 200 percent of base salary.

- Tesoro Corporation: The oil company provided a base salary of $1.2 million for CEO Bruce Smith, plus 165,000 stock options and 27,000 restricted shares of common stock.

exchanges, putting it into their treasuries. This is usually done as an investment in the company, expecting that the amount of money used to purchase the stock could be no better spent on anything else. It is also a way for a corporation to signal to the investing public that its own management values the company's stock very highly, thus giving an endorsement for the company by its own management. Wall Street analysts greet buyback announcements as a very positive sign of a company's health and a forecast of robust future earnings.

GENERAL ELECTRIC

In 2004, GE was the fifth largest company in the United States and ninth largest in the world with sales of $152 billion, profits of $16.5 billion, and its stock had a market value (called market capitalization) of $375 billion. How well did this behemoth pay its top five executives? Table 4.5 spells out the compensation mix each of the top five executives received.

In addition to cash compensation, each of these top executives received stock awards in GE stock of two types: restricted stock and stock options. The aggregate dollar values of holdings by each individual of both types of stock were as follows: Immelt $22.3 million, Dammerman $38.0 million, Wright $58.6 million, and Heinemann $19.0 million. Sir William Castell,

TABLE 4.5
Executive Compensation at General Electric, 2004* ($ in millions)

Name/Position	Salary	Bonus	Other Comp.	Total Annual Compensation	Long-Term Comp.	All Other Compensation
Jeffrey Immelt *Chairman and CEO*	$3	$5.3	$.235	$8.534	$0	$.279
Dennis Dammerman *Vice chairman and executive officer*	$2.3	$5.65	$.581	$8.531	$4.3	$.658
Robert C. Wright *Vice chairman and executive officer*	$2.5	$5.7	$.440	$8.640	$1.025	$.833
Benjamin Heineman *Senior Vice president, Law and Public Affairs*	$1.533	$3.1	$.83	$4.741	$1.084	$.461
William M. Castell *Vice chairman and executive officer*	$1.38	$2.9	$.71	$4.330	$.200 $0	$.38 $0

*General Electric Company, *Proxy Statement for 2005,* 33.

having only recently joined GE's executive team through the acquisition of his company Amersham, the large British health care company, had not yet received any GE stock as of the 2005 proxy report. The operating responsibilities of each of these five men were as follows:

Jeffrey Immelt, chairman of the board and chief executive officer, GE
Dennis Dammerman, chairman of GE Capital Services, Inc.
Robert Wright, chairman and CEO of NBC Universal, Inc.
Benjamin Heineman, chief counsel and head of public affairs activities
Sir William Castell, CEO of GE Healthcare

The total compensation in 2004 of Jeffrey Immelt was $31.1 million, the majority of which was GE stock. Yet, he was barred from cashing in most of his stock for a number of years, meaning that his real compensation in 2004 was something more than his cash salary and supplements of $8.8 million but nowhere near the total value of his stock holdings. There are many professional athletes, rock stars, and movie stars who make considerably more per year than these executives who run one of the world's largest and most successful corporations. Yet, by corporate standards, they are paid quite well.

BOEING COMPANY

In July 2005, Chicago-based Boeing Company announced the compensation package for its newly named chairman, president, and chief executive officer, James McNearney, who came to Boeing from these same positions at 3M Company in Minneapolis. (Prior to joining 3M Company McNearney had been an executive at General Electric, losing out for the CEO position to Jeffrey Immelt.) McNearney was hired by Boeing after a three-month search to replace Harry Stonecipher, who had been forced by the Boeing board of directors to resign several months earlier over a scandal involving a female Boeing executive.

McNearney's compensation package at Boeing included $1.75 million in base salary, an annual bonus of between $2.98 million and $4.00 million, and no signing bonus. An undisclosed amount of stock was also included, making the total package worth at least $52 million over several years. McNearney will have to remain at Boeing for at least six years to realize the full value of the package. The initial employment contract was for three years, automatically renewable for two-year periods. The package was designed to make McNearney "whole," his having given up a lucrative pay package at 3M Company.

Harry Stonecipher's pay package had included a salary of $1.5 million, a $2.1 million bonus, and he owned 1.76 million shares of company stock, which was then selling at around $55 per share.

JP MORGAN CHASE & COMPANY

The nation's second largest bank, JP Morgan Chase, is the result of the merger in 2001 of JP Morgan & Company and the Chase Manhattan Corporation, and subsequently the acquisition of Chicago-based Bank One Corporation by JP Morgan Chase. William B. Harrison, Jr. is the chairman of the board and chief executive officer of JP Morgan Chase; previously he held those positions at Chase Manhattan. James Dimon had been chairman and CEO of Bank One, and, following its merger into JP Morgan Chase, he became that company's president and chief operating officer. On a combined basis the total company's 2004 revenue was $57.0 billion and its profit was $10.2 billion.

Following these mergers, the new executive leadership team received the following compensation in 2004:

Name	Salary	Bonus	Perks	Stock	Stock Options	Other
Harrison	$1 million	$7.5 million	$368K	$0	$600,481 shares	$50,000
Dimon	$1 million	$6.5 million	$395K	$0	$600,481 shares	$86,512

The perks included personal use of company aircraft, life insurance premiums, and personal use of company cars. The Other category includes Dimon's moving expenses and certain tax reimbursements.[39]

MORGAN STANLEY

Sometimes top executives are paid well even if they fail to perform well and even if they are fired for poor performance.

An example is the once highly respected Wall Street investment bank Morgan Stanley. In 1997 Morgan Stanley merged with Dean Witter, a retail brokerage firm that also owned Discover credit card company, keeping the name Morgan Stanley for the combined firm. The new CEO of the combined company was Philip Purcell, Dean Witter's former CEO, who brought into the newly combined firm many of his former Dean Witter lieutenants and gave them top positions. As *Fortune* magazine put it, this merger was "toxic"; Morgan Stanley "choked on its own merger, [and] the ugliest civil war in recent Wall Street history broke out."[40]

During 2000–2005 Morgan Stanley underperformed its competitors by 10 to 15 percent, and profits were down 15 to 20 percent. Moreover, in 2005 the company paid out $125 million to settle charges of faulty stock research, it lost a judgment in a Florida court for $1.45 billion in a fraud case, it was stung by the SEC with an $8.5 million fine for securities infractions, and it paid out $6.1 million in settlements for overcharging 3,500 customers who held fee-based stock brokerage accounts. Dissident shareholders and former executives urged the board of directors to fire the top leadership and break up the company.[41]

Following a ten-week period of open warfare in mid-2005, the board fired the chief executive officer, Philip Purcell, and awarded him $44 million in exit pay, twice the $22 million he was paid in 2004. (Average Wall Street severance pay was *one* year's salary.) Purcell will also be paid $1.2 million a year for life. This was as "golden" a parachute as anyone could remember. As a *Wall Street Journal* headline said at the time, "At Morgan Stanley, It's Nice Work if You Can Get the Money When You Leave."[42]

The board also offered lucrative incentives to Purcell's principal deputies if they would leave the company within a month. For example, the co-president of the firm, Stephen Crawford, would receive a lump sum $32 million payout for a quick exit, or, if he chose to stay on and was later fired by the new CEO, John Mack, he would receive $16 million per year for the next two years anyway. Decisions, decisions. Other top Purcell lieutenants received similar, but smaller, exit awards.

Critics called these exit packages overly generous given these executives' poor performance. At that time the company's pretax earnings had fallen by 6 percent to a mere $3.4 million for the first half of 2005. A Wall Street analyst stated that Morgan Stanley shareholders were "frustrated that this much money is being handed out without [these executives] having to perform to get it."[43] Another Wall Street insider parodying *The Wonderful Wizard of Oz*, wrote, "There's No Place Like . . . Morgan Stanley."[44]

CONCLUSION

This chapter summarizes the major types of business entities, addressing the pros and cons of each. The corporation is the business entity that offers the most benefits, even though it is more difficult than the others to form and maintain. No other entity has proven itself so useful to the growth and expansion of business not only in the United States but also throughout the world.

The chapter also summarizes contributions corporations make to the over-all economy and benefits they provide to their own employees, including executive compensation and some examples from well-known companies. It addresses two of the pressing financial issues corporations face today stemming from these benefit packages, pensions and health care. How to establish a corporation is the topic of the next chapter.

NOTES

1. This discussion is based on Wesley B. Truitt, *What Entrepreneurs Need to Know about Government: A Guide to Rules and Regulations* (Westport, CT: Praeger, 2004), 89–94.

2. For information on the Federal Trade Commission's franchising rules, see www.ftc.gov.

3. Council of Economic Advisors, *Economic Report of the President, 2005*. Appendix Table B12, www.whitehouse.gov/cea/erpcover2005.

4. Ibid., Appendix Table B10.

5. Ibid., Appendix Table B14.

6. Ibid., Appendix Table B90.

7. *Fortune*, April 18, 2005, 232, F1, F19, F21.

8. *Los Angeles Times*, August 14, 2005, C4.

9. Ibid.

10. Alfred D. Chandler, Jr., *The Visible Hand: The Managerial Revolution in American Business* (Cambridge, MA: Harvard University Press, 1977), 17.

11. Alfred P. Sloan, *My Years with General Motors* (Garden City, NY: Doubleday, 1963).

12. ASTD 2004, "State of the Industry Report," cited in Jack Gregg's presentation to industry leaders, Beverly Hilton Hotel, April 21, 2005.

13. Jack Welch, *Jack: Straight from the Gut* (New York: Warner Books, 2001), Chapter 12.

14. Jack Gregg, dean, Space University, presentation to industry leaders, Beverly Hilton Hotel, April 21, 2005.

15. Roland Marchand, *Creating the Corporate Soul: The Rise of Public Relations and Corporate Imagery in American Big Business* (Berkeley, CA: University of California Press, 1998), 81–87.

16. For a discussion of types of pension plans, see Wesley B. Truitt, *What Entrepreneurs Need to Know about Government*, 147–149.

17. 29 U.S.C. Section 1001 et seq.

18. Adapted from *Wall Street Journal*, May 12, 2005, A10.

19. Ibid.

20. Ibid.

21. Ibid., January 12, 2006, C1.

22. Ibid., January 6, 2006, A3; February 8, 2006, A1.

23. Ibid., January 12, 2006, C1.

24. *Fortune*, July 11, 2005, 21; *Wall Street Journal*, December 16, 2005, B4.

25. U.S. Pension Benefit Guaranty Corporation, *2002 Annual Report* (Washington, D.C.: U.S. Government Printing Office, 2003); David Wessel, "The Politics of Pension Promises," *Wall Street Journal*, July 17, 2003, A2.

26. Melvin A. Brenner, "Is U.S. Deregulation a Failure? Here's How to Find Out," *Airline Executive*, September 1980, 22–23; Michael Wines, "Verdict Still Out on Deregulation's Impact on U.S. Air Travel System," *National Journal*, March 6, 1982, 404–409.

27. Cait Murphy, "A No-Fly Zone," *Fortune*, April 14, 2003, 56.

28. *Wall Street Journal*, July 6, 2005, C3.

29. *Los Angeles Times*, February 2, 2006, C3.

30. *Wall Street Journal*, July 6, 2005, C3.

31. *General Motors Corporation 2004 Annual Report*, 7.

32. *Wall Street Journal*, January 24, 2006, A1.

33. Ibid., June 29, 2005, B1, B3.

34. Ibid., November 8, 2005, C1, C4.

35. *Los Angeles Times*, July 20, 2005, C6.

36. Ibid.

37. Adapted from *Wall Street Journal*, February 13, 2006, B3.

38. Ibid., January 21, 2006, A7.

39. JP Morgan Chase Proxy Statement, 2005, 11; and *JP Morgan Chase Annual Report 2005*.

40. *Fortune*, May 2, 2005, 59–60.

41. *Wall Street Journal*, June 6, 2005, C1; June 15, 2005, A14; August 3, 2005, D3.

42. Ibid., July 13, 2005, C1.

43. Ibid., July 8, 2005, C3.

44. Andy Kessler, *Wall Street Journal*, June 15, 2005, A14.

RECOMMENDED READINGS

Council of Economic Advisors, *Economic Report of the President, 2005,* together with the *Report to the President by the Council of Economic Advisors, 2005,* www.whitehouse.gov/cea/erpcover2005.

Welch, Jack, *Jack: Straight from the Gut* (New York: Warner Books, 2001).

Five

Establishment of a Corporation

The process of incorporation is quite routine throughout the United States, and, even though each state has its own laws governing the process, the procedures are remarkably similar.

This chapter addresses the topics of what the legal basis is for a corporation, how is it established, where is it done, how is it done, and how the corporation is organized and financed.[1]

BASIS IN LAW FOR THE CORPORATION

Owing to the fact a corporation is a fictitious "person," it must be created by a government. This principle is firmly rooted in English common law as it was practiced in the thirteen American colonies while they were under British rule before the War of Independence, 1775–1783. Prior to independence, the British Crown issued royal charters to form corporations in England and in America. After independence, the power to grant charters of incorporation fell to the states as successors to the Crown, where it remains. Thus, in the United States the incorporation process for private business corporations can be performed only by states, not by the federal government.

The oldest corporation that has been in continuous existence in the United States is the Bank of New York, founded by Alexander Hamilton in 1784, five years before the Constitution was adopted.[2]

In 1819, in the earliest and most important U.S. Supreme Court decision regarding corporations, *Dartmouth College v. Woodward*, Chief Justice John Marshall laid out the basic precepts of a corporation in this landmark ruling:

> A corporation is an artificial being, invisible, intangible, and existing only in the contemplation of law. Being the mere creature of the law, it possesses only those properties which the charter of its creation confers upon it, either expressly, or as incidental to its very existence. These are such as are supposed best calculated to effect the object for which it was created. Among the most important are immortality, and, if the expression may be allowed, individuality; properties by which a perpetual succession of many persons are considered as the same, and may act as a single individual.[3]

Thus, under the laws of the United States, a corporation is a creature of law, has characteristics necessary to fulfill its purpose for being, has an individuality, has perpetual existence through the process of succession, and can act as would a natural person. Chief Justice Marshall's ruling, which remains the law of the land, provided a solid legal foundation for the concept of the corporation that enabled it to grow in use and value.

Marshall's ruling was later upheld and extended in another landmark case: *Santa Clara County v. Southern Pacific Railroad*. Following the Civil War, the Fourteenth Amendment was added to the U.S. Constitution with the intent of protecting newly freed slaves, "persons," from abuse. In 1886, in the *Santa Clara County* case the U.S. Supreme Court extended its protections to corporations. The court ruled that corporations are "persons," have the same standing before the court as a human being, and are therefore protected by the Constitution to have a right to "due process of law" and to have "equal protection of the laws."[4]

In the 1890s two states dramatically changed their corporation laws to the great advantage of corporations. New Jersey and Delaware both enacted laws that repealed rules that businesses can incorporate only for narrowly defined purposes, for a limited duration, and can operate only in particular locations. New laws also allowed corporations to buy and hold stock in other corporations, relaxing rules on mergers and acquisitions. John D. Rockefeller immediately reincorporated the Standard Oil Trust in New Jersey to take advantage of this new law. Other states quickly adopted the same regulations.[5]

The impact was to free corporations at last from the remaining vestiges of English common law that had restricted chartered companies. Now American business corporations were free to expand by acquiring others, operate in any state for any legitimate purpose, and have true perpetual existence. The great merger and acquisition boom that ensued was a direct result of this new legal framework.

CLASSIFICATIONS OF CORPORATIONS

Under American corporation law, there are three classifications of private corporations that may conduct for-profit business activities: domestic, foreign, and alien corporations.

Domestic corporations are those that are incorporated in the state in which they do business. For example, a corporation doing business in California that is also incorporated in California is a California domestic corporation, operating under the laws of the state of California. This is the typical case for most small and middle-size businesses.

Foreign corporations are those that are doing business in states other than the one in which they are incorporated. For example, a company incorporated in Delaware that is doing business in New York is viewed in New York as a foreign corporation.

An *alien corporation* is one that is incorporated in a country outside the United States. A Swiss company doing business in Pennsylvania is an alien corporation in Pennsylvania. For the most part, alien corporations are treated as foreign corporations throughout the fifty states.

It is very important to understand that all three types of corporation have a right to do business in any of the fifty states once they are legally incorporated in their domestic jurisdiction. All foreign and alien corporations, however, must obtain a certificate of authority to conduct business in all states in which they wish to do business—other than the state or nation in which they are incorporated.

THE PROCESS OF INCORPORATION

Forming a corporation is a straightforward process. The entrepreneur needs to identify which state is the most attractive for doing so. For convenience, most start-up companies incorporate in the state in which they intend to do business. So, if your business will be based, for example, in California, the state that has the largest number of start-up corporations primarily because it has the largest population, it is likely that you will choose to incorporate in that state, under California law. It thus becomes a domestic corporation in the state of California.

Again, once your company is incorporated in any state, it can do business in all states—after filing a certificate of authority with the secretary of state of the other states. California's secretary of state charges a $30 fee for the certificate of authority from foreign corporations.[6]

Later, if your business grows and prospers, if you wish you can re-incorporate in another state to take advantage of benefits that certain states offer to companies incorporated under their laws. Two of the most popular states are Delaware and Nevada because both provide companies incorporated there particular benefits not offered elsewhere. For example, Delaware provides greater protections for management against hostile take-overs than any other state, and Nevada has no corporate income tax and wide-ranging privacy protection. More than half of the corporations listed on the New York Stock Exchange are incorporated in Delaware because its laws are so favorable.

REVISED MODEL BUSINESS CORPORATION ACT

There is a procedure and format that has to some extent standardized the incorporation process throughout the United States, but it is not mandatory that states follow it. The American Bar Association prepared this draft law, an act, as a guideline for states to adopt to gain a degree of consistency between states' corporation laws. This Revised Model Business Corporation Act was initially drafted in 1950 and revised in 1984. Most states use it as the basis of their corporation codes, some states use only portions of it, and a few states do not use it at all. Therefore, you will need to inquire what the specific incorporation process is in the particular state in which you intend to incorporate. This procedure can be found in the state's corporation code.

Under the Revised Model Business Corporation Act, the process has these steps. First, the people organizing a business that they intend to incorporate, called the incorporators, must choose a name for their corporation. That name must not have been registered and trademarked by another company anywhere in the United States. Even if the name is not currently in use, it might be protected by a trademark, and you could be sued by the trademark holder if you infringe on his or her intellectual property. To avoid infringement, you should search the roster of company titles at your state capital (usually the secretary of state's office) and also at the U.S. Patent and Trademark Office, U.S. Department of Commerce, 2021 Jefferson Davis Highway, Arlington, VA 22202, (800) 786–9199. The U.S. Trademark Office also maintains an Internet database.[7]

If your search finds no conflict, then you should register you company's name at the U.S. Patent Office and at the office of the secretary of state in which you intend to incorporate. Some states, such as California, have a procedure whereby the incorporators can reserve a name for 30 days while undertaking a search; the Name Reservation Request Form is submitted to the secretary of state with a fee of $20, along with your request for pre-clearance of your articles of incorporation.

This process is different from the one required for filing a patent to protect an invention or a trademark, or a copyright to protect the brand name you have chosen to represent that invention. For patent searches and for filing an application for patent protection, the U.S. Patent Office requires you to have a patent attorney or an agent who is registered with the U.S. Patent Office to perform this service for you. Be prepared to pay a fee. To register a patent, contact the U.S. Department of Commerce, Assistant Commissioner for Trademarks, Patent Applications, Washington, DC 20231, (800) 786–9199. To register a trademark, contact the Trademark Office, U.S. Department of Commerce, 2021 Jefferson Davis Highway, Arlington, VA 22202, (800) 786–9199.

Second, all states require that you include in the company's name the word *Corporation*, *Incorporated*, *Company*, or *Limited*, or an abbreviation of that word: *Corp.*, *Inc.*, *Co.*, or *Ltd.* This word signals to the world that the firm it will be doing business with is incorporated, carrying with it liability protection. As in the British tradition, this is a clear warning to creditors that the company's risk exposure is limited. Also the company name must not contain words that do not relate to the nature of the business for which the corporate charter is being issued. For example, if the company is to engage in the dry cleaning business, it may not have the word *pharmacy* in its name.

Third, after you are certain your company has clear title to its corporate name, you then prepare a document called the articles of incorporation, also known as the corporate charter. This will become the main governing document of the corporation. The articles of incorporation must be approved by the state government in the state in which you wish to incorporate. Once this approval is received, the document is filed with the secretary of state in that same state. In California, the filing fee is $100 for a general stock corporation. Once the document is filed, the corporation is established.

The approving and filing procedure is somewhat complex and must be followed precisely to avoid delays and rejection. To ensure compliance, you should retain the services of an attorney specializing in this area of practice, corporate law. These attorney fees can be considerable.

ARTICLES OF INCORPORATION

Under the Revised Model Business Corporation Act, the articles of incorporation, the basic governing document of the corporation, must contain the following items:

- The name of the corporation
- The address of the corporation—the initial registered office
- The name and address of the initial registered agent (usually a law firm)
- The name and address of each incorporator (the persons filing the articles of incorporation)
- The number of shares the corporation is authorized to issue
- The business purpose(s) for which the corporation is being formed
- The intended period of duration—a specific number of years or perpetual
- Limitations of the powers of the corporation
- Regulation of the affairs of the corporation

The articles of incorporation are first submitted to the state office that reviews corporate charters to ensure that your articles conform to law and will be acceptable for filing. In California, as in most states, this is the secretary of state's office. You can pay a preclearance/expedited fee to speed up the process at the California secretary of state's office; fees range from $250 to $500, depending on the speed you request.[8] Once that office approves them, the incorporators or their agent then files the articles with the secretary of state in the same state that gave the approval. The acceptance of the filing of the articles is the act of incorporation.

The California secretary of state offers an expedited filing service for an additional fee: Class A Service, based on preclearance approval, is 4 hours for a $500 fee; or Class B Service, without preclearance approval, is 24 hours for a $350 fee.[9] All special handling must be done in person at the State Capitol in Sacramento.

Later on, the articles of incorporation may require amendment for any number of legitimate reasons; if so, the shareholders must approve the amendment(s), and then the articles of amendment are filed with the secretary of state. Such amendments must consist of items that could have lawfully been included in the original filing of the articles of incorporation. In California, a certificate of amendment has a $30 filing fee. If the articles of incorporation require substantial changes (e.g., an entire rewrite to reflect major changes in the company's scope of business), the new articles are then filed with the secretary of state; in California the fee for restated articles of incorporation is $30.

An example of a restatement of a corporation's articles of incorporation is Dell Computer Corporation. When Michael Dell first incorporated in Texas in the early 1980s, this was the name he chose. Later, he re-incorporated in Delaware. Still later, after his business had expanded to include more items than personal computers—including such products as laptops, servers, printers, networking devices, and so on—he changed the company's name to Dell, Inc. and restated his articles of incorporation in Delaware.

Most states require domestic corporations, particularly nonprofit domestic corporations, to file biennially a statement of information with the secretary of state's office to update basic information regarding the corporation, even if the corporation may not be actively engaged in business at the time the statement is due. The filing fee in California is $20.[10]

Bylaws of the Corporation

All corporations have bylaws. Along with the articles of incorporation, the bylaws are the governing documents of the corporation. This document, simply called the bylaws of the X Corporation, is much more detailed than the articles of incorporation because it delineates the way the corporation's business affairs are to be conducted and provides the internal management structure of the corporation. The bylaws can be drafted, approved, and filed by the original incorporators, or they can be developed and approved by the board of directors of the corporation after it is established. The latter approach is most often used for convenience.

Bylaws typically include the following items:

- The time and place of the annual shareholders' meeting
- How special meetings of shareholders are to be called
- The time and place of the monthly meetings of the board of directors
- How special meetings of the board of directors are to be called
- The notice required for meetings
- The quorum needed to hold a shareholders' or board of directors' meeting
- The required vote needed to enact a corporate matter
- The committees of the board of directors and their duties
- The corporate officers and their duties
- Where the records of the corporation are to be kept
- Rights of inspection of corporation records
- Procedures for transferring shares of the corporation

The corporation's bylaws can be amended using the procedure stipulated in the articles of incorporation. This procedure usually provides that the board of directors can amend the bylaws, but under the law the corporation's shareholders always have the absolute right to amend the bylaws.

ORGANIZATIONAL MEETING

After the articles of incorporation are filed, meaning that the corporation is now in existence, the incorporators—the initial directors of the corporation—must hold an organizational meeting. At this meeting, the directors adopt the bylaws, elect the officers of the corporation, and transact any other business that is appropriate to initiate business activities.

The types of decisions that the directors usually make at the organizational meeting to initiate business activities include the following:

- Approve the form of the stock certificate
- Authorize the issuance of shares of stock
- Accept share subscriptions
- Choose a bank
- Choose an outside auditing firm
- Establish committees of the board—including an audit committee
- Hire company employees
- Determine the salaries of company officers
- Authorize the officers to apply for government licenses to conduct business
- Empower corporate officers to enter into contracts on the corporation's behalf

The organizational meeting is the first step toward the company's actual launch into business. From this meeting forward, it is the officers of the corporation, led by the chief executive officer, who actually operate the business on behalf of the board of directors and the shareholders.

CORPORATE DIRECTORS AND OFFICERS

The directors of a corporation are the members of the board of directors of that company. They are all elected by the shareholders and serve until the next annual shareholders' meeting (usually one year), at which they can seek reelection for another year or vacate the board.

Under the Revised Model Business Corporation Act, if there are nine or more directors, they can be elected for staggered three-year terms of office, a third of them being elected (or reelected) each year at the shareholders' meeting. One purpose of having staggered terms, as in the U.S. Senate, is to preserve continuity and to prevent wholesale change in the membership of the board. Another purpose is to inhibit a takeover of the corporation by preventing the company threatening the takeover from packing the board with its supporters to gain a majority.

The principal duties of the directors are to (1) elect the officers of the corporation and determine their compensation; (2) oversee the work of the officers of the corporation to safeguard the interests of the shareholders; (3) establish broad policy direction for the corporation, such as what businesses to enter and exit; (4) determine the number of shares to issue and decide if, when, and how large a dividend to pay out to shareholders; (5) decide when and where to hold the next board meeting (unless this is stipulated in the bylaws); and (6) initiate any action that will require the shareholders' approval by passing a resolution of the board authorizing the action—such as a merger or acquisition, an amendment to the articles of incorporation, and other major transactions that would fundamentally affect the life and health of the corporation.

There are two kinds of directors: inside and outside. *Inside* directors are those individuals who are also officers of the corporation. Typically, the officers who sit on the board of directors include the chief executive officer (who may also be the chairperson of the board of directors), the chief operating officer (who is often also the president), and the chief financial officer, who is also the corporation's treasurer. These directors are called inside directors because their principal employment is inside the company.

Outside directors are those directors who are not employed by the corporation. These independent directors are asked to serve on the board because of their business skills and experience, such as attorneys, bankers, experienced heads of other companies, and so forth. Precise rules determining the meaning of outside versus inside directors have been developed by the New York Stock Exchange and other major exchanges; these are presented in chapter 9, Corporate Governance.

OFFICERS OF THE CORPORATION

The officers of the corporation are individuals who are elected by the board of directors, under procedures defined in the articles of incorporation and the bylaws, to hold the various executive positions the board has created to operate and manage the firm. These people are the top executive employees of the corporation. The key officer positions that are typically created and filled by qualified individuals are chief executive officer, chief operating officer, chief financial officer, secretary of the corporation, and any other top-level position the board decides is needed to manage the day-to-day business affairs of the company effectively.

The officers are chosen and elected by the board of directors for a term of office decided by the board, which could be for a specific number of years (usually defined in an employment contract), until terminated, until the individual voluntarily vacates the position, or until the individual reaches mandatory retirement age, which is set by the board.

All employees of the company, including elected officers, hold their positions on the basis of good behavior, meaning they will break no laws or company regulations. If they do, the board can terminate them *for cause*, meaning there is a good reason for doing so. Violations of law would include such acts as theft, embezzlement, and discrimination in hiring or firing. Violations of company policy could include such actions as sexual harassment of an employee, use of illegal substances on company property, and misuse of company assets (using a company plane for personal purposes).

Duty of Care

All directors and officers have two overarching duties to the corporation, in addition to the specific duties and responsibilities stipulated in the articles of incorporation and the bylaws. These two duties are *of care* and *of loyalty*.

The duty of care simply means that all directors and officers must use care and due diligence when they act on behalf of the corporation. They must perform their duties in good faith, with the care that an ordinary prudent person would use in this position in similar circumstances, and in a way that the person honestly believes would be in the best interests of the corporation. Honest mistakes of judgment—decisions made at the time and under the circumstances they were made—are *not* punishable, according to the *business judgment rule*.

A director who fails to exercise his or her duty of care is said to breach the duty. A breach of the duty of care can result in the director being *personally* liable to the corporation and its shareholders for any harm, called an *injury*, that may result to the company. A typical breach of care is caused by the negligence of the director to be properly informed about the business of the corporation and to intervene in a timely manner to prevent an action by an officer or by the company as a whole that may cause it an injury.

How is negligence created? A director may fail to attend board meetings regularly to keep informed of unfolding events, may fail to investigate a company matter that appears suspicious, may fail to properly supervise a company officer who later is found to have committed a crime, such as embezzlement, and so forth. Breaches of duty of care are brought before courts to adjudicate them case by case.

Duty of Loyalty

The duty of loyalty provides that directors and officers subordinate their own personal interests to the corporation and its shareholders. The officer or director must put his or her allegiance to the corporation's welfare above his or her personal interest or gain. In the event a director or officer makes personal profit on a transaction involving the corporation, the corporation can sue that director or officer for recovery of the illicit profit.

FINANCING THE BUSINESS

Among the first issues the directors and officers of a newly formed corporation face is how to finance the business of the corporation. There are two principal ways for doing so: issuing stock and undertaking debt.

Classes of Stock

Stock in the corporation represents an equity ownership in the corporation. Stock is called an equity security. Holders of the company's stock are the owners of the corporation because when they purchased the stock they purchased an ownership right in the corporation.

There are two types or classes of stock: common stock and preferred stock. Common stock is the type of equity security that most people refer to when they say they own stock in a certain company. Preferred stock is an equity security that has rights and preferences associated with it that put its owners ahead of common stockholders if the company fails. For example, at the time of liquidation of the firm, or its bankruptcy, preferred stockholders and creditors of the corporation are first in line to receive payment out of the assets of the company for the value of their preferred stock and their loans. Common stockholders are then paid for the value of their stock, if there are any assets remaining.

Common stock derives its name from the fact that it has no preferences, unlike preferred stock. A share of common stock represents "the residual value" of the corporation, meaning that holders of common stock get paid what is left over—the residue—after preferred stockholders and creditors are paid out of the assets of the corporation at the time the corporation is liquidated.

Anyone who owns common stock is known as a common stockholder. That person's investment in the corporation is represented by common stock certificates. The value of a share of common stock is determined by the price other individuals are willing to pay for it on a stock exchange on any given day; it has no intrinsic value of its own.[11] A number of factors go into the calculation of the market value of a share in a particular company's stock: the dollar value of the corporation's revenue as reported each quarter and each year, the earnings (profit) of the corporation each quarter, the outlook for the growth of the company's business, overall economic conditions affecting the sales of the company's products and services, the amount of debt the company may have undertaken, and so forth.

Common stockholders may or may not be paid dividends for their investment in the company. Dividends are payments to stockholders made from the corporation's profits after paying taxes. The board of directors makes the decision whether to declare dividends and, if so, how much, based on the company's earnings. Many start-up companies do not declare dividends for a number of years, using earnings to invest in the company's growth, rather than paying them out to investors. Investors buy shares in such companies in the hope that the company will perform well in its markets and the value of its stock will rise.

Common stockholders also have voting rights because they own the company. It is the common stockholders, not preferred stockholders, who elect the members of the board of directors, and they also have the right to vote on critical issues affecting the corporation, such as mergers and acquisitions.

Debt Financing

The second major way corporations have of financing their activities is to borrow money, which is called debt financing. If a corporation borrows money from others, it becomes the debtor and the lender of the money is called the creditor.

Debt financing is quite different from *equity* financing, such as issuing stock or selling a portion of a privately owned company to another person. In the case of debt financing, the creditor does not own any of the company and therefore has no right to claim any of its revenues and profits, except, of course, to receive interest and principal payments on the loan in accordance with the terms and conditions of the loan agreement. An equity owner is just that: another party who owns a portion of the company, for example, 25 percent, in exchange for a major investment in the company. That person then shares with the other equity owners the risks and rewards of ownership.

Most start-up companies prefer debt financing rather than equity financing because they want to keep the future rewards of ownership for themselves—future profits. However, some start-ups are not viewed as creditworthy, and so have no choice but to seek equity investors to finance their activities.[12]

Corporations use three types of debt securities to finance their operations: bonds, debentures, and notes.

Bonds are long-term debt securities that are secured by *collateral* of the corporation. Collateral is a tangible asset of some type: buildings, land, equipment, and so forth. Holders of bonds can foreclose on the collateral if the corporation fails to pay interest or principal as required by the terms and conditions of the bond. At the end of the maturity period, the corporation must pay off the face value of the bond to the bondholders. Often this is done by issuing a new bond.

Debentures are long-term debt securities that are *unsecured*, meaning there is no collateral backing them. Debentures often have a maturity of at least thirty years. Their value at the time of issuance is based on the corporation's general credit rating as given by a major credit rating service, such as Moody's Investors Service or Standard & Poor's. In the event the corporation is forced to liquidate, holders of debentures are treated like any other creditor holding an unsecured note.

Notes are debt securities having a shorter maturity than debentures, no more than five years. Notes may or may not be secured by collateral. Note holders are usually banks.

CONCLUSION

This chapter addresses the legal basis for corporations, how and where they are established, the initial organization of the corporation, election of directors and officers, what their general responsibilities include, and how they finance the activities of the business. Anyone interested in forming a corporation should contact a corporation attorney who is licensed to practice law in the state in which he or she wishes to incorporate.

NOTES

1. As a reference and guide, this chapter is largely based on Frank B. Cross and Roger LeRoy Miller, *West's Legal Environment of Business,* 5th ed. (Mason, OH: Thomson South-Western, 2004), Chapter 18; and Henry R. Cheeseman, *The Legal and Regulatory Environment,* 2nd ed. (Upper Saddle River, NJ: Prentice Hall, 2000), Chapter 13.

2. www.Fortune.com/500/archive.

3. 4 Wheaton 518, 636 (1819); cited in Henry R. Cheeseman, *The Legal and Regulatory Environment,* 2nd ed., 352. The *Dartmouth College* ruling also established the sanctity of contracts in American law.

4. 118 U.S. 394 (1886), *Santa Clara County v. Southern Pacific Railroad Co.*

5. Roland Marchand, *Creating the Corporate Soul* (Berkeley, CA: University of California Press, 1998).

6. www.ss.ca.gov/business/corp/corp_formsfees.htm.

7. www.uspto.gov/web/menu/tmebc/index.html.

8. www.ss.ca.gov/business/corp/corp_precexp.htm.

9. Ibid.

10. www.ss.ca.gov/business.

11. The Revised Model Business Corporation Act did away with the concept of par value of stock; this was the minimum value assigned to a share of common stock by the corporation's board of directors at the time of initial public offering of its stock. All stock today is issued as no par value, meaning that the securities markets will determine its value.

12. For a discussion of the pros and cons of debt versus equity financing, see Wesley B. Truitt, *Business Planning: A Comprehensive Framework and Process* (Westport, CT: Quorum Books, 2002), 155–157.

RECOMMENDED READINGS

Cross, Frank B., and Roger LeRoy Miller, *West's Legal Environment of Business* 5th ed. (Mason, OH: Thomson South-Western, 2004).

Marchand, Roland, *Creating the Corporate Soul: The Rise of Public Relations and Corporate Imagery in American Big Business* (Berkeley, CA: University of California Press, 1998).

Six

Operating a Corporation

Now that the corporation has been established, it is time to operate it as a business. This chapter addresses such operational issues as what duties the corporation's directors and officers perform, the requirement to hold board and annual shareholder meetings, how these meetings are noticed and quorum requirements, and reporting requirements of minutes of meetings. Also addressed are other corporate requirements such as the procedures for issuing stock, financial reports, paying dividends and corporate taxes on profits, and disclosure requirements.

This chapter also addresses day-to-day operations of the corporation: organizational structures for start-up and established companies, staff versus line responsibilities, and generally how a corporation's business is managed. Public perceptions of the identity of the corporation must be managed, and sometimes management may need to change the company's name. Managing the corporate image is a tricky task.

DUTIES OF DIRECTORS AND OFFICERS

The principal duties of the members of the board of directors of the corporation are the following:

- Elect the officers of the corporation.
- Oversee the work of the officers as they perform day-to-day management.

- Make decisions regarding fundamental aspects of the corporation, such as decisions to acquire or merge with another company or to change the nature of the business (add or delete product lines).
- Terminate officers if their performance fails to meet board requirements.

Under American corporation law, directors have a *fiduciary duty* to the shareholders to oversee the work of the officers, who are the top executives of the firm. This means that there is a legal requirement on the part of the directors to protect the investment of shareholders, to make every effort to see that it is used properly and legally.

All employees in the company ultimately report to the officers, and it is they who are responsible to the directors for the successes and failures of the company. If the directors fail to properly perform their supervisory duty, they can be sued individually by shareholders for a breach of fiduciary duty. This is one of the very few instances in which the personal liability protections of the corporation can be set aside; this is called *piercing the corporate veil*. This does *not* mean that the officers and directors must always be right, and that all their decisions prove profitable; it *does* mean that directors must adequately perform their oversight responsibilities consistent with their duties of care and loyalty.

Top Officers

Corporate officers are elected by the board of directors and given the responsibility to manage the business affairs of the company. They are in effect the generals and admirals who command the company. The bylaws of the corporation delineate their specific responsibilities in the job descriptions of each office. Officers typically hold their positions for as long as they perform their duties effectively, or until they are promoted, decide to take a position with another firm, or retire.

CEO

The chief executive officer (CEO) is responsible for every aspect of the performance of the firm. All other officers report to him or her, and the CEO reports to the board of directors, which collectively represents the owners of the corporation—the shareholders.

The American CEO is quite different from the chief executive/administrative officer of corporations outside the United States. According to the late Peter Drucker, "the CEO is an American invention—designed first by Alexander Hamilton in the Constitution in the earliest years of the Republic, and then transferred into the private sector in the form of Hamilton's own Bank of New York and of the Second Bank of the United States in Philadelphia." What makes the CEO of American firms so unique is that "he or she has *distinct and specific* work" to perform and as the clearly-defined leader of the enterprise carries the full responsibility for its success or failure.[1]

In large corporations the CEO is usually given an employment agreement, developed by the board's compensation committee, that states his or her duties (from the bylaws), spells out compensation and other benefits (stock, bonus, and perquisites), and sets the number of years of service under the current contract. Some employment contracts also have a *morals clause*, a provision that states if the CEO performs an immoral act (a violation of law or of the company's code of ethics), the board can terminate the agreement and fire the individual. These agreements are, of course, renewable through a renegotiation process at the end of the term, provided the CEO is performing his or her duties to the board's satisfaction. Otherwise, this is a convenient time for the board to let the individual go gracefully, by not renewing the agreement.

COO

In large corporations there is often an officer who holds the title chief operating officer (COO). This position, as defined in the bylaws, typically carries with it the title of company president, unless the CEO also has that title. In that event, the COO might have the title executive vice president, being the number-two person in the chain of command after the CEO/president. If the firm has a COO, that person is usually responsible for day-to-day operations of the company's business, leaving the CEO to deal with larger issues of strategy, expansion, and public affairs activities. The CEO and the COO must be compatible and work well together in an atmosphere of trust and confidence.

CFO

The chief financial officer (CFO) is responsible to the CEO and possibly also to the COO for the finances of the corporation. This officer also may carry the title of company treasurer, handling the company's cash, investments, paying the bills, making financial reports, filing income tax returns, and so forth. In large corporations, these duties are assigned to individual senior officials who report to the CFO, and each may have a large department beneath him or her—such as accounting, accounts receivable and payable, financial reporting, comptroller, tax, and so forth.

These three positions—CEO, COO, and CFO—are the top jobs in the corporation. In large corporations the individuals holding them are all located at the company's headquarters, called the corporate office, which may be in a location different from the firm's operating units such as factories and distribution centers that are probably located in industrial areas of a city. For example, Boeing's corporate headquarters is in Chicago, where the company has no plants.

Demographic Profile. What is the profile of the top managers of major American corporations? Looking across a wide swath of the largest U.S.-based corporations, the *Fortune* 500 in 2003, a recent study indicates that management ranks and boardrooms remain almost exclusively white male enclaves. Although African-Americans represent 13.8 percent of the U.S. workforce, they held only 6.5 percent of manager positions. Hispanics were 11.1 percent of the workforce but were just 5 percent of managers. Whites made up 69.9 percent of the workforce, and they held 84.5 percent of manager positions—and even more of the top management jobs. Only 7.9 percent of top earners at *Fortune* 500 companies in 2003 were women.[2]

BOARD MEETING REQUIREMENTS

All corporations are required to hold meetings of their boards of directors and to keep minutes of those meetings, which are periodically filed with state authorities, usually the office of the state's secretary of state. It is primarily in these meetings that the directors perform their role as overseers of the corporation. The date and time of these periodic meetings is usually set in the bylaws or by vote of the board, such as the second Tuesday of each month at 9:00 A.M., and so there is no need to provide formal notice of the meetings. Special meetings can be called at any time to address specific, usually urgent, topics, provided sufficient notice is sent to all directors. Most boards of large corporations meet monthly except for two summer months and sometimes December is also skipped. Committees of directors can meet at any time.

For a board meeting to be official and valid, it must have a quorum; that is, a minimum number of directors in attendance. The quorum varies by state law and by corporate articles of incorporation and bylaws, but it is at least a majority of the members. Voting is usually done in person by each board member, though there are provisions for proxy voting in some states. The rule is each director has one vote, including the CEO and the chairperson of the board. The bylaws may require a greater than majority vote for certain critical matters such as a merger, usually a two-thirds vote.

ANNUAL MEETING REQUIREMENTS

Corporations must hold an annual meeting of their shareholders. The purpose of this meeting is to elect the members of the board for the next year (or if the board has staggered terms, the vote is for the next one-third of directors to serve for the next two years) and to conduct other business that the directors choose to bring before the shareholders. These items typically include a vote to approve the outside accounting/auditing firm, any changes in compensation arrangements for board members, and other business matters that the board chooses to discuss. Typically, this is also an opportunity that the CEO utilizes to make a report to the shareholders on the condition of the company.

Annual shareholder meetings must comply with Securities and Exchange Commission regulations regarding how much notice is provided to shareholders before the meeting is held, giving the date, time, and place of the meeting and an agenda of what will be covered. Shareholders have a right to address the chairperson and the entire board at these meetings. Some large corporations hold their annual meetings in different cities throughout the country to enable greater numbers of shareholders to attend. Other companies choose to hold their meetings in company-owned facilities that are less easily accessed (versus a large hotel's ballroom) to discourage attendance by disgruntled shareholders in a bad year. These meetings are subject to quorum requirements (at least a majority of the shares must be represented in person or by proxy) and conformance to company bylaws.

STOCK

Directors authorize the corporation's officers to undertake the issuance of stock. This is done, of course, to raise capital to operate the business and possibly to expand it through either internal growth or acquisition. The procedure for issuing stock, particularly the initial public offering (IPO), is prescribed by law and by regulations issued by the Securities and Exchange Commission (SEC). These procedures must be followed precisely to the letter; otherwise there may be delays in granting permission to issue the stock, or there may be penalties if the SEC concludes that fraud or other deviant behavior is present.

If a corporation wishes to make an IPO of its stock, this becomes a *federal* government matter. Up to now, the corporation has been created and acted solely within *state* laws and regulations. Stock issuance triggers federal involvement. The company must file a registration statement with the SEC, comply with other SEC regulations for issuing stock, and later must file periodic financial reports with the SEC.[3]

REGISTRATION

The IPO registration statement to the SEC contains the following items:

- a description of the securities intended to be offered for sale, such as common or preferred stock
- the business the company is in
- names of the company's officers and the amounts of stock each person is to receive
- any pending litigation
- purposes for which the money to be raised by the stock will be used
- pertinent government regulations with which the company must comply
- extent of competition within the industry
- any special factors or issues that might have a material effect on the performance of the firm

The registration statement must be accompanied by a financial statement certified by a certified public accountant (CPA) and a copy of the proposed prospectus, which is a summary of the information contained in the registration statement that will be sent to the prospective buyers of the stock. After filing these papers, there is a twenty-one-day waiting period before registration becomes effective, unless an earlier date is requested.

There are precise regulations regarding what the company may and may not do before filing the registration materials, during the waiting period, and after the SEC approves the registration. A firm specializing in stock registration and underwriting of securities should be consulted regarding these activities because violations of regulations are subject to penalties and no registration. The Securities Act of 1933, as amended, governs initial public offerings of securities.

REPORTING

The Securities and Exchange Act of 1934 also governs the initial offering of securities and their trading. The SEC, established by this act, is the regulatory agency of the federal government for stock trading and reporting. The SEC requires corporations to issue financial reports if the company has registered securities, has assets of $5 million or more, has five hundred shareholders or more, or if its securities are traded on a national exchange. Companies falling under any of these criteria are called *reporting* companies.

All reporting companies must file the following with the SEC: form 10-K, an annual financial report; form 10-Q, a quarterly financial report; and form 8-K, a monthly report when a material event occurs, such as a merger. The SEC stipulates the form and precise content of each report. All the reports become a matter of public record.

Once all the necessary SEC approvals have been received, the company's underwriters, major securities firms such as Merrill Lynch & Company and Goldman, Sachs & Company, will help the firm establish an initial stock price based on their valuation of the firm's current business and future potential. The underwriters will also help prepare and distribute a pro-spectus to advertise the new stock to the investing public.

The lead underwriters will then publish a notice in major newspapers of the intention to sell the selected number of shares of the stock at the initially determined price per share, giving the names of the lead underwriters and the subunderwriters (companies listed below the line in smaller print). This notice is known as a *tombstone* because it looks a bit like a headstone in a cemetery. As an example, see Figure 6.1 for the tombstone for the IPO of National Financial Partners Corporation, as published in the *Wall Street Journal* on September 21, 2005, p. C5. The moment trading in the stock begins, the market sets the stock price, which may be higher or lower than what the underwriters had forecast.

STOCK OWNERSHIP AND TRADING

Once the SEC approves the initial public offering, stock can be sold to the public and trading in the stock can begin. A stock certificate is issued to all purchasers of stock as evidence of their ownership of a specified number of shares, granting shareholders numerous rights of ownership: to vote for members of the board of directors, purchase future issues of stock, receive dividends, attend shareholder meetings, approve changes to the articles of incorporation and the bylaws, sell shares, and receive a proportionate share of corporate assets on dissolution of the firm. Specific rights of shareholders depend on provisions covering this in the articles of incorporation, cor-poration law in the state of incorporation, and SEC regulations.[4]

After stock is issued and sold, a new set of SEC regulations is triggered, all having to do with trading. One of the most important regulations has to do with *insider trading*, which the SEC strictly prohibits. Insiders are company officers, directors, and employees having access to privileged company in-formation. Insiders also include in-house or outside lawyers, accountants, and other financial professionals, such as bankers. Anyone having nonpublic information about the company and a fiduciary duty to the company wherever that person is located is an insider.

Persons falling into any of these categories who trade in the company's stock using nonpublic information to make a profit are liable for prosecution

FIGURE 6.1
National Financial Partners Corp. IPO Tombstone

This announcement is under no circumstances to be construed as an offer to sell or as a solicitation of an offer to buy any of these securities.
The offering is made only by the Prospectus.

August 17, 2005

7,353,733 Shares

National Financial Partners Corp.

Common Stock

Price $41 Per Share

Copies of the Prospectus may be obtained in any State or jurisdiction in which this announcement is circulated from only
such of the undersigned or other dealers or brokers as may lawfully offer these securities in such State or jurisdiction.

Merrill Lynch & Co.   **Goldman, Sachs & Co.**

JPMorgan   UBS Investment Bank   Keefe, Bruyette & Woods

CIBC World Markets
                Cochran, Caronia & Co.
                        Fox-Pitt, Kelton
                                Sandler O'Neill & Partners, L.P.
                                        Wachovia Securities

for insider trading. This is the case because such persons are taking advantage of the public to make personal gain.

It was precisely on this point that Samuel Waksal, CEO of ImClone Systems, was convicted in the highly publicized Martha Stewart case. Waksal sold his ImClone stock the day before the Food and Drug Administration announced it would not approve his new anticancer medicine.[5] Only certain days of the year are reserved for trading company stock by insiders, and Waksal violated that rule in an effort to profit personally.

Under the Sarbanes-Oxley Act of 2002, employees and agents of publicly traded companies can report suspected illegal acts in stock trading, financial reporting, or other aspects of corporate financial transactions without fear of retaliation by their employers. Anyone involved in stock transactions—brokers, advisors, attorneys, bankers, and so on—is liable under this law to criminal prosecution for retaliation against whistle-blowers.

Once the stock is issued and revenue from its sale flows into the corporation's treasury, the directors and officers are free to use those funds for the purposes stated in their filings to the SEC—internal growth, acquisitions, and so forth.

CORPORATE PROFITS AND TAXES

When a corporation makes a profit, it will pay tax on that profit at the prevailing *corporate tax rate*. Taxation of corporate profits is required by the federal government and by the majority of state governments. These taxes are paid quarterly to the federal government and are accompanied by form 10-Q. The profit left over after the corporation pays its federal and state taxes is called *net profit*.

When a corporation has net profits, its board of directors has two choices of what to do with them. They can either distribute all or part of the net profits to their shareholders in the form of dividends, or they can retain them.

Dividends are distributions of profits or income that are ordered by the directors and paid to shareholders in proportion to their number of shares held in the corporation. The corporation receives no tax deduction for paying dividends. When individual shareholders receive dividends, which represent income to them, they will pay a tax on that income on their individual income tax returns.

This is the so-called *double taxation* drawback of corporate taxes: both the corporation and the individual dividend-receiving shareholder pay tax on the corporation's profits. The one exception to this rule is when corporations

Corporate Income Tax Rates

The United States imposes the highest corporate income tax rate among the 30 wealthiest countries. The combined federal and state corporate tax rate of 39.3 percent is 10 percent higher than the average among countries in the Organization of Economic Cooperation and Development (OECD) as shown below.

U.S.	39.3%
Japan	30.0
Germany	38.9
France	35.0
Britain	30.0
Australia	30.0
Sweden	28.0
Switzerland	24.1
Ireland	12.5
OECD Average	29.2

The United States ranks well below average on *total* tax burden because most other wealthy nations also impose high value-added, capital gains, gasoline, and payroll taxes.[6]

pay distributions of capital; these distributions to shareholders result from the sale of fixed assets (versus earnings) and are not taxed by the government.

When corporations choose to retain all or part of their profit, these are called *retained earnings*. Many young companies pay no dividend at all, even if they earn a handsome profit, choosing to retain earnings to reinvest in the business for its growth. Larger corporations retain earnings for various legitimate corporate purposes: to fund research and development, make acquisitions, buy equipment, pay down debt, and so forth. Retained earnings, if invested wisely by the directors and officers, can grow the value of the corporation and generate greater future earnings and stock value. Individual shareholders can sell their stock later at a higher price, reaping the capital gains from the higher selling price of their shares. As of 2004, the capital gain federal tax rate on stock held one year or longer is 15 percent.

ORGANIZATIONAL STRUCTURE

As a company grows from infancy to maturity, its business goals will expand. As this process unfolds, the firm will need to organize and periodically reorganize its people and activities to achieve its expanding strategic goals in the marketplace. This requires structure. Suffice it to say that strategy drives structure, as Alfred Chandler instructed decades ago.[7] Decide first on your strategy and then on a structure to support that strategy.

Keeping focused on the execution of its strategy is a major challenge for many of today's medium and large corporations. Sometimes their structure inhibits that task, as could have been the case with Unilever, with its traditional dual structure of two headquarters, one in Britain and the other in the Netherlands.[8] Unilever lost market share to its archrivals Procter & Gamble and Nestlé, who were highly focused on strategy execution using simple structures organized around product groups and individual brands.

Similarly, another dual-based multinational corporation lost focus and in the process developed a scandal. For nearly 100 years Royal Dutch/Shell was based in both the Netherlands and in Britain as a result of the 1907 merger of Royal Dutch Petroleum Company and Shell Transport & Trading Company, based in London. Beginning in 2002, the company repeatedly overstated its crude oil reserves by approximately 23 percent. British and American regulators discovered this illegal reporting and later fined the company $150 million. The board of directors fired the CEO. The deliberate overstatement of reserves partly resulted from the duel responsibility situation, which was rectified in 2004 in a corporate restructuring in which the company was combined into a single new entity called Royal Dutch Shell PLC, based in London.[9]

The structure of a modern corporation is largely a function of its age and size. Young start-up companies have very different structural needs than do large, established corporations. The organizational structure of each is unique to its stage of growth.

ENTREPRENEURIAL START-UP COMPANIES

Entrepreneurial start-up companies have very small structures usually centered around the owner(s). All the members of the leadership group operate as a single team whose captain is the owner. Owing to the fact of their newness, start-ups are typically small in size, not yet having developed a diverse product line necessitating a large number of employees, nor the resulting need for large organizational structure. Keeping the structure simple and straightforward also keeps it inexpensive to operate. Owners need to keep in mind a fundamental principle: people and structure add cost and complexity. Simplicity, not complexity, is a key to successful performance and profitability.

Figure 6.2 depicts a notional structure for a twenty-first century entrepreneurial start-up company having a single owner. GM's Alfred P. Sloan

FIGURE 6.2
Organizational Structure for a Modern Start-up Company

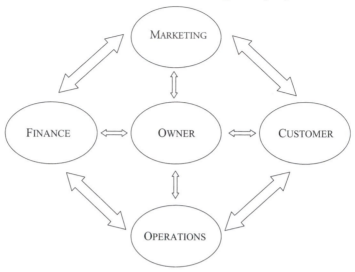

would be startled to see such a nonhierarchical structure. Notice that all the members of the leadership team deal with each other as well as with customers, except for the person handling the finances. Keep him or her away from customers.

As a company expands its sales and perhaps also its product offerings, it will need to grow internally. Growth requires additional people, which requires additional structure. As the structure and staff grow, the team leader will want to retain the team atmosphere—the team spirit—the company had when it was small. This collegial spirit, if retained, becomes part of the DNA of the firm, a core feature of its personality. If the team spirit is lost, the firm changes and becomes something different.

Apple Computer

This happened at Apple Computer. When Steve Jobs and Steve Wozniak, both at age twenty, founded the company in the mid-1970s, they did so in the Jobs family's garage, always wore casual clothes, and treated each other and their small growing staff as teammates. When they incorporated, the company's stock soared.

Ten years later, after the company had become highly successful with the introduction of the Macintosh computer, Jobs and the board of directors decided that "professional" management was now needed to handle its larger size. They brought in as CEO John Scully, who had been CEO of Pepsico North America. Scully was from the old school of corporate structure and style with which Apple's conservative board members were more comfortable.

Jobs's and Scully's visions of the future diverged, they had a falling out, and the board backed Scully, who fired Jobs and Wozniak, having tired of their casual, undisciplined style. Scully immediately removed the beanbag chairs, put in walls between offices, and set up a hierarchical chain of command. The company nearly went under. The board soon fired Scully and eventually brought back Steve Jobs, who restored the creative DNA and brought out exciting new products, such as the iPod.[10]

STRUCTURES OF ESTABLISHED CORPORATIONS

When a company has grown to a size that requires a significant number of employees to produce its products and services, it will need to reorganize its expanding workforce while continuing to focus its activities to achieve the company's goals.

As companies grow with their success, their leaders must be constantly vigilant to keep the creative juices flowing and not bureaucratize the firm. To achieve this, many large corporations reorganize themselves in one of two ways: (1) keep the company intact but restructure and reinvigorate it with a spirit of dynamism and entrepreneurship; or (2) split up the company into smaller operating units, each having profit and loss responsibility, to reinvigorate them and restore competitiveness.

Caterpillar Inc.

This $30-billion corporation, the world's largest manufacturer of earth-moving equipment, is an example of the first approach.[11] "Cat," as it is known throughout the world, had fifty years of uninterrupted profitability until 1982 when it posted its first loss. It was facing bankruptcy with losses mounting in the millions of dollars a day. The underlying problems were the worldwide recession, intense competition from Komatsu, its Japanese arch-rival, and high operating costs resulting in high prices. Cat's price for a piece of equipment comparable to Komatsu's was typically 20 percent higher—a premium that Cat demanded because of its extraordinary quality and service, as well as its high cost base. The 1982 loss was a rude wake-up call.

Cat's management began to address its problems at their most fundamental level and in the process changed the company's DNA within a few years. The company decentralized decision-making, eliminated bureaucracy, empowered employees at all levels to innovate and contribute, reduced redundant staffs, and invested in new plant and equipment as well as R&D to develop new, more cost-effective products.

On one day in 1990 the entire corporation was reorganized, eliminating decision centers that were remote from both customers and operations. Then the CEO retired and a younger one took over. This 180-degree turnaround worked because Cat was a resilient company that could face abrupt changes and turn them into opportunities. Beginning in 1993, twelve straight years of profitability followed. In 2005, *Forbes* magazine listed Caterpillar as the best-managed industrial corporation in America. Its new DNA is clearly working.

General Electric

Another example of the first approach, keep the company together but restructure and add vigor, is General Electric under Jack Welch.[12] In 1981 when Welch at age forty-five became chairman and CEO of GE, he knew he wanted to change the company internally while holding it together. When Welch took over, GE had many strengths: its sales were $25 billion, its earnings were $1.5 billion, and it had 404,000 employees and a triple-A balance sheet. "Some employees proudly described the company as a 'supertanker'—strong and steady in the water. I respected that but wanted the company to be more like a speedboat, fast and agile, able to turn on a dime," wrote Welch. Without stating it as such, what Welch set out to do was to change GE's DNA.

In 1981 GE had a formal and massive bureaucracy, like much of American industry at that time, with too many layers of management and 350 business units, few of which were leaders in their markets. Welch observed,

It was ruled by more than 25,000 managers who each averaged seven direct reports in a hierarchy with as many as a dozen levels between the factory floor and my office. More than 130 executives held the rank of vice president or above, with all kinds of titles and support staffs behind each one.

Welch "knew the benefits of staying small even as GE was getting bigger." His strategy was to sort out the good businesses from the bad ones and eliminate the latter. "I wanted GE to stay only in businesses that were No. 1 or No. 2 in their markets. We had to act faster and get the damn bureaucracy out of the way," Welch said.

Over the next years, Welch, the change-agent, cut the bureaucracy down, reduced the layers between the shop floor and the CEO by half (from 12 to 6), reduced the number of managers and gave each 15 direct reports, up from 7. He broke down barriers between operating units with his "workout" and other innovations to reduce internal barriers and improve communications between operating units.

All this was accomplished as he grew the company six times larger and nearly ten times more profitable than it was when he had taken it over, earning *Fortune* magazine's coveted title "Most Admired Company in America," and the *Financial Times* named it "The World's Most Respected Company."[13] Welch made a fundamentally new GE internally, which is now the heart of its current success-oriented DNA culture.

Viacom

The second basic approach, splitting up large corporations into smaller operating units, is another way to achieve strategic focus and improve execution. An extreme technique is to split up the corporation itself. This is the approach Viacom decided to take in 2005 to improve sales and especially earnings, having lost $17 billion in 2004. Viacom is now two separate corporations—CBS Corporation and Viacom, Inc. Sumner Redstone, the chairman of both companies, anticipates that this new structure will better execute the strategies of each company.[14]

Cendant Corporation

This conglomerate, with a market value of $21 billion, had been cobbled together over more than a decade by its CEO Henry Silverman. Cendant announced that it would split into four separate companies by mid-2006, none of which had yet been labeled but none would carry the Cendant name. Each new company would focus on one of Cendant's main lines of business:

- Real estate would be composed of Century 21 and Coldwell Banker.
- Travel would include Orbitz, Galileo, and Cheap Tickets brands.
- The hotel company would include Ramada, Howard Johnson, and Days Inn brands.
- The car rental company would include Avis and Budget.

As Silverman stated, the conglomerate was "an artistic success but a commercial failure," the investment community seeing more value in the company in pieces than as a whole.[15]

Marriott

Some years ago, to stimulate growth and execute a new business model, Marriott split into two completely separate companies: Marriott International, the company that manages hotels, and Host Marriott, a real estate investment trust that owns hotel properties. In 2005, Host Marriott owned 107 hotels including properties with such brands as Ritz-Carlton and Four Seasons, plus convention center and resort properties in Hawaii, California, and Florida. Marriott International is the largest hotel management company in the world with sales in 2004 of $10 billion, more than twice those of Starwood Hotels, a chain of 140 owned hotels and 750 managed hotels whose brands include Sheraton, Westin, St. Regis, Le Meridien, and W hotels. Marriott was three times larger than Hilton before its acquisition of Hilton International of Britain. The same year Host Marriott had revenues of $3.7 billion.[16]

In large corporations that choose to remain intact, there is a clear tendency to internally restructure operations into smaller units that are highly focused on providing particular products and services to their specific customer groups. The operating units may still be called divisions, but increasingly they are called sectors or strategic business units. Figure 6.3 illustrates the organizational structure of a large corporation having a number of strategic business units, each of which has a highly focused product–customer relationship.

Line versus Staff

As is traditional in large corporations, there is a distinction between corporate and strategic business unit positions and also between *staff* and *line* positions. Staff positions are those both at the corporate office and the divisions that "support" the line activities. All corporate office executives' jobs (except the CEO and COO) are to oversee and to some extent coordinate the functional activities related to their positions' responsibilities in the company's various operating units, such as divisions.

For example, the corporate vice president for human resources (H-R) oversees all the human resource activities throughout the corporation—both at headquarters (the corporate office) and at the operating units—even though the heads of H-R at the divisions report directly to the division head. These H-R positions are all staff positions because they do not actually make or service the company's products, whether they are manufactured items or services.

Line positions are those that actually produce the company's products, as opposed to providing support for their production. The corporate vice president for operations, for example, would generally oversee and lend support for operations activities throughout the divisions; these include factory management, inbound and outbound logistics, and possibly purchasing of parts and materiel. The persons directly responsible for these tasks

FIGURE 6.3
Large National Corporation Having Strategic Business Units (SBUs)

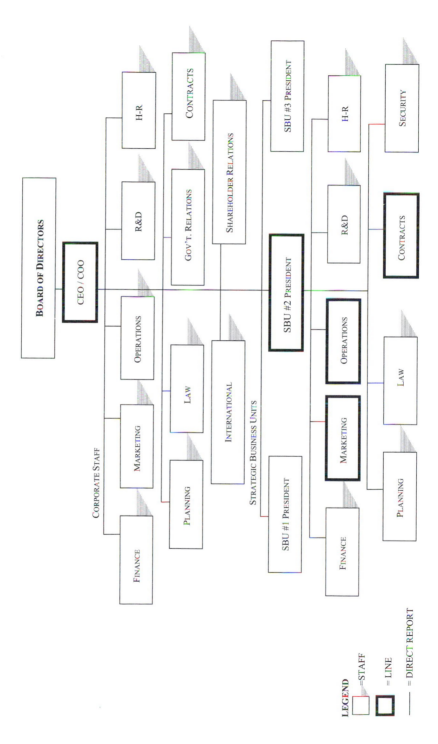

are the vice presidents or managers of these activities at the divisions, reporting to their division heads, usually called general managers or sector presidents. As in the case of the H-R situation, there is a "hard line" relationship between division executives and their general managers and a "dotted line" relationship between them and their functional opposite number at corporate headquarters. Dotted lines refer to coordination and hard lines (solid lines) refer to chain-of-command responsibility.

This same type of relationship with division executives exists for all corporate office executives whose titles relate to their functional areas of responsibility: corporate vice president of finance (who is also CFO), human resources, operations, marketing, contracts, research and development (sometimes called technical or product development), law (general counsel), and planning.

Activities unique to the corporate office, those that are not duplicated at the operating divisions, are government relations, shareholder relations, and international activities. These are all staff, not line, positions because these officers provide support services for the entire company that are best performed in a centralized location under a single executive. In large corporations each of these departments is headed by a corporate vice president. Sometimes there is also a separate security (or privacy) department, depending on the nature of the company's work. See Figure 6.4 for a typical organization chart of a major corporation showing line versus staff relationships, plus chain-of-command relationships versus coordination relationships.

CORPORATE IDENTITY AND PERCEPTIONS

How the public views a corporation may affect customers' decisions to purchase its goods in the marketplace and its decisions to invest in the company. If a corporation is generally considered to be trustworthy and honorable, its products, whatever they may be, may benefit from that overall perception and be purchased. Likewise, people will more likely be willing to invest in the company. If the reverse is the case, the firm's products may be rejected out of fear they may be tainted or of questionable quality and its stock price will likely suffer.

Public Perception of Corporate Identity

Corporate identity and public perceptions of that identity are critical factors that companies need to take into account not only in their product marketing strategies but also equally importantly in their corporate communications

FIGURE 6.4
Typical Organization Chart of a Major Corporation Showing Line versus Staff

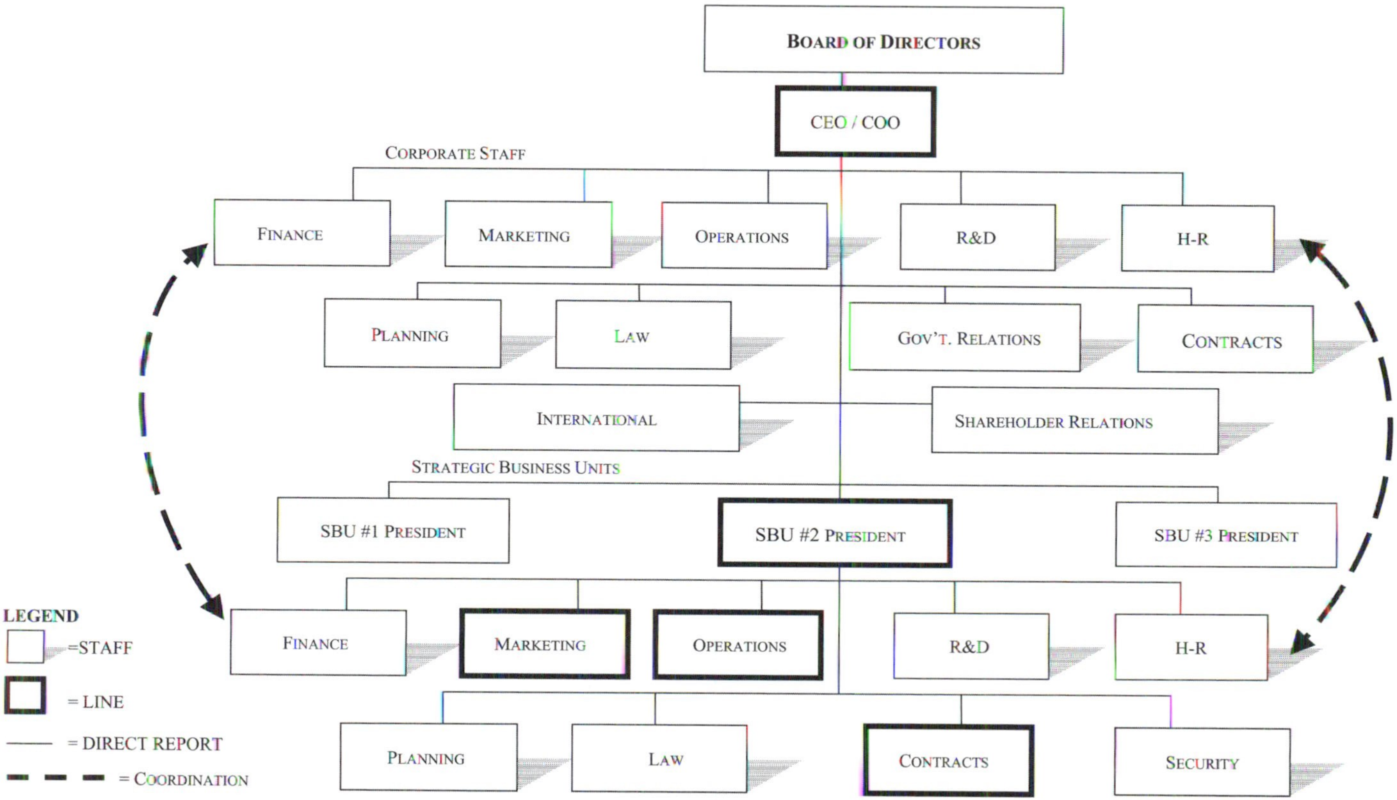

LEGEND
= STAFF
= LINE
= DIRECT REPORT
= COORDINATION

in general. Some experts refer to this as perfecting an image, whereas others simply state that this is the company's reputation.[17]

A clear example of the impact of corporate identity on consumers' purchasing decisions is designer clothes. Fashions come and go, but Ralph Lauren and Calvin Klein jeans for teens and young adults, Chanel and Armani clothes for affluent middle-age and older women and men, and Ferragamo and Stewart Weitzman shoes for middle-age and older women are almost always a must because their wearers want to project the same image as their corporations—sexy, chic, and with it.

Regarding jeans, this became a serious problem for Levi Strauss & Company, which invented blue jeans 150 years go. Its stodgy old brand lost its cache to hip newer designers, and along with it Levi's lost half its market share to them in the 1990s.[18] Designer brand products project a self-image of their wearer that is constantly reinforced by the corporate image advertising of their makers.

In sports, Nike and Adidas work hard and spend countless millions of dollars developing a perception that their sports apparel and shoes will enhance a person's success in athletics. Having Michael Jordan or Tiger Woods wear the Nike swoosh, or having David Beckham, the great English soccer player, wear the Adidas logo is a celebrity endorsement of success that the average sports-minded consumer longs to emulate.

Nike also spends millions in advertising for the nonathlete to gain a certain recognition, as summed up by a mid-twenties youth counselor in New York: "People wear Jordans to look cool." Nike's sales are more than twice those of Adidas and nearly five times Reebok's, motivating those smaller players to merge.[19]

Merck

In some industries a product failure can have a toxic effect on a company's entire reputation. Take the example of Merck, the giant pharmaceutical company based in New Jersey.[20] One of its most important and largest selling drugs was Vioxx, a painkiller. Some customers who used Vioxx alleged they were harmed by it, and a number of people assert family members died from it and sued Merck. In August 2005, in the first such case to reach a verdict, a Texas jury found in favor of a family that had sued Merck. Interviewed after the trial, jury members said they thought Merck had concealed the risks of the drug. At that time there were 4,200 pending U.S. Vioxx lawsuits against Merck having a total value of $30 billion, plus hundreds more cases from British plaintiffs awaiting trial.

The Texas plaintiffs argued that Merck had been aware for seven years before it withdrew Vioxx from the market that it increased heart and stroke risks (based on internal company e-mails). The jury apparently believed them and awarded the deceased's family a staggering $253 million judgment, mostly punitive damages. That same day Merck's stock lost 7.7 percent. Merck appealed the jury's award, of course, but where does Merck go to appeal the damage this entire episode has had on its overall reputation?

"The decision against Merck...is a clear statement that ... we're losing the battle for consumer trust," said an industry spokesman.[21] For a drug company to be forced to withdraw a key high-profit product from the marketplace because it has the perception—and worse if it has the reality—of being harmful or fatal to its users is as bad as it gets.

Johnson & Johnson

The reverse was the case in the famous Johnson & Johnson Tylenol case, when J&J withdrew the medication from stores' shelves at great expense to itself after it was discovered that an individual had tampered with the containers by putting cyanide inside. For its quick, proper response safeguarding the public's health, the public's perception of Johnson & Johnson was enhanced, adding to its luster of trust.

Years later, fearing the Merck Vioxx cases would further tarnish the entire drug industry's image and knowing the public's distrust of the pharmaceutical industry in general, Johnson & Johnson dramatically increased its advertising to enhance its corporate image and provide general information on diseases, instead of ads for specific drugs. J&J's advertising budget for the first five months of 2005 was $190 million, and during that period it allocated 25.3 percent of the total to corporate image and general information ads, up from 8.7 percent. This was partly sparked by a January 2005 *Wall Street Journal*/NBC News survey in which only 3 percent of people polled thought drug companies were working for the public good and 76 percent thought they were mostly interested in making profits.[22]

Annual surveys are taken of the public's perception of major corporations. The result is a ranking of corporate reputations, as determined by these Harris Interactive Inc. polls. In the 2005 survey, number 1 in reputation was Johnson & Johnson, number 2 was Coca-Cola Co., and number 3 was Google, Inc. J&J and Coca-Cola are each over one hundred years old, but Google was founded only in 1998 in a Stanford University dorm room. It usually takes decades to establish a positive reputation, but Google jumped up high in the rankings because it is viewed as indispensable to many Internet users. Merck & Company placed 45th on the survey, being denounced by some respondents as greedy and dishonest. Companies involved in scandals ranked in the cellar, with Enron last at number sixty.[23]

Having a positive reputation for reliability and ethical behavior is essential for a modern corporation. Gone are the days when sharp practices could be gotten away with because worldwide media coverage hungers for examples of corporate misbehavior and worse. It took years for Ford Motor Company to overcome the Pinto disaster of exploding gas tanks from rear-end crashes. WorldCom, a telecom company, Enron, an energy company, and Arthur Andersen, its accounting firm, were destroyed by their deliberate unethical behavior, which juries found to be illegal also.

Corporate Identity

Every organization, like every individual, has an identity associated with its name. For corporations, the identity "articulates the corporate ethos, aims and values and presents a sense of individuality that can help to differentiate the organization within its competitive environment."[24] A corporation carefully crafts the way its name appears in print, the color and shape of its corporate logo if it has one, and the selection of publications and other media in which its name and logo will appear.

Coca-Cola is the most widely recognized brand in the world; it is also the corporation's name: the Coca-Cola Company. This name symbolizes the company's main product, which stands for refreshment. Linking refreshment in the public's mind with the brand Coca-Cola is an achievement that took decades of advertising, promotion, and *brand management.*

Especially since the mid-1990s, corporations have spent a great deal of effort and resources to create a carefully crafted corporate identity. Having a clearly defined, positive public identity has become a critical part of a company's strategic management.

In essence, corporate identity is the reality and uniqueness of an organization which is integrally related to its external and internal image and reputation through corporate communication.... Corporate communication is the process through which stakeholders perceive the company's identity and image and reputation are formed.[25]

A number of factors in the external business environment that have emerged in recent years have accentuated the need to manage corporate identity strategically for competitive advantage.

These ten factors in the environment require middle-size to large corporations to strategically manage their corporate images just as carefully as

Ten Driving Forces for Managing Corporate Identity

There are ten such driving forces in the environment causing corporate identity and communications to have ever greater importance:[26]

1. *Acceleration of product life cycles*—particularly in consumer durable goods such as consumer electronics, in which customers want the latest technology

2. *Deregulation*—which has affected banking, telecommunications, and airlines dramatically

3. *Privatization*—such as British Airways and Lufthansa, which are now viewed as customer-friendly as well as reliable

4. *Increased competition in the public and nonprofit sectors*—especially public versus private colleges and universities, most of whose appeal rests on reputation

5. *Increased competition in the services sector*—such as Hong Kong & Shanghai Banking Corporation changing its name to HKSB for global appeal

6. *Globalization and the establishment of several free trade areas*—enabling a company based in one country to expand easily to others within the free trade zone

7. *Mergers, acquisitions, and divestitures*—a successful acquirer such as British Petroleum changing its corporate name to BP because of its new global reach

8. *Shortage of high-quality people*—can be overcome by having a solid corporate reputation that will attract and retain skilled people

9. *Public expectations of corporate social responsibility*—companies like Target Corporation advertising their commitment to the environment or gifts to charities to gain customer goodwill

10. *Blurring of boundaries between internal and external aspects of organizations*—Nestlé's joint ventures with General Mills and Coca-Cola for cereal and beverages

they manage the images of their products or brands for the purpose of gaining or maintaining a competitive advantage. This management process is centered in these companies' corporate communications departments.

NAME CHANGES

There are times when a company's name is no longer appropriate and has to be changed. This results from its product line having changed over the years, because one of the industries it is in is viewed as less desirable than others, or because the name has simply been outgrown, possibly because of acquisitions. Examples of each of these abound.[27]

Uniroyal

This name was adopted when management realized that its long-time name, U.S. Rubber, no longer fit. The company had grown to serve world markets, not just the United States, and it had expanded into products other than tires such as chemicals, fibers, plastics, and so forth. U.S. Royal had been its most important tire brand in the United States.

United Technologies

This name was adopted by United Aircraft Company, a corporation that decided its aircraft industry affiliation was hurting its investment potential and depressing its stock price at a time when aircraft manufacturing was viewed as a less than desirable investment. Often there had been mistaken identity with United Airlines. Moreover, the company had a major position in other industries as exemplified by some of its brand names: Otis elevator, Carrier air conditioning, Hamilton Standard (military electronics), Sikorsky helicopters, and so forth.

Exxon Mobil Corporation

This largest U.S.-based oil company's name reflects the merger of the previous number-one and number-two oil companies in the United States. Their joining was billed as a merger of equals at the time, and the joint name appears to reflect that. Of critical importance is the fact that the combined company decided to continue marketing its products under both brand names, and so it wanted the corporate name to reflect that decision.

Pfizer

This is the world's largest pharmaceutical company, which gained that status following a series of acquisitions, the largest of which were Warner-Lambert and American Home Products Company. It had always been Pfizer's policy not to add to its corporate name acquired companies' names. In contrast, the world's second largest pharmaceutical company has taken the other approach: GlaxoSmithKlein is the corporate name that resulted from the acquisition by GlaxoWelcomen of SmithKleinBeecham.

FMC

The former name of this conglomerate was Food Machinery Corporation. It had a number of famous brand names: Link-Belt, John Bean, American Viscose, and Niagara Chemical. All these brand names obscured the corporate parent's name, which was less well known. Moreover, only one of the company's brands was food machinery: John Bean tractors. Finally, FMC had expanded into military hardware, developing the Bradley fighting vehicle for the army—hardly a food machine. Hence, its management adopted the acronym of the old corporate name to label the parent company of the expanded product line better.

RCA

This famous brand, which was the acronym of Radio Corporation of America, is a company that began during World War I as a joint venture of General Electric, AT&T, and Westinghouse. In the 1920s RCA was split off as a separate company. RCA remained independent with a well-recognized logo for its televisions and radios, and it also owned the National Broadcasting Company (NBC).

General Electric acquired RCA in 1985 for $6.3 billion, primarily to get NBC to enable it to expand into commercial broadcasting. A few years later, GE traded the RCA logo and its television set manufacturing to Thomson of France for its medical system business. Thomson, now the world's largest manufacturer of television sets, wanted a product logo recognizable in the United States and throughout the world for its televisions and other consumer electronics products. The RCA logo itself was one of the most valuable parts of the entire multi-billion-dollar transaction.[28] In this case the RCA name was not changed; its ownership was.

Bank of America

When Nations Bank changed its name to Bank of America following its 1998 acquisition of BofA for $57 billion, thousands of branch banks had to have new signage, new stationery, new deposit slips, new ads in the Yellow Pages, and so forth. The cost was in the tens of millions of dollars. Moreover, an expensive advertising campaign was launched to acquaint the public with that name change and to tout the now truly nationwide bank that Bank of America had become, coast to coast.

Acquisitions continued, including FleetBoston Financial in 2004 for $48 billion with its branches throughout New England and MBNA in 2005 for $35 billion to obtain its huge credit card business. More sign changes were made with each purchase. As of 2005, Bank of America had the largest branch banking network in the country with nearly 6,000 branches, seven times the number with Citigroup's name over the door.[29]

Every company name change is the result of a major management decision. Philip Morris & Company changed its corporate name to Altria to reduce the stigma of being a tobacco company. A firm's identity in the marketplace, on Wall Street, and in the minds of individual customers and investors is a critical factor that has to be approached with the greatest care because of the cost and consequences of that change. The cost can be staggering.

Repositioning corporate identity to change the public's perception of the company needs to be approached strategically and must be managed effectively to achieve the positive impact on the public that the company intends. Its name may be one of the company's major assets, as the RCA example illustrated, and tampering with that asset is risky, unless it is handled most carefully.

CONCLUSION

The operation of a corporation is a complex matter. Directors and officers are required to conform to the company's own articles of incorporation and bylaws as well as with the law of the state in which it is incorporated. With respect to stock, the company must also comply with federal laws and regulations as administered by the SEC.

Internal organizational structures vary with the stages of growth of companies. They have fairly simple structures when they are new and become more complex as they grow and expand their product lines and diversify their customer base. Structure should follow the strategy the top management has chosen with great rigor. It is easy for large companies to lose their competitive edge as they become large, and it is a constant struggle to retain it—or regain it—when they are huge. The chapter offers examples of both successes and failures.

Managing the corporate identity is a vital function of management. Once a company's image has been established, it is reinforced with a consistent use of its logo, its color scheme, and its overall business approach. Changing a company's name is a risky undertaking because it can alter public perceptions, unless that is the reason motivating the change.

NOTES

1. Peter F. Drucker, "The American CEO," *Wall Street Journal*, December 30, 2004, A8.

2. Carol Hymowitz, "Globalizing the Boardroom," *Wall Street Journal*, November 14, 2004, R1.

3. For a discussion of financial matters, see Wesley B. Truitt, *What Entrepreneurs Need to Know about Government: A Guide to Rules and Regulations* (Westport, CT: Praeger, 2004), 120–124.

4. For a discussion of shareholder rights, see Frank B. Cross and Roger LeRoy Miller, *West's Legal Environment of Business,* 5th ed. (Mason, OH: Thomson South-Western, 2004), 429–437.

5. *Wall Street Journal*, June 10, 2003, A1; June 11, 2003, A2.

6. Tax Foundation, 2005, cited in *Wall Street Journal*, December 28, 2005, A14.

7. Alfred D. Chandler, Jr., *Strategy and Structure: Chapters in the History of Industrial Enterprise* (Cambridge, MA: MIT Press, 1962).

8. *Wall Street Journal*, June 18, 2004, A3.

9. *Wall Street Journal*, November 2, 2004, A1, A14.

10. Steve Jobs, "Stay Hungry. Stay Foolish," *Fortune*, September 5, 2005, 31–32. For a discussion of Apple, see Jeffrey S. Young and William L. Simon, *iCon Steve Jobs: The Greatest Second Act in the History of Business* (New York: Wiley, 2005).

11. This discussion is based on Gary L. Neilson and Bruce A. Pasternack, "The Cat That Came Back," *Strategy + Business,* Fall 2005, 32–45.

12. This discussion is based on Jack Welch, *Jack: Straight from the Gut* (New York: Warner Books, 2001), 92–93.

13. Cited in Wesley B. Truitt, *Business Planning: A Comprehensive Framework and Process* (Westport, CT: Quorum Books, 2002), 41–42.

14. *New York Times*, November 2, 2005, C3.

15. *Wall Street Journal*, October 24, 2005, A3.

16. *Fortune*, April 18, 2005, F9, F19; *Wall Street Journal*, September 1, 2005, A12.

17. For a discussion of image versus reputation, see John M. T. Balmer and Stephen A. Greyser, *Revealing the Corporation* (London: Routledge, 2003), 173–185.

18. For Levi Strauss, see Wesley B. Truitt, *Business Planning*, 76–77, 191–192.

19. *Wall Street Journal*, August 4, 2005, A1, including the quotation.

20. *Wall Street Journal*, August 22, 2005, A1; August 23, 2005, C4, D3; *Los Angeles Times*, August 23, 2005, C4.

21. *Wall Street Journal*, August 26, 2005, B1.

22. Ibid.

23. Ronald Alsop, "Ranking Corporate Reputations," *Wall Street Journal*, December 6, 2005, B1, B14.

24. Statement on corporate identity by the International Corporate Identity Group, 1995, quoted in John M. T. Balmer and Edmund R. Gray, "Corporate Identity and Corporate Communications: Creating a Competitive Advantage," in John M. T. Balmer and Stephen A. Greyser, *Revealing the Corporation* (London: Routledge, 2003), 134.

25. John M. T. Balmer and Edmund R. Gray, "Corporate Identity and Corporate Communications," in John M. T. Balmer and Stephen A. Greyser, *Revealing the Corporation*, 126.

26. Ibid., 127.

27. The Uniroyal, United Technologies, FMC, and RCA examples are from Walter Margulies, "Make the Most of Your Corporate Identity," in John M. T. Balmer and Stephen A. Greyser, *Revealing the Corporation*, 68–75.

28. This RCA discussion is based on Jack Welch, *Jack: Straight from the Gut*, Chapter 10.

29. *Fortune*, September 5, 2005, 109–116.

RECOMMENDED READINGS

Balmer, John M. T., and Stephen A. Greyser, *Revealing the Corporation: Perspectives on Identity, Image, Reputation, Corporate Branding, and Corporate-level Marketing* (London: Routledge, 2003).

Grunig, J. E., ed., *Excellence in Public Relations and Communication Management* (Hillsdale, NJ: Erlbaum, 1992).

Lechem, Brian, *Chairman of the Board* (Hoboken, NJ: Wiley, 2002).

Malone, Thomas W., Robert Laubacher, and Michael S. Scott Morton, eds., *Inventing the Organizations of the 21st Century* (Cambridge, MA: MIT Press, 2003).

Post, James E., Lee E. Preston, and Sybille Sachs, *Redefining the Corporation: Stakeholder Management and Organizational Wealth* (Stanford, CA: Stanford Business Books, 2002).

Van Riel, C. B. M., *Principles of Corporate Communication* (London: Prentice Hall, 1995).

Seven

Corporations in Other Countries

Understanding how American corporations work is essential, and understanding how businesses operate in other countries is equally important. Why? Economic globalization is the answer. World trade, worldwide capital flows, interdependent economies, and regional integration, such as the North American Free Trade Area and the European Union, are forces that are pulling the world's economies more tightly together. Responding to those trends, corporations are operating more and more on a global scale.

This chapter discusses how corporations are organized and operated in countries outside the United States. But first, a summary of the globalization of economic activity puts worldwide corporate activity into its global context.

ECONOMIC GLOBALIZATION

Economic globalization as a phenomenon can be examined from several perspectives. The ratio of world trade to world output is one key measure.[1] Right after World War II it was approximately 10 percent, meaning that about 10 percent of the world's total gross domestic product (GDP) was produced by international trade. By the 1980s the ratio had doubled, and by the end of the twentieth century it exceeded 35 percent and was still growing. More than half of this trade was intracompany transfers; that is, trade between divisions of the same company operating in different nations.

World trade during the past half century was growing at about 7 percent per year, much faster than the average GDP growth of the most advanced industrial nations. This is the story regarding *merchandise* trade, the exporting and importing of goods of all types.

International trade in *services*, although still a smaller amount in dollar value compared with merchandise trade, is growing at an even faster rate. Services include such important items as travel and tourism, financial and engineering services, freight, telecommunications, and insurance.

Of still greater importance are international capital flows. Capital is flowing across national borders at an unprecedented rate. This category includes portfolio investments (such as buying shares in foreign corporations) and foreign direct investment (FDI), which includes funds companies in one country spend for building plants, refineries, and other such facilities in other countries. By the end of the twentieth century, annual capital flows exceeded $600 billion, up from less than $40 billion twenty years earlier. Interdependence of economic activity is stunningly illustrated by the fact that, according to United Nations survey data, sales by major multinational firms' foreign affiliates exceeded $12 trillion in 1998, twice the volume of world merchandise trade.

A good example of this is the General Electric Company. In the early 1980s GE's total annual sales were approximately $25 billion. GE then embarked on a strategy of global expansion, focusing first on Europe and later on Asia, building facilities and buying existing plants and businesses in those areas. By 2004, GE's European sales alone were $25 billion out of total worldwide sales of $152 billion.[2]

Regional groupings have become a major factor in business throughout the world. The United States, Canada, and Mexico formed the North American Free Trade Area (NAFTA) in 1994 to stimulate higher rates of economic growth within the three countries by eliminating tariffs and opening the three countries' borders to trade and travel. This grouping had a population of approximately 425 million people as of 2005. In the same year the European Union, composed of 25 nations, had a population of 455 million and a GDP roughly the same size as NAFTA's. Other regional economic groupings can be found in Central America (CAFTA), the Caribbean, South America (Mercasor), Southeast Asia, and Africa.

Concurrent with this phenomenal expansion in world trade and investment, there has been an increase in the number and type of businesses engaged in the world's commerce. New technologies (particularly the Internet), new regional groupings (especially the European Union with its new currency, the euro), new countries joining in world trade in a major way (especially China and India), and new business strategies (especially outsourcing) have all contributed to the rapid expansion of worldwide trade and commerce. No other period in the modern history of the world can compare with the size, scope, and expanse of our global economy today.

A former secretary of labor, Robert Reich, predicted that by 2010 a majority of Americans would be working directly or indirectly for global companies that would have no particular nationality, the multinational corporation.

Leading this global expansion is the modern corporation. Whether it is based in the United States or some other country, corporations are the business entities that have led and are leading this phenomenal growth in the world's economy, bringing with it improved living standards for people in virtually every country it touches.

BASIS OF CORPORATION LAW

What is the basis of corporate organization? All business organizations are based on national law; that is, the law of a particular nation and the jurisdiction within that nation that has the authority to authorize the formation of businesses, such as states in the United States. This is true of corporations as well as partnerships, limited liability companies, sole proprietorships, and all other types of business entities.[3] There is no international law permitting the establishment of corporations or any other type of business.

Even though a company may operate internationally, its corporate governance is nevertheless based on the laws of the country of its incorporation, called the *home country*. The organizational form a business takes usually depends on the place where it began. Its choices for the type of entity it may adopt are limited, and it turns out they are remarkably similar from country to country.

News Corporation

It is rare that a corporation chooses to change nationalities. News Corporation, the media giant that owns the Fox television network, Fox News Channel, 20th Century Fox movie studio, a string of newspapers around the world, and satellite broadcasting channels in Europe and Asia, moved its corporate home from Australia to the United States in 2005, incorporating in Delaware. It made this move because the bulk of its business activities had come to be centered in America, and it wanted to be closer to them and have easier access to the capital markets of the United States, the largest in the world.

When a company chooses to operate outside its home country, it also has a limited set of choices as to the form its foreign operations may take: representative offices, agencies, branches, and subsidiaries. These forms are based on the laws of the foreign country in which it chooses to operate, called the *host country*. The host country cannot regulate the parent company (the corporate headquarters) any more than the parent company's nation can regulate the company's operations in host countries.

Nestlé

An example is Nestlé, the multinational food corporation headquartered in Switzerland under Swiss corporate law. Nestlé has offices, factories, and subsidiaries in dozens of countries throughout the world, all of which operate under host country law, such as Carnation Company, one of Nestlé's many American subsidiaries.

Carnation Company is governed by the laws of the United States and each state in which Carnation operates, particularly its subsidiary headquarters in Los Angeles, which operates under California law. Swiss corporate law has no effect on Carnation's activities, any more than California corporate law has any effect on Nestlé's corporate activities in Switzerland. This is the same case throughout the world for all of Nestlé's foreign holdings, which are in the hundreds.

Two Exceptions

There are two major exceptions to the general rule that national laws have no force and effect on businesses outside their domestic jurisdiction.

Antitrust Activities

One exception involves antitrust activities, whereby, for example, European Union (EU) antitrust regulators can prevent or modify the merger of two U.S.-based companies, provided one or both have significant business activities within the EU. Outside the United States, antitrust regulations are called *competitiveness* laws to prevent or regulate *anticompetition* behavior. An example is one of the largest attempts at a merger ever made: General Electric's 2001 proposed $44 billion acquisition of Honeywell International, which the EU turned down on antitrust grounds ending the merger, even though U.S. antitrust regulators had already approved the merger.[4]

Foreign Corrupt Practices Act

The other exception relates to bribery of foreign government officials. The United States is the only nation that has laws that carry its rules of behavior (in this instance, its statutory principles of good conduct) to other countries. This is called *extraterritoriality*, extending one's rules of behavior beyond one's own territory into that of other nations.

When the Foreign Corrupt Practices Act of 1976, amended in 1988, was first enacted, there were numerous scandals involving corporate officials (not only U.S. corporations) attempting to gain business from foreign governments by paying bribes to those governments' officials. This statute carries U.S. antibribery prohibitions beyond U.S. territory into the domestic spheres of other nations, even though all nations have their own laws prohibiting the payment of bribes to their own government officials. In some nations these laws are vigorously enforced, whereas in others they are completely ignored, giving way to local customs and standards of conduct.

The act prohibits American individuals, companies, and foreign subsidiaries of U.S. firms from promising, offering, or paying anything of value to any foreign government official or political party to obtain or retain business.[5] No other country has a law like this, which many American executives believe handicaps U.S. firms, knowing foreign firms covertly engage in this practice.

The most famous bribery case is that of Lockheed bribing the prime minister of Japan to gain his influence in picking Lockheed's airplane over those of competitors from Europe.[6] More recently, in a strange twist of fate, in 2004 Lockheed exposed the largest foreign bribery scandal ever: Titan Corporation's bribes to six West African nations' officials on a telecommunications deal. Lockheed was performing due diligence to acquire Titan when it discovered the bribes and reported them. Titan subsequently paid $28.5 million in 2005 to settle the case. The largest previous penalty under the Foreign Corrupt Practices Act had been Lockheed's own $24.8 million payment ten years earlier.[7]

This law does *not* prohibit *express payments*, sometimes called *facilitation payments*, to foreign government officials. These payments involving relatively small amounts of money are used to speed goods through foreign customs inspections, gain approvals for exports, expedite passport inspections, and so forth. They are perfectly legal under U.S. law and the laws of the countries in which these practices are considered normal and routine.

CORPORATIONS ARE "PERSONS"

In every country corporations are *juridical* entities. This means that corporations have a legal identity of their own, separate from that of their owners. A corporation is a *person* before the courts, as defined in the Fourteenth Amendment to the U.S. Constitution,[8] as corporations are in all countries under their own legal systems. This separate juridical identity has four important consequences in all countries that have corporations:

1. Corporations, like a person, can own property, sign contracts, borrow money, sue, be sued, and have separate standing in a court of law, under the direction of their boards of directors and company officers.

2. The owners' (stockholders') liability is limited to the amount of their investment in the company, meaning that the company's owners are not required to pay the company's obligations (debts, fines) from their own personal funds and assets.

3. The rights, benefits, and assets of the company belong to the company, not to its owners.

4. The owners of the corporation cannot make decisions or commitments for the company, cannot act as its agent, cannot contractually commit the company, nor can they impose any liability on the company. Only the directors and officers of the corporation can do these things, consistent with the corporation's charter and bylaws.

TYPES OF LAW

Most nations have one of two main types of law on which their legal systems and their businesses are based: (1) English common law and (2) civil law. Civil law is sometimes known by other names: codified law, continental law, or Napoleonic Code. Civil law is partly derived from Roman codes of law.

This type of law will be called civil law here, but remember it goes by other names also. Civil law is the type of law practiced on the continent of Europe and also in non-European countries that were once members of the empires of these continental-based countries: France, Spain, Portugal, Germany, Italy, the Netherlands, and Belgium. For example, all countries in Latin America except Belize and the former British Guiana practice civil law, having once been part of the empires of Spain, Portugal, and France.

English common law is the basis of law for all countries that were once part of the British Empire, the British Commonwealth of Nations, and other countries that modeled their legal systems on that of England. This includes almost all English-speaking countries: Britain, Ireland, India, Pakistan, Bangladesh, Australia, and New Zealand. The United States and Canada are part of the common law tradition, having also been under British rule. Within the United States only the Commonwealth of Puerto Rico, once part of Spain, and the state of Louisiana, once a part of France, have civil law as the basis of their state law.

Mexico is part of the civil law tradition, having been part of Spain's empire. Thus, legal issues within NAFTA, which includes Mexico, the

United States, and Canada, have to be approached carefully. A key decision for incorporating as well as litigating an issue is choosing which country's law (and courts) is most appropriate and advantageous to you, provided you have such a choice.

In addition to common law and civil law, there are two other types of law: Islamic law and Communist law.

Islamic Law

Islamic law, sometime called Muslim law, is practiced in some Muslim countries, largely found in the Middle East and in certain countries in Southeast Asia (Indonesia and Malaysia are the largest) and is based on the Koran. However, many of these countries were once members of European states' empires, which brought to those countries the type of law practiced in their homeland, leaving a mixed tradition of European law with elements of Muslim law.

Muslim countries having an English common law element include Egypt, Jordan, and Malaysia because these countries were once controlled by Britain. Countries having civil law are former French-controlled countries (Morocco, Algeria, Tunisia, Lebanon, and Syria) and former Dutch-controlled Indonesia. The only countries with pure Muslim Law are Saudi Arabia, Yemen, Kuwait, Iran, Oman, and the small Persian Gulf states—Qatar, Bahrain, and the United Arab Emirates. Iraq's law is under revision.

Communist Law

Communist law, originally developed in the Soviet Union in the 1920s, is being dismantled in the fifteen former member countries of the Soviet Union (Russia, Ukraine, Latvia, Lithuania, Estonia, Kazakhstan, Armenia, etc.) and other East European countries (Hungary, Poland, Czech Republic, Slovakia, etc.) that were once under Soviet domination. These countries are all adopting civil law, consistent with the majority of European Union countries.

Today, only Cuba, North Korea, and a few Communist countries in Africa still practice this type of law, which provides for no private property rights for individuals or companies and has severe limitations on individual civil liberties. China is rapidly dismantling its Communist law heritage and is developing a Western legal system, especially for commercial law, based on civil law.

ENGLISH COMMON LAW CORPORATIONS

Under English common law there are two major types of corporations: public corporations and private corporations. Both types must register with the government.

Some common law countries also recognize two other types of corporations: unlimited liability corporations, a company whose members are not liable in the event the firm's assets are insufficient to cover its debts at its termination; and no liability corporations, a company whose shareholders are not required to pay any of the firm's debts but who do not receive any dividends if the firm's debts are unpaid. These two types are such special cases that they will not be addressed further here.

PUBLIC CORPORATIONS

Public corporations are recognized throughout the common law world.[9] In England, where they originated, they are known as public limited corporations (PLC) or simply limited (Ltd.). *Limited* is used in Canada, also. In the United States this is the type of corporation most commonly used, and companies that are incorporated must have one of the following words in their formal titles: *corporation, incorporated, Inc., Ltd.,* or *company*. These U.S. corporations are technically known as C corporations, as opposed to S corporations, which are a very special type established mostly for tax purposes and are not widely used.[10]

Definition

Under common law, a public corporation is a separate juridical entity owned by its shareholders who have limited liability, that can raise money in the public marketplace through the sale of freely transferable stock (shares in the ownership of the company), and whose financial activities and performance must be disclosed through periodic reports to its shareholders and to the government (e.g., the Securities and Exchange Commission).

Procedures

In England a public corporation is organized by filing two documents with the registrar of companies in London: a memorandum of association and articles of association. The memorandum of association describes the firm: its name, the address of its registered office, its business purpose, a statement as to the limited liability of its members, and the capital shares subscribed.

The articles of association are provisions describing the internal regulations of the corporation, the directors' duties, voting rights, and so on. The English Companies Act of 1985 established a default set of articles of association; if a company does not register its own articles of association, the roster of articles in the act apply.

Capital

The act also requires a minimum of two subscribers (or shareholders) and a minimum of £50,000 to be paid into the firm before the government will issue a certificate of incorporation. This requirement for paid-in capital is consistent with European Union regulations, of which the United Kingdom is a member, in which other member countries have a strong belief that a commitment of capital is important for the protection of creditors.

By comparison, in the United States there is no minimum requirement for paid-in capital and only one member (shareholder) is needed to incorporate.

Shares of Stock

The memorandum of association authorizes the issuance of a larger number of shares than those needed to start the business. Only those shares actually issued constitute the corporation's capital; the rest of the shares are "authorized but unissued shares," meaning that they can be issued later if necessary to raise additional capital. (In civil law countries, all authorized shares must be issued.)

In England and in most common law countries, par shares (those having a specified face value) are the only type that public corporations can issue, thus establishing the capitalization of the company. This means that a certain dollar value, or pound sterling value, is assigned to each share, typically one pound sterling per share. In the United States, no-par-value shares are issued; that is, shares are issued with no specific face value, leaving it up to the board of directors to determine the initial dollar value of each share of stock at the time of the stock's initial public offering. That price per share may go up or down during the first day's trading.

In most common law countries shares of stock may be issued in exchange for cash, property, or services. When cash is not received, a description or contract must be filed with the English registrar clearly describing the noncash items and assigning a good-faith monetary value to them. In the United States, it is left up to the board of directors and management to determine the value of property or services exchanged for shares.

Registration

In England, no business can be conducted by a public corporation until the registrar of companies issues a certificate certifying that the firm has complied with all legal requirements, including minimum share capital requirements set by law. In the United States, a corporation can begin doing business when it files its articles of incorporation with the appropriate governmental authority, typically the office of the secretary of state in the state in which the incorporation occurred.

Types of Stock

There are two types of stock in England and the United States: common and preferred. Common stock, the most widely used and the type typically referred to as a company's "stock," is issued by the corporation to its shareholders at the time of initial public offering (IPO). In England, common stock is based initially on the par value of the shares, and after trading in the stock begins it is based on the trading price of the stock. Voting rights of common stock shareholders is straightforward: one vote per share.

Preferred stock in English and American companies gives its owners a guaranteed dividend, priority position to receive the value of the corporation's assets at the time of liquidation of the company, and some other preferences over common stock shareholders. Preferred stock is more widely used in the United States than in England.

Stockholder Meetings

In England, formal meetings of stockholders are required to elect the board of directors and to carry on other business specified in the articles of association. A quorum is achieved when two shareholders are present (unless the articles specify otherwise). In the United States, shareholders are allowed by most states' rules to take virtually all actions by written consent or proxy, rather than by holding a formal meeting. Most states require a quorum for the meeting when a simple majority of the shareholders are present in person or by proxy, but there are some states and some articles of incorporation that permit the establishment of a quorum by a third or a quarter of all shareholders in person or by proxy.

Powers of the Board

The English Companies Act does not specify who declares dividends, though the act does provide that the board of directors must recommend a dividend (and the amount), and a quorum of the shareholders at the annual meeting must authorize it. A dividend is the amount of current or accumulated earnings distributed to shareholders in proportion to the number of shares each owns. The shareholders may not declare a dividend in an amount larger than that authorized by the board of directors. In the United

States the board of directors declares dividends. The criteria are that the company must be solvent, the issuance of a dividend does not violate the articles of incorporation, and the source of the dividends must be of a certain type—from earnings, a surplus, and so forth.

Management System

England and the United States each have a one-tier management system. The shareholders elect the board of directors, which in turn elects the top officers of the corporation. Some of those officers, especially the CEO, the chief operating officer, and the chief financial officer, typically sit on the board of directors. Thus, a small group of directors/officers actually runs the corporation. The board of directors is the ultimate authority and has the ultimate responsibility for the corporation's affairs, even though it delegates to the CEO and his or her top executives the day-to-day management of the firm. Beginning in 2002, a growing number of large American companies split the role of CEO from that of chairman of the board, increasing from roughly one-quarter to one-third of the companies in the *Fortune* 500.[11]

In England and throughout most of Europe, the board of directors is called the supervisory board, which in England the CEO can chair, but today an outside director typically chairs it. Throughout Britain, having a separate chairman and chief executive has become standard practice over the past decade; 95 percent of the FTSE 350 companies (like the *Fortune* 500) have the split system.[12] The Financial Services Authority, Britain's equivalent of the Securities and Exchange Commission, frowns on boards chaired by CEOs, but nevertheless the law permits it.

PRIVATE CORPORATIONS

The major advantage of private corporations is they have much the same legal standing as public corporations and the same liability protections for shareholders, but they also dispense with many of the formalities required of public corporations. An advantage of private corporations over limited partnerships is that shareholding directors assume the management of a private corporation without the risk of having unlimited liability for the debts it may incur.

In England, under common law, a private corporation is a legal entity that cannot ask the public to subscribe to its shares, bonds, or other securities, and it is subject to disclosure requirements less stringent than those of public corporations. Most private corporations are small in size, and their governing documents restrict the transfer of shares, giving transferability powers exclusively to the board of directors. A single director may be appointed, rather than a full board, and shareholders may grant to others by proxy the right to attend and speak for them at meetings.

In the United States, private corporations are called *close corporations* or *closely held corporations*. They are required to meet conditions similar to those in England, after which they are modeled. The board of directors of an American closely held corporation may be dispensed with entirely, and the corporation can be managed directly by its shareholders, of which there are few. These companies typically have only close friends or family members as their shareholders.

A variant of the closely held corporation, found only in the United States, is the professional corporation. All fifty states permit this corporate form. Professionals, such as doctors, lawyers, accountants, and so forth, form professional corporations to give themselves better tax treatment, retirement planning, and disability options. Each member of a professional corporation is liable for the professional malpractice of all the members, but none is individually liable for the nonprofessional obligations of the corporation, such as its debts.

CIVIL LAW CORPORATIONS

In civil law countries every type of business entity or business organization is a company, and all companies must register with the government of their country.[13] France and Germany are featured here, France being the home of civil law and Germany being the largest European Union country practicing it.

It is important to note that there is no overriding European Union law on corporations or any directive requiring any particular corporate form. Corporate law and corporate forms of governance are reserved for each member nation in the twenty-five-member European Union to determine for itself.

In France, companies are called *sociétés*, and all companies of any type are regarded under the law as juridical entities that are independent of their owners. A French public corporation is known as a *société anonyme* (S.A.). In Germany a company (*Gesellschaft*) must register with the government, but only corporations are juridical entities, not partnerships or any other type of entity. In Spain and Spanish-speaking countries a corporation is a *sociedad anonyme* (S.A.), in Italy a corporation is *societa per azioni* (SpA), and in Japan corporations are *yugen-kaisha* (Y.K.). Russia's Civil Code of 1994 recognizes four main types of company structures, including a joint stock company (open or closed), which is its main type of corporation.

In all civil law countries, like public corporations in common law countries, a corporation is a company of capital whose owners have limited liability, meaning that investors are liable only to the limit of their financial investment. Two basic types of corporations exist: stock corporations and limited liability companies.

STOCK CORPORATIONS

Stock corporations are the only type that can raise money in the public marketplace. In France this type of public corporation is a *société anonyme* (S.A.), and in Germany it is *Aktiengesellschat* (AG). Formal company names have S.A. or AG after their titles, comparable to the use of Inc. in the United States (e.g., Dell, Inc.). L'Oréal S.A., the giant French cosmetics company, is an example. The great Swiss food company, Nestlé S.A., is another example because Switzerland largely follows French corporate practice. Daimler-Chrysler AG is a German example.

Procedure for Incorporation

A stock corporation is initiated by preparing articles of incorporation and then finding subscribers (investors) to purchase shares. The articles of incorporation contain the same type of information as those of common law corporations: name of the company, registered office address, the purpose of the firm, and the capital invested. In France, the articles of incorporation also must include the term of existence of the corporation (limited or unlimited), the address of the corporate office (not just the registered office address), the par value and type of shares to be issued, and the number of shares directors must own to be eligible to be directors.

Capital

Laws in each country require a minimum amount of capital (money) to be raised before a corporation can be formally organized. Capital is raised by subscription for a new corporation in one of two ways. First, *simultaneous incorporation* is the most typical approach. The promoters of the corporation, usually venture capitalists or bankers, form a syndicate that purchases the shares of the corporation; these are the *subscribers*. After the business is incorporated, the subscribers then sell shares to the general public.

Second is incorporation by *stages*, whereby the promoters of the corporation issue a prospectus describing the terms and conditions of the sale of stock in the new company and invite the public to subscribe. Subscribers are then invited to a meeting to approve the draft of the articles of incorporation, ratify the issuance of shares, and approve other corporate arrangements needed to start the company operating.

Stock

After the minimum amount of capital is paid in, an organizational meeting is held at which the board of directors is appointed or elected. The articles of incorporation are then registered with the appropriate government office. Some countries require that a notice of registration be published in an official government publication. After registration and publication, the stock corporation officially comes into existence.

The number of shareholders required varies from country to country. In France, a stock corporation can never have fewer than seven shareholders, and if the number falls below that the corporation may be forced to dissolve. In Germany, after incorporation, the shares can be transferred to a single owner, permitting a wholly owned stock corporation to be set up.

Typically, the only type of shares subscribers may purchase are par shares, those that have a specified face value. In France, the corporation's bylaws must specify a minimum par value per share. Only a few civil law countries, such as Brazil, permit no-par-value shares, those having no specified face value. Payment for shares can be made by cash or property, but an independent appraiser must establish the value of the property. In France, there is a two-year waiting period after incorporation before shares purchased in exchange for property can be negotiated or sold.

The right to transfer ownership of stock from one party to another is permitted in civil law countries. To make transfer easier, most corporations issue their stock certificates in the form of bearer instruments. In France, shares are no longer issued in paper form as certificates; ownership is shown by the entry of the shareholder's name in an account maintained by the issuing corporation or a financial institution approved by the government.

Operating Procedures

Owners of common stock are entitled to vote on the operation of their corporation; preferred stockholders are not. The use of preferred stock, which was a rarity until recently, has grown in popularity. France and Germany now authorize corporations to issue preferred stock that confers special rights regarding dividends and preferred status at the time of dissolution of the company, like common law public corporations do.

The common stock shareholders of stock corporations elect the board of directors, review the annual financial statements, and declare dividends, if any. Formal meetings are required, and quorum requirements (minimum number of shares' owners who must be present for a meeting to be held) are enforced, though they vary widely from country to country. No quorum is required in Germany for ordinary matters, but in France and other countries a quorum must be met at the first meeting, and, if not, a reduced quorum number is required for a second meeting to take place.

Financial statements are prepared annually in advance of the stockholder annual meeting. Outside auditors or government auditors are employed by the corporation to examine the books. Once examined, the financial statements are then released to the shareholders and the public, and in some civil law countries they must be published.

Management Systems

There are two types of management structures in civil law countries: one tier and two tier. The one-tier type is used exclusively in common law countries. In this situation, the board of directors, which has ultimate responsibility for the corporation, is elected by the shareholders, and the board in turn elects the operating officers, some of whom may also serve on the board of directors, such as the CEO.

One-Tier Management System. The one-tier system is used in certain civil law countries, though the titles of various positions are different. France, for example, is a one-tier country in which the members of the board of directors delegate operating authority to a managing director or a director-general. The term *chief executive officer* is not used, nor are there any *officers* in the American sense of the term. In France, the director-general is typically chairman of the board and, if the company is large, there may be two directors-general. For some of France's very largest companies, the two positions are increasing being split in an effort to improve corporate governance: Alcatel, L'Oréal, Renault, and Carrefour are examples of corporations having split roles.[14]

Even though it is a civil law country, Japan's corporate law is strikingly similar to that of the United States: corporations have a single board of directors elected by the shareholders, and the board has a duty of care to the shareholders and the corporation. In Japan, however, the largest corporations' boards are very large, some with as many as fifty members, being composed of current and former managers as well as creditors, employees, and other stakeholders. Mixing these groups' representatives on the board is far different from the strict independence of American boards, focusing on shareholder interest.

Japanese boards, therefore, do not seek only to enhance shareholder interests, as do American boards; they traditionally operate to benefit a small group of owners, managers, and other stakeholders. Their corporate governance system protects employees and creditors as much as or more than shareholders and provides little incentive to maximize shareholder value.[15]

China is also a one-tier country in which shareholders' interests dominate corporate decision-making. The Chinese Company Law stipulates that large companies establish a supervisory committee of shareholders that has the power to oversee the financial affairs of the company. Shareholders may pass their own resolutions, which must be implemented by the board of directors. Shareholders also approve acts of the board of directors, such as their business plans and investment decisions. Thus, shareholder power pervades the day-to-day decisions and operations of Chinese corporations.[16]

Two-Tier Management System. Germany is a two-tier country, wherein management of the corporation is vested in two main bodies: a supervisory board and a management board. The supervisory board, composed of representatives of shareholders and workers, performs the functions of the board of directors in one-tier countries: it elects and removes the executive board's members, approves financial statements, and handles all matters relating to shareholders. It is chaired by an outside director, and the CEO is a member of the board.

The management board, chaired by the CEO, manages the day-to-day activities of the firm, much like the CEO and other board-elected officers of American corporations. Members of the management board report to the supervisory board.

Although the two-tier system is intended to diffuse power, to make the management board responsible and accountable to the supervisory board, in practice, however, the management board has the real clout. For example, in 1998, Jurgen Schrempp, CEO of Daimler-Benz's management board, told his board in early April of the impending merger with Chrysler, creating DaimlerChrysler AG, but he waited until early May, one day before the merger was announced to the public, to inform the supervisory board. Chrysler's CEO, Robert Evans, told his board of directors about the merger as soon as the deal was struck in early February 1998. Without information, boards cannot supervise!

Switzerland

Switzerland is also a two-tier country in which 77 percent of the blue-chip companies (the 26 member companies on the SMI index) have a separate chairperson and chief executive. In January 2005, the supervisory board of the country's largest company, Nestlé, ran against this tide and decided that its CEO, Peter Brabeck-Lethathe, would also become chairman of the supervisory board when the chairman, Rainer Gut, retired. In the company's long history, the two roles had been merged for only 12 years. Under Brabeck-Lethathe's 8-year leadership, Nestlé's sales had doubled, becoming the world's largest food company.[17]

The Nestlé board's decision received harsh criticism from many shareholders' groups, but at its April 2005 annual shareholders meeting a motion to reject that decision was defeated by a narrow 51 percent vote. The closeness of this vote, combined with the bitter dissent generated by the proposal for combining the two positions and a statement that Brabeck-Lethathe would hold the two positions for only a couple of years, gave encouragement to the growing investor rights movement in Europe.[18]

Some one-tier countries permit the two-tier arrangement for very large corporations. In France, a two-tier management structure is allowed for a large stock company but not for a limited liability company. In recent years, as already noted, some of France's largest companies have split the chairman and chief executive positions. In Brazil, instead of a supervisory board, shareholders may appoint an administrative council of shareholders to elect the management board.

Workers' Rights

Workers are represented on the supervisory boards of German companies and on the management boards in the Netherlands. This concept is most developed and far-reaching in Germany, however, dating back to a 1920 law requiring that at least two workers be members of corporate supervisory boards. Germany's Co-Determination Act of 1976 carried this concept even further: all companies of any type having five hundred or more employees are required to have a two-tier structure, and firms with two thousand or more employees must have a supervisory board of eleven members, five of whom represent the employees and five represent the shareholders, plus the chairperson. The balance of power still rests with the shareholders' representatives because, with respect to stock corporations, the chairperson is always elected by the shareholders and not the workers and has two votes if needed to break ties.[19]

All large German companies also have workers councils. These bodies provide that workers have an equal voice with management in determination of such issues as the workday (start and end times), distribution of work, wage policy, benefits, and other employee issues. These powers and responsibilities are over and beyond collective bargaining agreements that are negotiated between trade unions and industry councils or individual companies.

In other European countries workers councils and committees have only the power of recommendation to management on workers' issues. In almost all European countries management must at least consult with workers' representatives before making decisions affecting any employee issue, such as layoffs.

German corporation law is quite different from that of the United States, Britain, and even France. Various stakeholders are represented on German boards. The business corporation statute states: "the managing board, on its own responsibility, is to manage the corporation for the good of the enterprise and its employees, the common weal of society, and the State."[20] Thus, German law requires that managers operate the firm for the benefit of multiple stakeholders, not just shareholders, and these include workers, suppliers, and customers—all of whom may have representatives on the supervisory board. The interests of nonshareholder constituents are thus formally represented in all strategic decisions.

DaimlerChrysler AG. DaimlerChrysler AG is a good example of how this works. At the 2005 annual shareholders' meeting held at a Berlin convention center and attended by more than eight thousand shareholders, many openly expressed their disapproval of the company's performance since the merger with Chrysler in 1998. Under German law, any shareholder can have five minutes at the microphone to comment on management's performance, and this shareholders' meeting lasted for hours. Jurgen Schrempp, the CEO, had to sit there and take it.

The complaints ranged from quality problems at the Mercedes car unit of the company, having just had the largest recall in company history, to the loss of profitability of the Mercedes car unit, which plunged 97 percent in the prior quarter, to the losses at the new Smart Car unit of Mercedes, to the loss of half of the company's market cap since the Chrysler merger seven years earlier.

Despite the open frustration of individual shareholders and their call for Schrempp to step down, 95 percent of the shares voted to approve the board. The largest shareholders of DaimlerChrysler were Deutsche Bank AG and the governments of Kuwait and Dubai, all of whom supported the supervisory board.[21] A few months later Deutsche Bank sold a large amount of its DaimlerChrysler stock, and Jurgen Schrempp announced his retirement.[22] It appears that even in Germany CEOs are responsible to their shareholders!

LIMITED LIABILITY COMPANIES

Civil law countries also have a business entity known as a limited liability company. This corporation, owned by its members, does not issue negotiable share certificates and has minimal public disclosure requirements.

This business entity was initiated in Germany under the name *Gesellschaft mit bushranger Haftung* (GmbH) and has become quite popular, being adopted in other countries with different names. In France it is known as a *société à résponsabilité limitée* (SARL). This entity is used mostly to establish subsidiaries of corporations. It is a simpler form than a stock corporation, having the liability protections of a stock corporation but not its stringent public disclosure requirements because it cannot issue negotiable shares.

Procedure for Establishment and Operation

The way a limited liability company is set up is essentially the same as for a stock corporation. Articles of incorporation are drafted, capital is subscribed, an organizational meeting is held, an initial supervisory board is appointed or elected, and the articles are registered with a government office.

The minimum amount of capitalization needed varies from country to country but is generally less than that needed for a stock corporation. Investors are called members, rather than shareholders, and they own a *participation* rather than shares. The number of members is restricted in most countries; in France and Mexico, the maximum number is fifty. Meetings of the members to approve actions of the company are routine and vary from formal to informal depending on the country.

In Germany, the Co-Determination Act of 1976 requires limited liability companies, as well as stock corporations, to have worker representation on supervisory boards of companies having two thousand or more employees: five out of eleven members. The ultimate power in limited liability companies is vested in the shareholders.

The transfer of members' interest in a limited liability company to another person is permitted, yet the process is cumbersome compared to stock corporations and highly restricted. The transfer is usually by a formal notarized act. In some countries participation certificates are permitted, but they must be registered with the government in the form of nonnegotiable instruments. There is no open trading of certificates on a stock exchange.

U.S. LLCs

The United States also has limited liability companies (LLCs) that are similar to those in civil law countries.[23] It is the only common law country that has LLCs. The owners of American LLCs, those contributing capital, are called members, and the members have no personal liability for the business beyond their capital contributions.

Any type of business can be organized as an LLC as long as two or more persons are members. The LLC pays no taxes because its profits flow through to the members, who pay them on their individual tax returns. Forming an LLC is quicker, easier, and less expensive than forming a corporation, and yet it has many of the same benefits, particularly liability protection. Unlike corporations, American LLCs have a restriction on their life span (established for a certain number of years), and there are restrictions on transferring members' interests, just as in civil law countries.

CONCLUSION

This chapter summarizes the two major types of corporations, public and private, found throughout most of the world, each based on the type of law present in countries where they operate: English common law and civil law. Presented here is a summary of the procedures for establishing and operating these types of corporations. It is essential for Americans to understand this information because of the increasing globalization of business and commerce.

NOTES

1. This section is largely drawn from José de la Torre, Yves Doz, and Timothy Devinney, *Managing the Global Corporation: Case Studies in Strategy and Management*, 2nd ed. (New York: Irwin/McGraw-Hill, 2001), xi–xii.

2. *Fortune*, April 18, 2005, F1.

3. For a discussion, see Ray August, *International Business Law*, 2nd ed. (Upper Saddle River, NJ: Prentice Hall, 1997), Chapter 4.

4. Jack Welch, *Jack: Straight from the Gut* (New York: Warner Books, 2001).

5. See www.usdoj.gov/criminal/fraud/fcpa.

6. For a discussion, see Ray August, *International Business Law*, 2nd ed., 197–201.

7. *Wall Street Journal*, March 2, 2005, A3.

8. 118 U.S. 394 (1886), *Santa Clara County v. Southern Pacific Railroad Co.*

9. This discussion is based on Ray August, *International Business Law*, 2nd ed., 157–163.

10. For a discussion, see Wesley B. Truitt, *What Entrepreneurs Need to Know about Government: A Guide to Rules and Regulations* (Westport, CT: Praeger, 2004), 93–94.

11. *The Economist*, April 16, 2005, 57.

12. Ibid., 56.

13. This discussion is based on Ray August, *International Business Law*, 2nd ed., 148–154.

14. *The Economist*, April 16, 2005, 56.

15. Larry A. Dimatteo, *The Law of International Business Transactions* (Mason, OH: Thomson South-Western, 2003), 71.

16. Ibid., 70.

17. *Wall Street Journal,* March 24, 2005, C1, C4.

18. Ibid., April 15, 2005, B3.

19. Ray August, *International Business Law,* 2nd ed., 160.

20. Larry A. Dimatteo, *The Law of International Business Transactions,* 71.

21. *Wall Street Journal,* April 7, 2005, A10; *Los Angeles Times,* April 7, 2005, C3.

22. *Wall Street Journal,* July 29, 2005, A1. Schrempp was succeeded by Dieter Zetsche, who headed the Chrysler Group.

23. Wesley B. Truitt, *What Entrepreneurs Need to Know about Government,* 92.

RECOMMENDED READINGS

Denis, Diane K., and John J. McConnell, *Governance: An International Perspective* (Northampton, MA: Elgar Publishing, 2005).

Dimatteo, Larry A., *The Law of International Business Transactions* (Mason, OH: Thomson South-Western, 2003).

Eight

Multinational Corporations

This chapter addresses multinational corporations: what are they, why study them, and how important are they? It covers the characteristics of multinational corporations, along with examples of multinational corporations and special features that set them apart from other large corporations. A case study of Nestlé is presented.

It is important to understand multinational corporations because of the enormous influence they have on the world's economy and on our lives as consumers, employees, and investors, given the fact that 80 percent of the world's industrial production is generated by the one thousand largest multinationals. Over one-third of total U.S. international trade is conducted by and within U.S.-owned multinational corporations; these are called intercompany transactions.

IMPORTANCE OF MULTINATIONAL CORPORATIONS

Business transactions between companies in different nations is nothing new. International trade in goods is as old as the nation-state system itself. Moreover, some businesses have had foreign direct investments and foreign operations for centuries; the British Hudson's Bay Company and the Netherlands' East India Company are clear-cut examples. A surprising number of American-based companies in the nineteenth century were multinational manufacturing companies.[1]

Characteristics of Multinational Corporations

At the end of World War II in 1945, numerous companies based in the United States and Western Europe began to establish large-scale operations in foreign countries to take advantage of emerging international political and economic opportunities. These firms were not only trading goods with foreign firms but also investing in and operating their own businesses in multiple foreign locations with strategies directed from their central headquarters.

Thousands of businesses across many nations thus developed into multinational enterprises with ownership, majority control, or other links crossing many national boundaries, treating the world as though it had no national boundaries. This was a dramatic shift in the way the world had conducted its business, and it has largely happened over the past half century.

When a large corporation makes foreign direct investment in more than two or three different nations, thus establishing ownership or control over businesses in those countries, and when that firm takes a global view of its markets and its resources to integrate production and distribution across national borders, it becomes a *multinational corporation* (MNC). These are the essential characteristics of an MNC. Some writers also assert that MNCs should also have international management.

While international trade between essentially domestic firms has continued to grow in dollar value, its relative importance to the total international business picture has declined. Its position was eclipsed as early as the 1960s by the rising dollar value of MNCs' trade and business operations.[2] So large were the businesses and production facilities owned by U.S.-based firms in France in the 1960s that these American-owned companies had become the largest generators of GDP in France at that time.[3]

MNCs' Size

Looking at individual MNCs today, one is immediately struck by their sheer size. Exxon Mobil Corporation in 2005 was the world's largest company in terms of market capitalization, having annual revenue ($270 billion in 2004) that exceeded the gross domestic product (GDP) of all but the top twenty countries in the world.[4] Wal-Mart Stores, Inc. was the world's largest company in terms of sales, with $288 billion in 2004.[5]

Looking at the top 100 *economies* in the world, only 47 of these are in fact nation-states; the other 53 are MNCs. The 1,000 largest MNCs throughout the world today account for 80 percent of the world's total industrial production.[6]

By any definition, the ten largest U.S.-based corporations in terms of revenue (sales) in 2004 are all multinational corporations. See Table 8.1.[7] All of these corporations have far-flung activities in the United States and throughout the world. Whether it be Wal-Mart Stores in Germany, Britain, Canada, Mexico, Japan, and China; Exxon Mobil's oil pumping, refining, and retailing in the Middle East, East Asia, Africa, North America, or Latin America; GM's and Ford's car and truck factories in Europe, Russia, Latin America, East and Southeast Asia; GE's factories and financial services in Europe, Asia, or Latin America; Citigroup's financial services (insurance and banking) throughout the world; or American International Group's insurance activities also throughout the world—all these companies have global reach from their U.S. headquarters. Thus, MNCs are product-producers, service providers, retailers, and firms with a mix of products and services.

Market value (current share price multiplied by the number of outstanding shares) is a key measure of size. This is often called *market capitalization*, or simply market cap. In 2004, Exxon Mobil's was $392 billion and General Electric's was $374 billion; these were the number-one and -two companies in the world in market cap. Combined, these two companies had much greater value ($766 billion) than the GDPs of Australia and New Zealand combined, which was $704.2 billion for the same year.[8]

INTERNATIONAL MANAGEMENT

Most large U.S.-based MNCs have non-Americans serving in their top management and on their boards of directors. For example, a few years ago a Lebanese-born Australian, Jacques Nasser, was CEO of Ford Motor

TABLE 8.1
Ten Largest U.S.-Based Corporations, 2004 ($ in millions)

Rank	Company	Revenue	Profits	Assets
1	Wal-Mart Stores	$288,189	$10,267	$120,624
2	Exxon Mobil	270,772	25,330	195,256
3	General Motors	193,517	2,805	479,603
4	Ford Motor Co.	172,233	3,487	292,654
5	General Electric	152,363	16,593	750,330
6	Chevron	147,967	13,328	93,208
7	ConocoPhillips	121,663	8,129	92,861
8	Citigroup	108,276	17,046	1,484,101
9	American International Group	98,610	11,050	800,000
10	IBM	96,293	8,430	109,183

Company, and an Englishman, Alex Troutman, had preceded him in that role. A Canadian and an Englishman have been CEOs of Exxon. Serving on IBM's board of directors in 2005 were a Mexican, a Frenchman, a German, and a Japanese, in addition to nine Americans.

For the largest global MNCs the criterion for leadership selection has little to do with the individual's nationality. Instead, it has everything to do with the person's skills and competence and the contribution he or she can make to the company's success. This is especially true for U.S.-based MNCs, as well as those based in Canada, Britain, the Netherlands, Belgium, and certain other countries.[9]

Approximately 90 percent of Europe's largest companies have one or more directors from outside their home country. In a 2005 survey of 99 large companies, 49 percent had at least one American on the board, up from 35 percent in 1999. By contrast, another survey of 149 large non-MNCs in the United States found only 35 percent had at least one non-American director, up a mere 31 percent from 1999. Not having an international presence on a board may put U.S.-based companies at a disadvantage in the global marketplace.[10]

In most other countries nationals of those countries usually get the top jobs. Two major exceptions in Japan are Nissan and Sony: a Brazil-born Frenchman, Carlos Ghosn, is CEO of both Nissan Motor Company, Ltd., Japan, and Renault S.A. of France, Nissan's parent company; and a Welsh-born American is the first non-Japanese CEO of Sony, Ltd.[11] These are the only examples of non-Japanese heading Japan-based MNCs. No non-Chinese head major Chinese firms.

Typical of the United States and the United Kingdom is Cadbury Schweppes, a London-based MNC that markets sodas and confections globally. It has been headed since 2003 by Todd Stitzer, its first American CEO, a Harvard-educated lawyer. Stitzer joined Cadbury Schweppes in 1983 and worked his way up. The company's brands include Cadbury chocolate; Dr. Pepper, 7-Up, and Schweppes soft drinks; and Trident and Adams gum.[12]

FOREIGN DIRECT INVESTMENT

A critical feature of multinational corporations is that they make investments in foreign countries. These investments can take many forms. Sometimes MNCs buy all or part of an existing foreign company, or they might establish a factory or distribution center in a country to make or distribute an existing product locally. At other times they launch a start-up company in another country, and occasionally they establish a refinery or research and

---

FDI in the Automobile Industry

Foreign direct investment most typically is in the form of an equity investment (a purchase) by a firm in one country of a firm in another country. The automobile industry in the 1990s provides examples. In 1990 Ford Motor Company, United States, purchased of all the stock of Jaguar Motor Company, Britain. After the deal closed, Ford installed its own management at Jaguar and integrated the company and its products into Ford's extensive European and U.S. procurement, marketing, and management systems.

Similarly, General Motors purchased Saab of Sweden; BMW of Germany purchased Rolls-Royce of Britain; Daimler-Benz AG purchased Chrysler, to form DaimlerChrysler AG; and in 1999 Renault S.A., France, purchased controlling interest (44 percent) in Nissan Motor Company, Ltd., Japan.[13]

---

development center in a country to capitalize on local resources, talent, or business conditions, such as low labor costs or favorable tax laws.

Whatever the reason for making such investments, they are all grouped under a single title: *foreign direct investment* (FDI). It is *foreign* because the investment is made in a country that is not the MNC's home country. It is *direct* because it is made straightforwardly by the MNC (not by a government agency or through one). And it is an *investment* because the MNC hopes that by putting its money to work in a foreign location it will generate a financial return to the parent company.

UNITED STATES AND FDI

Foreign direct investment into the United States (or any country) occurs under two major categories: acquisitions of American companies by firms based abroad and equity investments by foreign firms in productive assets in the United States. Good examples of the former are the acquisitions of Miller Brewing Company, Milwaukee, by South African Brewery to form SABMiller[14] and of Ben and Jerry's ice cream company by Unilever, an Anglo-Dutch multinational. Acquisitions of existing companies provide instant entrée into a foreign market and are often less expensive than developing from scratch a business that can become competitive.

The second type, equity investments, often involves *greenfield* projects, such as Nissan Motor Company building an enormous assembly plant for several models of its cars, light trucks, and SUVs in Alabama. The idea is that a firm buys a green field and builds a factory on it. Other foreign auto companies' greenfield projects include BMW's in South Carolina, Toyota's in Kentucky and elsewhere, DaimlerChrysler's Mercedes-Benz plant in Mississippi, and so forth.

Foreign direct investment flows outward from one country and inward to another. In 2004, FDI outflows from the United States totaled $285 billion. This dramatically low dollar value of outward FDI reflected the weakness of the dollar (relative to other major currencies) that year yet "it also confirmed continuing strong interest among US companies in acquiring corporate assets abroad," according to the Organization of Economic Cooperation and Development (OECD).[15] Inward FDI to the United States in 2004 was a staggering $580 billion. Looking at the twenty-five largest cross-border mergers and acquisitions in 2004, only five had a U.S.-based company as the acquirer.

Table 8.2 summarizes FDI transactions in and out of the United States over the past four decades.[16]

According to the U.S. Department of the Treasury, by 2003, the total market value of U.S. private assets directly invested abroad was $2.7 trillion, compared with the market value of foreign-based private direct investment in the United States of $2.4 trillion.[17] The income from foreign affiliates of U.S. companies in 2001, the latest year statistics are available, was $126 billion, compared with payments to foreign owners of U.S.-located investments of only $23 billion. Capital has always flowed into the United States seeking safety and acceptable returns, based on high-productivity growth of the U.S. economy and its historic tradition of safety and stability.[18]

U.S. operations of foreign-based corporations employed 5.4 million American workers in 2002, which represented nearly 5 percent of total private sector employment, up from 3.9 million workers a decade earlier.

TABLE 8.2
U.S. International Transactions, 1960–2003 ($ in billions)

Year	U.S.-Owned Private Assets Sent Abroad	Foreign-Owned Private Assets Sent to the United States
1960	$ 5.1	$.821
1965	5.3	.607
1970	10.2	.555
1975	35.3	10.14
1980	73.6	47.11
1985	38.0	147.2
1990	81.3	107.6
1995	341.5	328.6
2000	568.5	1,004.0
2003	285.4	580.6

FDI is an employment stimulator in both the outbound and the inbound country; overseas investment stimulates investment at home at a ratio of 1:3.5. In other words, for every $1.00 a domestic company invests abroad, it also invests an additional $3.50 in its home country operations. This finding is in a report by the president's Council of Economic Advisors.[19]

What states receive the most foreign direct investment? Table 8.3 lists the top ten states receiving FDI in 2002, showing the employment levels of foreign-controlled companies and the percent of that employment in that state's workforce. The national average percentage of employment in foreign-controlled companies is 4.8 percent.[20]

Looking at California, the state with the largest number of employees of foreign-controlled companies, nearly one-fourth of these jobs (149,400) were in manufacturing, representing 9.1 percent of total manufacturing employment in that state in 2002. The five largest countries of origin of these foreign-controlled companies were the United Kingdom, Japan, Switzerland, Germany, and France. Financial institutions, such as banks, that are affiliated with foreign companies are excluded from these data.

Taking a snapshot of national data for just one year, 2004, see Table 8.4 for a list of the countries that sent and received the most foreign direct investment to and from the United States.[21] China was number eleven on the outbound list with $4.2 billion and was far down on the inbound list.

The staggering amounts of investment by American corporations scattered in countries around the world produced another dramatic statistic: over one-third of total U.S. trade is conducted inside of U.S.-based multinational corporations. "In 2002, 35% of total U.S. international trade in goods was

TABLE 8.3
Top Ten States by Employment of
Foreign-Controlled Companies, 2002

Rank	State	Number of Jobs	% of State Workforce
1	California	616,400	4.9
2	New York	394,700	5.5
3	Texas	351,400	4.4
4	Illinois	268,400	5.2
5	Florida	244,900	3.8
6	Pennsylvania	233,400	4.6
7	New Jersey	228,600	6.7
8	Ohio	212,800	4.5
9	North Carolina	212,700	6.5
10	Michigan	204,100	4.4

TABLE 8.4

Top Ten Countries Sending/Receiving FDI to/from the United States, 2004

FDI Inbound to United States		FDI Outbound from United States	
Country Sending	$ in Billions	Country Receiving	$ in Billions
Canada	31.8	United Kingdom	$22.9
United Kingdom	19.4	Canada	22.4
Japan	16.1	Netherlands	12.5
France	9.2	Japan/Switzerland (tie)	10.6
Netherlands	6.1	Ireland	10.4
Switzerland	4.7	Germany	9.9
Australia	3.6	France	9.7
Sweden	3.3	Mexico	7.4
Germany	1.5	U.K.-Caribbean Islands	5.0
Panama·	1.4	Luxembourg	4.5

accounted for by trade within components of firms with operations in two or more countries," reported the Council of Economic Advisors.[22] This includes dollar flows in both directions, inbound and outbound.

FDI also includes transactions having both inflows and withdrawals between foreign-invested enterprises and their foreign-based parent companies. For example, in 2004 inward FDI to Germany and France, the two largest economies in the European Union, fell sharply. For France, inward investment was cut almost in half, falling from $43 billion in 2003 to $24 billion in 2004. For Germany, foreign investors withdrew about $39 billion from the country in 2004, reversing the inflow of $27 billion recorded the year before. Poor business conditions in these countries, including high labor costs and chronic unemployment depressing consumer confidence, were contributing factors.

DEVELOPING NATIONS AND FDI

At an increasing rate developing countries are investing in the United States, just as European, Canadian, and Japanese companies have for decades. Though these dollar amounts are comparatively tiny, they nevertheless show a rising trend as the global economy reaches into these developing nations providing them with the means and the need to be part of the globe's largest economy.

Table 8.5 summarizes the dollar value of acquisitions of U.S. companies by firms in the ten less developed countries making the largest U.S. acquisitions over an eight-year period.[23] The value of these acquisitions accounted for less than 2 percent of all acquisitions in the United States during this same

TABLE 8.5
Value of Acquisitions of U.S. Firms by Firms in
Developing Countries, 1997 to Mid-2005 ($ in billions)

Country of Acquiring Companies	Value of U.S. Acquisitions
Israel	$12.7
Mexico	11.2
Brazil	7.8
Singapore	6.5
Hong Kong	5.0
Bahrain	3.2
Hungary	2.5
China	1.8
Saudi Arabia	1.3
Taiwan	1.2

period, reflecting the fact that developing nations are still bit players in the global investment league.[24]

During just the first seven months of 2005, there were seventy different acquisitions of U.S. companies by firms in developing nations, having a total value over $10 billion. Leading this group was one deal in which the Israeli company Teva Pharmaceutical Industries Ltd. acquired Ivax Corporation, a generic drugmaker, for more than $7 billion.

In the category of *developing countries*, some are greater beneficiaries than others of foreign investment. The People's Republic of China continues to receive a large share of direct investment from all sources, having inbound FDI of $60 billion in 2005, up from $55 billion in 2004.[25] The Asian financial center countries of Singapore and Hong Kong (part of China but recorded separately) received a combined total of $50 billion of inward FDI in 2004, reflecting continuing good business conditions. "India is making steady progress in establishing itself as an attractive destination for FDI," according to the OECD; since the late 1990s, inward FDI has trended upward, reaching $4.3 billion in 2003 and $5.3 billion in 2004. In 2004, Argentina received FDI totaling $4 billion, Brazil $18 billion, and Chile $8 billion, all approximately double what they had received the year before.[26]

Some countries in the developing category are beginning to make outward FDI, though by the standards of *developed countries* (United States, Western Europe, Japan) these foreign investments are still small. Large corporations in Brazil and Mexico are in the process of engaging in regional integration through investment and are also moving to develop truly multinational corporate networks. Chinese companies, some state owned or partially state owned, are also increasingly undertaking strategic investments abroad, mostly related to raw materials, especially energy.

India's largest company is the Tata Group, a conglomerate having major businesses in steel, autos, chemicals, and consulting. In recent years this multinational corporation has begun making foreign direct investments on a fairly large scale, beginning in 2001 with the acquisition of Britain's Tetley Tea Company for $432 million. Next, in 2004, Tata acquired NatSteel of Singapore for $289 million, and in 2005, it acquired Teleglobe, a Bermuda-based wholesale telecommunications company, for $239 million. Tata's chairman, Ratan Tata, is positioning the Tata Group for global competition by transforming its operations at home and by plugging it into the world economy. As India's government continues its market-driven economic reform program, the company had to become more competitive with other world-class players.[27]

WHAT IS A MULTINATIONAL CORPORATION?

Multinational corporations are large companies that compete on a global basis often in a single industry, such as Exxon Mobil in energy and Nestlé in food; have size or scale requirements that exceed the size of a single national market; treat the world as though it were a single market; and have centralized strategic leadership but decentralized operational management that is indifferent to national origin.[28] Other MNCs, such as General Electric, have major businesses in several unrelated industries: such as power systems, plastics, medical equipment, entertainment, and financial services. MNCs compete both locally and globally.

MNCs can consist of a network of loosely organized national companies, competing locally against others in a single country setting. They can also behave like global companies pursuing centrally directed strategies that take advantage of their global power and resources to compete successfully in domestic markets in which they have operations.[29]

There is no universally agreed-upon definition of MNCs. Various scholars have offered suggestions, but none seems to have been fully accepted. Part of the problem stems from the complex nature of global activities: there are *international* companies, *global* companies, *global industries*, *transnational* companies in *global industries*, and *multinational* companies. The critical distinction is whether the company is more than just an importer/exporter into and out of a single or multiple domestic markets. That would be an international or transnational company, whatever its size.[30]

MNCs, on the other hand, must be large enough to have actual business operations that are locally managed in several countries, treating the world as a single marketplace, and also have centralized leadership setting company-wide strategy and policies. One precise definition of an MNC is a firm "that engages in foreign direct investment and owns or controls value-adding activities in more than one country."[31]

In addition to owning or controlling assets in various countries, MNCs also buy resources or raw materials in various countries, ship them to other countries for processing, and then ship the finished goods to still other countries to sell them. All this activity is managed from a central headquarters that permits its local managers to align their activities as appropriate to local conditions. The flow of goods and services through a supply chain from raw materials to finished products to be sold in a marketplace is a major management challenge, the successful design and execution of which sets profitable companies apart from marginal performers. MNCs are masters of this art.

Airbus Industrie

The construction of the new Airbus Industrie super jumbo airliner, the 555-seat A380, is an example of how an MNC works, even though Airbus Industrie itself is not an MNC; it is an international company, importing parts from 30 countries and exporting finished aircraft to a number of countries. Airbus is adding this new super jumbo to its existing offering of several smaller size models, all of which directly compete globally with the world's only other maker of large commercial airliners, the Boeing Company, based in Chicago.

The supply chain for one part (the wing) of the A380 is illustrative of the global reach of this one company. Bauxite ore is mined in western Australia, shipped to a smelter in the United States, where it is turned into large aluminum sheets that are then transported to Britain, where they are shaped and formed into wings by BAE Systems Ltd. Wings are then shipped by boat to a port in France, where they are trucked to Toulouse, Airbus's final assembly plant, to be joined to the fuselage, manufactured by EADS in Germany. All this activity involving hundreds of thousands of parts is managed by Airbus Industrie from its headquarters in Toulouse, France. This large-scale transnational operation involves hundreds of companies all around the world.

Boeing

Airbus Industrie's only rival is the Boeing Company, America's largest exporter. Like Airbus, Boeing is not an MNC but an international company. It imports parts from firms owned by others and exports airliners. Boeing's newest aircraft, the 787, a 200- to 300-seat fuel-efficient long-range passenger jet, is a model of international cooperation. Its first delivery is scheduled for 2008. Between 60 percent and 70 percent of the airplane is being built overseas, parts being shipped to Seattle for final assembly by Boeing. Foreign partners are based in Britain, Italy, France, China, and Japan.[32]

Three Japanese companies, Mitsubishi Heavy Industries Ltd., Kawasaki Heavy Industries Ltd., and Fuji Heavy Industries Ltd., are designing and will build 35 percent of the new airplane, primarily the wings and part of the passenger cabin. The wings are not made of aluminum but of composite materials to reduce weight. Mitsubishi built a $400-million, 500,000-square-foot factory in Japan to assemble the wings, which will be "stuffed" with electronics and wiring, plus fuel tanks. Once built, the wings will be flown to Seattle in a modified 747 for assembly with the fuselage, the midsection of which is being built by Kawasaki and Alenia Aeronautica of Italy. Boeing's Japanese partners previously built 15 percent of the 767 and 20 percent of the 777 airliners.[33]

Crislu

On a smaller scale, the American company Crislu, which makes fashion accessories specializing in cubic zirconium, designs its jewelry in the United States, outsources the manufacturing to firms in China, where the jewelry is also packaged, and then ships the finished goods to distribution centers in the United States and Europe. It markets its products through upscale retail outlets such as Nordstrom in the United States and Galleries Lafayette in Paris. Crislu is an example of an international company (exporting and importing), not a multinational corporation, because it is not large and has no equity investment overseas.

Regardless of their size and global reach, MNCs begin in a home country and expand their operations outward from there. MNCs are incorporated under the laws of a single country, their home country. Therefore, Exxon Mobil, a U.S.-based MNC, is incorporated under the laws of the United States, which means it is incorporated in a particular state; in Exxon Mobil's case, Delaware. Nestlé is a Swiss-based MNC that is incorporated under the laws of Switzerland, though it has 400 factories and other operations in over fifty countries throughout the world.

WHERE ARE MULTINATIONAL CORPORATIONS BASED?

The explosive growth in the number of multinational corporations is a recent phenomenon, occurring since 1970. In 1969 there were 7,258 MNCs

TABLE 8.6
Distribution by Home Country of Global Top Fifty Industrial Firms,
1964–2004

Year	United States	Europe	Japan	Other	U.S. Firms' Share of Total Sales %
1964	39	11	—	—	79
1974	24	20	4	2	57
1984	22	18	6	4	45
1993	15	19	13	3	37
2004	18	21	7	4	36

and by 2000 there were 63,000 of them, a ninefold increase. In the hundred years before 1970 the world's population of MNCs had barely tripled.[34]

Where are these MNCs based? Most are based in the United States, Western Europe, and Japan. Looking at the last four decades, the percentage of the world's largest MNCs headquartered in the United States declined by more than half as more and more companies with home bases in Europe and Japan grew into MNCs. The global distribution by location of the world's fifty largest industrial MNCs' headquarters is summarized in Table 8.6.[35] The percent of sales of these MNCs made by U.S.-based MNCs is also indicated. Interestingly, in the "Other" category, two new countries appeared on the top fifty list in 2004: China with three companies and South Korea with one, Samsung Electronics, number thirty-nine on the list with sales of $71.5 billion.

The country-by-country distribution of the largest European-based MNCs in 2004 is as follows: Germany six, France five, Britain three, Italy and the Netherlands two each, and one each for Switzerland, Britain/ Netherlands, and Belgium/Netherlands.[36]

The ten largest corporations in the world in 2004 by revenue are all multinational corporations; they are listed in Table 8.7.[37] BP is the new name for British Petroleum. Four of the top ten companies are oil companies (BP, Exxon Mobil, Royal Dutch/Shell, and Total), and another four are auto manufacturers. The revenue for these ten corporations totaled $2.132 trillion, making them larger than all but six nations in the world in 2004, as measured by their gross domestic product (GDP).[38]

CASE STUDY OF AN MNC: NESTLÉ S.A.

Nestlé S.A. is a classic example of a multinational corporation operating successfully in nearly every country on Earth. It is the forty-third largest company in the world with sales in 2004 of $70 billion.[39] As is usually the

TABLE 8.7
Ten Largest Companies in the World by Revenue, 2004 ($ in billions)

Rank	Company	Country of Headquarters	2004 Revenue ($ in Billions)
1	Wal-Mart Stores	United States	$287.9
2	BP	Britain	285.0
3	Exxon Mobil	United States	270.7
4	Royal Dutch/Shell	Britain/Netherlands	268.6
5	General Motors	United States	193.5
6	DaimlerChrysler	Germany	176.6
7	Toyota Motor Co.	Japan	172.6
8	Ford Motor Co.	United States	172.2
9	General Electric	United States	152.8
10	Total S.A.	France	152.6

case, the company began with a single product invented by its founder and then grew into a multiproduct company with operations first in its domestic market, then expanding internationally and later moving to a global scale.

Nestlé grew primarily by acquisition, consolidating its leading position in each national market with a focus on a single industry, in Nestlé's case, food. The brand names of the acquired companies were retained, and their operations (procurement of raw materials, manufacturing and processing into finished products, distribution, and marketing) were coordinated either by the acquired company, if large enough, or by a national corporate entity, such as Nestlé USA or Nestlé Germany.

As a matter of long-standing company policy, its operations in each country are usually managed by nationals of that country (for example, Carnation Company is managed by Americans) because they best understand the local marketplace. Its global operations are managed from corporate headquarters in Switzerland. This is where strategic decisions are made, such as the policy to purchase raw materials (agricultural products) and not own agricultural production property. Two key product decisions were made at corporate headquarters in the 1990s: to become a global player in both pet food and bottled water, Nestlé becoming the largest company in the world in both categories.

Its top management has in recent years been non-Swiss, having had a German and now an Austrian CEO. For MNCs other than those based in Japan and China, nationality at the top is unimportant; skill and leadership are what counts, regardless of the passport the person holds.

The Nestlé S.A. case study illustrates many of the features of the typical growth, expansion, and governance of large multinational corporations. See the Appendix to this chapter for the story of this company.

CONCLUSION

Multinational corporations are a major economic force in the world, the thousand largest of which account for 80 percent of the world's industrial production. These enormous corporations are headquartered throughout the world and do business in almost every country. A case study of the rise and development of one of the world's largest MNCs, Nestlé S.A. of Switzerland, is presented, illustrating its strategies for growth, operations, and reasons for its success.

APPENDIX: NESTLÉ S.A., PROFILE OF A MULTINATIONAL CORPORATION

The world's largest food company with sales in 2004 of $70 billion was founded by Henri Nestlé, a German born in Frankfurt in 1814, who moved to the small town of Vevey, Switzerland, when he was twenty-nine. Nestlé's world headquarters is still in Vevey.[40] Today, Nestlé has hundreds of brands and does business in almost every country. Some of its familiar brands in the United States are Nescafé coffee, Nestea, Stouffer's frozen foods, Carnation milk, Friskies and Alpo pet food, Häagen-Dazs and Dreyer's Grand Ice Cream, Perrier and Arrowhead water, Baby Ruth and Rolo candy, Libby's canned foods, Beringer wine, and Buitoni pasta.

Nestlé has over 400 production centers in 50 countries throughout the world, more than 200,000 employees, and 100,000 Swiss and foreign shareholders. With no more than one-third of its sales from any one continent, Nestlé is truly a global company. In 140 years, Nestlé S.A. became one of the world's leading companies by becoming one of the world's largest and most successful multinational corporations.

Humble Beginnings

In 1865, through trial and error, Henri Nestlé, now in his fifties, invented a milk-based packaged cereal for infants and young children called *Kindermehl* (infant cereal). He put his own name and his own logo on the package: a small bird's nest, which in the Swiss-German dialect is the word *Nestlé*. His baby food quickly caught on and Henri Nestlé's company grew. To this day, the company uses his original bird's nest logo.

Nestlé quickly expanded his small company with his major success coming in 1868 when he exported his baby cereal to the larger markets of Germany, France, and Britain. He worked day and night to fill the avalanche of orders coming in from his sales agents, with expansion interrupted only by the Franco-Prussian War (1870–1871).

Nestlé's marketing strategy was simple: to bring the product within everyone's reach, he priced it low to generate volume. He never advertised ("it cost too much and yielded too small a return") but instead shipped samples of his cereal to pharmacists and physicians, asking them to examine it and test it themselves.[41]

Within five years, his baby cereal was marketed in 17 countries, including the United States, Mexico, Argentina, Australia, the Dutch East Indies (Indonesia), Russia, and throughout much of Europe. His sales doubled between 1871 and 1873, achieving a production rate of 500,000 cans per year. Henri Nestlé was proud of the fact that his baby cereal reduced infant mortality in many countries and provided a highly nutritious and easy-to-use food for mothers to use in large parts of the world.

New Owners

At his age, Nestlé knew he was unable to manage the continuing rapid expansion of the firm. In 1875, he decided to sell the business and was immediately made two offers at the same price: Sfr. 1,000,000. At the time, this was an immense sum of money. He accepted the offer made by people from his own town, who threw in a splendid coach and team of horses. Nestlé retired and had nothing more to do with the company, dying in 1890.

The new owners had bought the Nestlé name, his recipes, his factory, his machinery, his patents, his worldwide distribution network, and everything associated with the company. They quickly incorporated the new company with initial capitalization of Sfr. 1,000,000 under the name Farine Lactee Henri Nestlé, with a three-person board of directors who were also the active managers. The firm prospered, expanded production facilities and sales of the baby cereal, achieving ever higher rates of market penetration from big cities to small towns and villages throughout the world.

In 1878, just three years later, a competitor showed up: the Anglo-Swiss Condensed Milk Company, a neighboring Swiss firm that began marketing its own baby cereal along with condensed milk. Nestlé's managers counterattacked by expanding their product line to include condensed milk also. The competition was fierce, but Nestlé's expansion strategy worked: it built two additional factories in Switzerland and, in 1898, bought a condensed milk plant in Norway. This worked well, and the company continued expansion, building more plants within the next few years in Britain, Germany, the United States, and Spain. These local plants were needed partly to overcome high tariffs on food imports by these countries.

In 1903, a German plant was built in the town of Hegge. The German company was incorporated as Nestlé Kindermehl GmbH, with its head office in Berlin. This was the first of what became a global pattern of locally incorporated subsidiaries of the Nestlé company.

MERGER AND ACQUISITION STRATEGY IS ESTABLISHED

In 1904–1905, another pattern for the company was set: alliances and mergers. First, Nestlé's board decided to expand its product line by adding milk chocolate. Not wanting to undertake the time and expense of developing its own formulas and facilities, Nestlé formed an alliance with Peter & Kohler Swiss General Chocolate Company to produce milk chocolate under the Nestlé trademark. This was the first in a long list of business alliances, leading to the merger of the two firms in 1929.

In 1905 Nestlé merged with its longtime rival, the Anglo-Swiss Condensed Milk Company. This firm had been founded in 1866 by two American brothers, Charles and George Page. Charles had been American consul in Zurich and was familiar with Swiss industry. Both brothers had observed Gale Borden's invention of condensed milk in 1856 and believed Switzerland was an ideal location for a condensed milk factory. They chose the name Anglo-Swiss to flatter the British, their intended target market. The company prospered, greatly expanded, and opened plants in the United States, Britain, and other countries. In 1902 Anglo-Swiss sold its U.S. holdings to Borden Company and was in a stronger financial and market position than Nestlé, though it had the same number of factories.

The 1905 merger of Nestlé and Anglo-Swiss was treated as a merger of equals, though in fact Anglo-Swiss absorbed Nestlé. The merger was brokered by two Swiss bankers who each sat on one of the company's boards. After the merger, the Nestlé and Anglo-Swiss Condensed Milk Company was well on its way as a major player in the global packaged food industry.

LOCAL INCORPORATION STRATEGY CONTINUES

During the 1910–1920 period, Nestlé expanded globally, buying plants and milk production sites first in Australia and then in United States, Argentina, Brazil, Chile, Cuba, Mexico, and elsewhere. The U.S. activities were so large the company decided to incorporate in New York City with the name Nestlé's Food Company. A similar local incorporation strategy was soon followed in Australia, Brazil, Argentina, and Cuba. During the 1920s, the company overextended itself and, in the face of the worldwide financial crises, retrenched and reorganized its finances to improve cash flow.

In the 1930s Nestlé invented instant coffee, giving it its now famous brand: Nescafé. Brazilian coffee producers had approached the chairman of Nestlé, who had once lived in Brazil, asking him if Nestlé could develop an instant coffee to help use the surplus of coffee beans grown there. After a few years of experimentation at Nestlé's now-famous research center in Switzerland, Nescafé instant coffee was invented and was soon produced in plants in the United States, Britain, and France.

World War II Split Management

On the eve of World War II, Nestlé had over one hundred factories around the world, producing instant coffee, condensed milk, and chocolate. In 1939, realizing that war was imminent, Nestlé decided to split its management in two: half of the senior executives moved to Nestlé's U.S. headquarters, now in Stamford, Connecticut, from where they would direct the company's non-European operations. The other half remained in Vevey, Switzerland, to manage the company's operations in Europe. The two management groups were able to continue close coordination even after the United States entered the war against Germany and Italy because Switzerland remained neutral.

World War II, of course, interrupted deliveries of supplies and finished product in Europe and much of Asia. To overcome these disruptions, Nestlé accelerated its policy of local production, setting up plants in several more Latin American countries. In Panama, needing to shift production from milk to sugar and other more profitable products, Nestlé began production of canned tomatoes, thus extending its product line to vegetables. Nestlé's policy was always to employ local managers and labor whenever possible, averaging 95 percent local workers.[42]

Nescafé, which had been invented just before the start of the war, really caught on during the war in the United States and elsewhere in the world. A second American plant was built in Illinois, the total production of which, along with that of the first plant, was bought by the U.S. government during the war to supply the armed forces.

Postwar Situation: Consolidation and Growth

Nestlé came out of World War II in better shape than most European businesses, largely because Switzerland had remained neutral and Nestlé's operations were on a global scale. One of Nestlé's plants in France and another in Germany had been damaged, as was the office in London, but by and large Nestlé survived the war intact. Shortages of all types affected the company after the war ended, especially in raw materials and transportation in Europe. Getting the European businesses back on their feet was a major challenge, but the thriving businesses in North and South America provided much of the means for doing this. The plants in Czechoslovakia and Poland were nationalized in 1948 by their new Communist governments, and the plant in Berlin (in the Soviet zone) was dismantled. Nestlé received some compensation for the loss of these facilities.

In 1947 Nestlé recombined its corporate management in Vevey, Switzerland, and embarked on a horizontal expansion by acquiring Maggi, an old-line Swiss firm that made soups, other types of canned foods, and bouillon cubes. Maggi came out of the war in worse shape than Nestlé, with most of its markets and eleven factories being in war-torn Europe, which was slow to recover. The merger maximized the value of Nestlé's worldwide distribution system and instantly expanded the company's European product line for the first time from milk products, cocoa, and instant coffee. With the Maggi acquisition, Nestlé's sales went from Sfr. 833 million to Sfr. 1.34 billion a year later. The merged company was named Nestlé Alimentana S.A., dropping the Anglo-Swiss name and the name Maggi, preferring to use Maggi's holding company's name, Alimentana.

The 1950s saw economic recovery in Western Europe and the continuing expansion of Nestlé's research and development activities, along with its product line.

In 1960 the next large acquisition occurred: Crosse & Blackwell, a respected British firm that manufactured and marketed canned soups, canned vegetables, fish, jam, and chocolate. At the same time Nestlé also acquired La Gragnanese SpA and Locatelli SpA, both Italian companies, and Cain's Coffee in the United States. In 1962 Nestlé acquired 80 percent of Findus International S.A., a Swedish firm that specialized in frozen foods, and soon began manufacturing and distributing ice cream as well as frozen food in Europe, adding two new lines of business for the growing firm. The remaining 20 percent of Findus was acquired a few years later.

Nestlé at One Hundred

By 1966, at its centennial, the company had more than 214 factories in 36 countries and marketed its products in virtually all parts of the non-Communist world. Its product line had expanded to include condensed and powdered milk, Nescafé, Nesquick, baby food, chocolate, and many other food products, both canned and frozen. Nestlé had become a fully integrated global food company.

In 1968 the company published its financial report for the first time. That year sales totaled Sfr. 8.4 billion, having doubled in a decade. The new chairman of the board announced that Nestlé would continue its fifty-year tradition of self-financing its operations, meaning that it did not borrow money.

Having achieved this level of economic growth, Nestlé was truly a multinational corporation. It had global reach with its production capacity and markets, and it had an international management organized in a decentralized management system. Switzerland, its home country, having only 6 million people, represented a mere 2.5 percent of Nestlé's annual sales, necessitating the company's multinational character to successfully compete in the global packaged food industry.

To maintain competitiveness, the company continued to expand its product lines. In 1969 it acquired a minority interest in Vittel, the third largest French mineral water company, and in 1974 it fully acquired the second largest German bottler of mineral water, Blaue Quellen AG. In 1987, Nestlé acquired a majority of Vittel.

MAJOR EXPANSION IN THE UNITED STATES

In 1970, Nestlé already owned a small interest in the large American food producer Libby, McNeill & Libby and faced the fact that that company, and its investment, were in trouble. Nestlé decided to increase its ownership stake to enable it to take over the management and turn the company around. That year Libby's sales were $350 million. Once it had a controlling interest and installed its own management, Nestlé quickly achieved its turnaround objective.

In 1975 Nestlé acquired 100 percent of Libby, the Chicago-based company that was nearly as old as Nestlé itself with products similar to Nestlé's and with factories and markets in North America and Europe. The key difference was that Libby's sold its fruit, juice, and meats exclusively in cans, and it owned its own can-making factories and some agricultural land, such as a large pineapple plantation in Hawaii. Nestlé's philosophy was never to own the package-making capability or agricultural land but to purchase these items. This was a hundred-year-old management strategy that is known today as outsourcing or buy, not make.

Nestlé quickly sold Libby's landholdings and its packaging factories and consolidated its operations into other Nestlé-owned activities. After these sell-offs, Libby's continued as a Nestlé company, selling the canned meat, fish, vegetables, and fruit juices it made, plus distributing in the United States the products of Crosse & Blackwell and Maggi.

CHEESE BECOMES A BIG PLAYER

Cheese was a product in which Nestlé had had a longtime interest, beginning decades earlier in the Netherlands. In 1947, Nestlé made several minority acquisitions of French cheese companies, and in 1961 it acquired Locatelli, an Italian company. In 1967, Nestlé faced the decision either to exit the cheese business or to consolidate its various holdings in the cheese industry and expand them.

Nestlé decided to make cheese a major company product line and to focus that activity in France, from where it began to rationalize its cheese product management throughout Europe. In 1968 Nestlé acquired three French cheese producers, adding them to the two it already owned in France. This newly combined firm, headed by the CEO of one of the acquired firms, formed the basis for Nestlé's presence in the soft cheese market. French cheeses were then exported to Italy, Italian cheeses exported to France, and cheese from both these sources was exported to Britain, Germany, and other European countries.

Nestlé's next major acquisitions were in 1971. First, Beringer vineyards in Napa, California, were purchased, and, second, Nestlé bought another old-line Swiss company that had just acquired a new name: Ursina-Franck S.A. This was the ninth largest firm in Switzerland. Nestlé had long been the largest Swiss company with sales in 1970 of Sfr. 10.2 billion, making it the thirty-ninth largest company in the world. After the acquisition of Ursina-Franck, in 1972, Nestlé's sales were Sfr. 14.6 billion, 53 percent of which were in Europe, with worldwide employment of 111,800 people. The two firms were competitors in many product areas, enabling the combined firm to rationalize production and distribution to its markets. Nestlé quickly sold off all of Ursina-Franck's nonfood assets: companies in real estate, printing, ink, varnish, banking, and small computers.

FROZEN FOOD GETS A MAJOR FOCUS

In 1972 Nestlé's management decided it was time to increase its position in the world's largest frozen food market: the United States. Its largest U.S. holding at that time was Libby's, which had a small portion of the U.S. frozen food business, and it was concluded that it would take at least five years and additional funds to grow Libby's frozen food business to the level Nestlé desired to be genuinely competitive in that category. Nestlé also marketed through Nestlé USA its products produced elsewhere in the world. What Nestlé now wanted was more production to be based in the United States.

The opportunity arose to acquire Stouffer Corporation, based in Cleveland, a large frozen food manufacturer with annual sales of $124 million, which also owned a chain of hotels and institutional catering services. Litton Industries, a conglomerate based in Beverly Hills, wanted to divest Stouffer's, and the management of Stouffer's wanted to reacquire their own company and take it public. The current Stouffer's president, James Biggar, was the son-in-law of the last heir of the company's founder.

Nestlé decided to pursue this acquisition directly, its Libby's subsidiary and Nestlé USA being too weak financially to make the acquisition. Therefore, Nestlé Alimentana S.A. made the offer. The president of Nestlé made five trips to the United States in as many months to close the deal for $105 million in March 1973. All of the Stouffer's management remained onboard, and the prior Stouffer president, James Biggar, stayed in that position and later became head of all Nestlé operations in the United States. Uncharacteristically, Nestlé did not divest Stouffer's hotel and institutional catering business because they were closely tied in to its frozen food business. The hotels were sold later, however.

DIVERSIFICATION IN THE UNITED STATES

At this point, Nestlé declined to attempt further expansion of its food business in the United States, fearing a possible antitrust reaction and the negative publicity that would generate. Therefore, its next move was in the pharmaceutical industry. In 1977, Nestlé USA acquired Alcon Laboratories, Inc., in Ft. Worth, Texas. This acquisition of a pharmaceutical company that specialized in products for eye surgeons and dermatological research to develop skin care products expanded on Nestlé's recent 25 percent investment in L'Oréal, the French company that developed and marketed cosmetics and skin care products. The two companies would now share their distribution systems. Alcon had sales of $81.0 million and a profit of $8.9 million (11 percent of sales). After the takeover, Alcon's management and all its employees remained at their jobs.

Alcon, with Nestlé's backing, began a series of strategic acquisitions to expand its leading role in ophthalmic research and medicines: Burton & Parsons, Texas Pharmacia, Allercreme Dubarry, and Person & Covey, plus a pharmaceutical laboratory in Brazil.

Not wanting to ignore its core food business, Nestlé acquired the American Beech-Nut Corporation in 1979 to reenter the American baby food business, which it had long ago abandoned. This acquisition was to last only a decade.

To strengthen and rationalize its position in the European cheese and milk product industry, in 1978, Nestlé began the phased acquisition of the French company Chambourcy S.A. Chambourcy's main product was yogurt, which was beginning to be popular in Europe, and it had a leading position in France, Italy, and certain other countries. Chambourcy's management wanted to expand globally and lacked the resources to do so. Nestlé provided the means and added this high-value product line to its ever-expanding fresh food division. Refrigerated shipping permitted the worldwide distribution of soft cheese and yogurt.

The oil shocks of 1973–1974 and again in 1979 and the worldwide recession that followed impacted Nestlé, along with most global companies. In 1980 the company faced problems stemming from deflationary policies pursued by certain governments, rising interest rates, the rising cost of fuel, and a global economic slump. These factors impacted the company's profitability that year.

A NEW LEADER POSITIONS NESTLÉ FOR MAJOR GROWTH

In 1980 Nestlé's situation was this: total sales were Sfr. 25 billion, of which 46 percent was generated in Europe, 18 percent in North America, 16 percent in Latin America, 12 percent in Asia, and the rest in Africa and Oceania. Nestlé employed 150,000 people, had 309 factories, and had fixed assets totaling Sfr. 1.2 trillion.

Nestlé decided changes were in order. First, in 1977 Nestlé's corporate name was changed from Nestlé Alimentana S.A. to simply Nestlé S.A. Second, new management was brought in. A German named Helmut Maucher, who had been CEO of the German Nestlé Company, became CEO of Nestlé S.A. in 1981. He was the first non-Swiss to run the company in a very long time. Maucher set out to strengthen Nestlé's internal structure, streamline its operations, and reduce operating costs. At the same time he increased R&D expenditures, marketing, and management training. Even though the early 1980s were a difficult time for every firm, with rising interest rates and growing international tensions, Nestlé increased its profitability during this period of time.

Consistent with Nestlé's long-standing philosophy of remaining mostly a food-oriented company, Nestlé resumed its acquisition strategy, focusing on the United States. In 1983–1985, Nestlé spent Sfr. 9 billion partially or wholly acquiring Hills Brothers Coffee, MJB Coffee, Warner Cosmetics, Paul Beich Company, an Illinois chocolate company, Ward Johnston chocolates, and in 1985 the largest acquisition in the food industry up to that time, Carnation Company, Los Angeles, for $3 billion. This was also Nestlé's largest acquisition ever. Carnation's management remained onboard and sold off its nonfood businesses and its primary production activities, such as dairy farms and cattle ranches.

Through the rest of the 1980s Nestlé continued its expansion program. Herta Group, a German maker of refrigerated cold cuts, was acquired in stages, as was Nestlé's custom, and a Swedish coffee company, Zoegas, was acquired by Nestlé's German subsidiary. Dr. Ballard's Pet Foods, based in Canada, was then added, extending Nestlé into the pet food market in Canada. Nestlé then established a 50 percent stake in Life Savers, an Australian candy company. The acquisition of Buitoni-Perugina, Italy's third largest food company, consolidated its presence in that country, much like Carnation had in the United States. Buitoni produced pasta, olive oil, cold cuts, and chocolates, as well as canned and frozen foods in France. The world's fourth largest confectionery company, Rowntree, maker of Kit Kat and Rolo candies, was acquired in Nestlé's first hostile takeover attempt against a rival Swiss company. Rowntree secured Nestlé's leading position in Great Britain.

R&D is a Major Focus

In 1987 Nestlé inaugurated its newly expanded Nestlé Research Center in a town near Vevey, its Swiss headquarters.[43] This center, with almost 400 scientists, performs basic scientific research regarding food and nutrition. Nestlé also operates an international network of eighteen R&D/development centers located in various parts of the world: China, Ecuador, France, Germany, Great Britain, Israel, Italy, Singapore, Spain, Sweden, Switzerland, and the United States, where it has six product technology centers.[44] The development centers do not undertake basic research, but rather they have clearly defined commercial objectives of developing new products for market using new technologies and improving existing ones.

Nestlé in the 1990s: Growing the Product Line

In 1990, Nestlé and General Mills formed a joint venture called Cereal Partners Worldwide to produce and market breakfast cereals. They chose to use the Nestlé brand for the packaging. Today, Nestlé brand cereal is sold in

80 countries outside of North America, where it is not sold, so as not to compete with General Mills's brands.

Another major joint venture is with the Coca-Cola Company. After an earlier attempt at joint marketing and distribution of cold beverages in Asia had been discontinued in 1994, the two companies came back together in 2001 to form Beverage Partners Worldwide, a Coke/Nestlé joint venture to market cold Nescafé and Nestea in cans, using Coca-Cola's massive distribution system in thirty-five countries. This new corporate entity is headquartered in Zurich with a senior Coca-Cola executive as CEO.

During the 1990s, Nestlé expanded its bottled water business to the point that, by 2004, it constituted nearly 10 percent of total company sales. The origin of its involvement in water began in 1969 with its 30 percent acquisition of Vittel, the French water company. Seeing bottled water as a major growth industry, Nestlé acquired controlling interest in Vittel in 1992, and in the same year acquired 100 percent of Perrier Group, which sells bottled water around the world under such brands as Perrier, Arrowhead, and Poland Springs. The Italian firm San Pellegrino was acquired in 1997; in 1998 Nestlé Pure Life water was established to sell bottled water in the Middle East, Latin America, and parts of Asia. In 2000, Nestlé acquired Aquarel, a major water company in Europe. By 2002, Nestlé Waters, the new group name, had 77 brands sold in 130 countries.

Pet food was also seen as a growth market. In 1982 Nestlé had acquired Fancy Feast cat food, and its 1985 acquisition of Carnation brought with it Friskies brand pet food sold in the United States and parts of Europe. Nestlé expanded that product area in 1995 by buying Alpo, in 1998 by acquiring Spillers, a major European brand, and in 2001, the largest of all, by acquiring Ralston-Purina Company, the dominant U.S. player. Today, this product area is called Nestlé Purina PetCare and is the world's largest pet food company with such brands as Friskies, Fancy Feast, and Alpo.

Divestitures are also part of Nestlé's growth strategy, selling off brands that are marginal performers or companies that are in areas of activity that Nestlé believes have limited growth potential. Such sales generate funds for acquisitions in more promising areas. For example, in 1999, Nestlé sold a large piece of its coffee business, including such brands as Hills Brothers, MJB, and Chase & Sanborn. In 2004, it divested Crosse & Blackwell to Smuckers, and it sold the nectar juices of its Kerns and Libby's brands.

Ice Cream Becomes a Big Player

Wanting to expand its presence in the $21 billion ice cream business in the United States, in 2003 Nestlé acquired for $2.8 billion the country's largest ice cream maker, Dreyer's Grand Ice Cream, Inc., based in Oakland, California, whose sales that year were $1.4 billion. To gain Federal Trade Commission approval for the purchase, Nestlé had to divest three of Dreyer's superpremium brands: Godiva, Whole Fruit, and Dreamery. With the Dreyer's acquisition completed, Nestlé controlled 17 percent of the U.S. ice cream market, which was the same as its archrival Unilever, the Anglo-Dutch food giant.[45]

Häagen-Dazs, which Nestlé came to control, was introduced into the United States in 1960 by a New York City family of Polish descent who gave it a totally made-up Danish name.[46] It was a recipe rich in egg yolks, fresh cream, and the finest fruit ingredients. It contained 15 percent to 20 percent air versus 50 percent to 60 percent typical of supermarket packaged ice creams, giving it a dense, rich flavor and creamy taste. It was designer ice cream for the yuppie generation of the 1970s and 1980s when its sales took off, selling at a 75 percent premium over its rivals; sales grew by 25 percent per year. In 1983 the company was sold to Pillsbury, which already owned strong brands and planned to make Häagen-Dazs a global brand. Five years later Pillsbury was itself acquired by the British conglomerate GrandMet, which split off Häagen-Dazs into a separate company under the GrandMet umbrella.

GrandMet decided to reintroduce Häagen-Dazs into Europe, beginning in Britain in 1990 and then, if successful, expanding on to France. A decade before, Häagen-Dazs had tried and failed in Europe because it had lacked the clout of a major distributor such as GrandMet. By 1993, the brand was profitable in Europe and held an 80 percent market share in the two targeted countries, but experts wondered for how long, given the heated up competition from Nestlé with its Chambourcy superpremium brand and Unilever's superpremium Maison Ortiz. Ben & Jerry's was introduced into Europe in 1994 and also posed a formidable threat, being second behind Häagen-Dazs in the United States in the superpremium category.

Later, GrandMet was dissolved, and Pillsbury reemerged as a separate company with Häagen-Dazs as one of its components. In 1999, Pillsbury and Nestlé formed a joint venture called Ice Cream Partners USA, which combined Häagen-Dazs with Nestlé's American ice cream businesses, with its headquarters at the Dreyer's Grand Ice Cream offices in Oakland. Ben & Jerry's was acquired by Unilever.

NESTLÉ AT THE MILLENNIUM

By 2002, Nestlé S.A. was the world's largest food company with sales of $57.2 billion. In 2004, Nestlé S.A.'s sales were Sfr. 86.7 billion (or $70 billion), net profit was Sfr. 6.7 billion (or 7.7%), and total assets were Sfr. 31.5 billion.[47] In 2004, it was the forty-third largest company in the world.[48]

In 2005, in a highly contentious move, Nestlé's supervisory board elected Peter Brabeck-Lethathe, an Austrian who had been CEO for the past eight years, to the additional position of chairman of the supervisory board, replacing Rainer Gut, who faced mandatory retirement at age 72. Brabeck-Lethathe is largely credited with Nestlé's dramatic expansion and high profitability.

Combining the two top jobs is most unusual at Nestlé and goes against a wave of corporate governance reform moving through Europe. Separating those positions is required by law in Germany but not in Switzerland. Most British firms and increasingly also French and Swiss companies have different people serving as chairman and CEO.[49] Brabeck-Lethathe is the second non-Swiss to run the company since Helmut Maucher, a German, had held both positions in the 1980s.

NOTES

1. Mira Wilkins, *The Emergence of Multinational Enterprise: American Business Abroad from the Colonial Era to 1914* (Cambridge, MA: Harvard University Press, 1970), ix.

2. Emile Benoit, "Interdependence on a Small Planet," *Columbia Journal of World Business*, spring 1966.

3. Jacques Servan-Schreiber, *The American Challenge* (London: Hamilton, 1968).

4. Medard Gabel and Henry Bruner, *Global, Inc.: An Atlas of the Multinational Corporation* (New York: New Press, 2003).

5. *Fortune*, April 18, 2005, F1.

6. George Melloan, "Global View," *Wall Street Journal*, January 6, 2004, A19.

7. *Fortune*, April 18, 2005, F1.

8. www.cia.gov/cia/publications/factbook.

9. Carol Hymowitz, "More American Chiefs Are Taking Top Spots at Overseas Concerns," *Wall Street Journal*, October 17, 2005, B1.

10. *Wall Street Journal*, October 31, 2005, B1.

11. *Los Angeles Times*, September 18, 2005, C1.

12. Ibid., May 9, 2005, C3.

13. "Hottest Car Guy on Earth," *Wall Street Journal*, January 14, 2006, A8.

14. *Fortune*, August 22, 2005, 26.

15. www.oecd.org/document/54/0,2340,en.

16. Council of Economic Advisors, *Economic Report of the President, 2005*, Appendix Table B103. www.whitehouse.gov/cea/erpcover2005.

17. Ibid., Appendix Table B107.

18. www.treas.gov/press/releases/po3643.

19. Council of Economic Advisors, *Economic Report of the President, 2005*, 180.

20. U.S. Department of Commerce, International Trade Administration, www.ita.doc.gov/td/industry/otea/state_reports. California data in the next paragraph is from this source.

21. U.S. Department of Commerce, Bureau of Economic Analysis, www.bea.gov/bea/newsarchive/2005/gdp.

22. Council of Economic Advisors, *Economic Report of the President, 2005*, 181.

23. Jon E. Hilsenrath, "Look Who Else Is Buying American," *Los Angeles Times*, August 15, 2005, A2.

24. Ibid.

25. *Wall Street Journal*, January 14, 2006, A2.

26. Jon E. Hilsenrath, "Look Who Else is Buying American," *Los Angeles Times*.

27. *Los Angeles Times*, August 8, 2005, C4.

28. David E. Lilienthal was probably the first person to use the term *multinational firm* in a 1960 paper, "The Multinational Corporation," in M. H. Anshen and G. L. Bach, eds., *Management and Corporations 1985* (New York: McGraw-Hill, 1990).

29. For a discussion, see George S. Yip, *Total Global Strategy* (Englewood Cliffs, NJ: Prentice Hall, 1995).

30. For a discussion, see José de la Torre, Yves Doz, and Timothy Devinney, *Managing the Global Corporation: Case Studies in Strategy and Management*, 2nd ed. (New York: Irwin/McGraw Hill, 2001) xiii.

31. John H. Dunning, *Multinational Enterprises and the Global Economy* (Wokingham, England: Addison-Wesley, 1993), 3.

32. *Los Angeles Times*, September 18, 2005, C1–C2.

33. Ibid., November 21, 2003, C5; May 9, 2005, C1, C3.

34. George Melloan, "Global View," A19.

35. Source for data prior to 2004: Carl Kaysen, "Introduction and Overview," in Carl Kaysen, ed., *The American Corporation Today* (New York: Oxford University Press, 1996), 25; source for data in 2004: *Fortune*, July 25, 2005, 119–126.

36. *Fortune*, July 25, 2005, 119.

37. Ibid.

38. *CIA World Factbook*, www.cia.gov/cia/publications/factbook.

39. *Fortune*, July 25, 2005, 119.

40. This discussion is based on the official history of Nestlé S.A. by Jean Heer, *Nestlé: 125 Years, 1866–1991* (Vevey, Switzerland: Nestlé S.A., 1992).

41. Ibid., 51.

42. Ibid., 198.

43. Arnoud De Meyer, "Nestlé, S.A." in José de la Torre, Yves Doz, and Timothy Devinney, *Managing the Global Corporation*, 2nd ed., 461–475.

44. Nestlé S.A. corporate website, www.Nestle.com.

45. *Wall Street Journal*, June 26, 2003, B1; *Los Angeles Times*, June 11, 2003, C2, June 28, 2003, C2.

46. This section is based on Karel Cool, "Häagen-Dazs and the European Ice-Cream Industry in 1992," in Jose de la Torre, Yves Doz, and Timothy Devinney, *Managing the Global Corporation*, 2nd ed., 80–98.

47. For more financial information, see www.Nestlé.com.
48. *Fortune*, July 25, 2005, 119.
49. *The Economist*, April 16, 2005, 56–57.

RECOMMENDED READINGS

Bartlett, Christopher, and Sumantra Ghoshal, *Transnational Management* (Homewood, IL: Irwin, 1992).

Gabel, Medard, and Henry Bruner, *Global Inc.: An Atlas of the Multinational Corporation* (New York: New Press, 2003).

Kaynak, Erdener, ed., *The Global Business* (New York: International Business Press, 1993).

Ohmae, Kenichi, "Putting Global Logic First," *Harvard Business Review*, January–February 1995.

Porter, Michael E., *The Competitive Advantage of Nations* (New York: Free Press, 1990).

Yip, George S., *Total Global Strategy* (Englewood Cliffs, NJ: Prentice Hall, 1995).

Nine

Corporate Governance

This chapter summarizes the responsibilities of board members based on federal and state regulations and internal rules governing corporations' activities. It also addresses issues of ethics including front page examples of unethical behavior by several major companies and reforms that have been sparked by these revelations. This recent federal legislation and its aggressive enforcement have significantly altered the operating rules for America's corporations. This chapter also addresses the issue of corporate social responsibility.

Understanding governance is important because corporations play a vital role in the U.S. economy, accounting for over 60 percent of our gross domestic product (GDP), and over half of all households own stock directly or indirectly, thus affecting their savings and investing for college, home purchase, or retirement. Governance enables stockholders outside the corporation to monitor decisions of the company's directors and officers and gives them the ability to influence their decisions to protect their investment by voting for or against board members.

RESPONSIBILITIES AND LIABILITIES OF THE BOARD

In the United States, responsibilities of board members, called directors, vary somewhat from state to state because there is no national corporation law as there is in other countries. Depending on the laws in the state in which the company is incorporated, directors' roles may be quite clearly defined or loosely defined. Directors must, of course, ensure that the company's management upholds the laws of the state under which the company is incorporated and that management upholds federal laws and regulations regarding issuing stock and other forms of securities.

The unifying theme for all states' rules is that directors have a duty to safeguard the interests of the owners of the company, who are the shareholders.

The directors' role is summed up by two terms: *duty of care* and *duty of loyalty*. Under the laws of all states, directors are responsible to the shareholders, as owners of the corporation, to oversee and direct—not to manage—the affairs of the company. They are to apply the principles of due care, that is, to conscientiously carry out their oversight duties; and duty of loyalty, meaning that directors' loyalty in the performance of their duties as directors is first and foremost to the shareholders, not to themselves or other interests. Should a director or the entire board of directors fail to act in accordance with these principles and as a result the corporation is harmed, the director or directors who failed in their duty of care and/or loyalty can be held *personally* liable for the harm done.

To insure directors against these and other liabilities, boards purchase directors and officers (D&O) insurance and pay the premiums. Lately, coverage has narrowed and premiums have escalated because of the growing number of violations of due care and loyalty by company officers and directors.

IMPORTANCE OF CORPORATE GOVERNANCE

Governance is the term used to describe the process by which corporations make decisions consistent with procedures required by external authorities and the company's internal governing documents, the corporate charter and bylaws. The president's Council of Economic Advisors defined it this way: "Corporate governance is the system of checks and balances that guides the decisions of corporate managers."[1] This means that governance concerns rules imposed on the company from outside and the entire decision-making system inside the corporation, from the board of directors on down. It is much more than simply who is on the Board.

Governance is (1) the term that describes the external regulations with which corporations must conform in their internal processes and activities, (2) the decision-making structures the company establishes to run its business, and (3) the overall process by which companies' managers make their decisions. Governance relates to all three of these areas, and it is therefore at the very heart of how corporations are managed because it relates to the board of directors, the company's management, and its shareholders in determining the performance and direction of the corporation.

Why Study Governance?

It is important to know how corporations are governed to gain a clear understanding of whether your investment in a company's stock is managed responsibly and ethically and, if you are an employee or retiree, if your job and pension are safeguarded. It is estimated that in recent years 10 percent of U.S. corporations have committed illegalities, had to restate their earnings, or have gone bankrupt because of illegal or unethical activities by their top managers.

These activities included criminal behavior by senior executives to hide from the public the real story of their company's financial condition to hype the firm's stock price or simply to steal from the company—all to enrich themselves at others' expense. These are clear violations of the duty of loyalty to the corporation.

Beginning in 1999, governance has been a front page issue when one after another of America's major corporations' top leaders were indicted, went on trial, or were convicted for violations of federal or state law. See Table 9.1 for a summary of high-profile convictions and sentences, some of which are on appeal.[2]

Convicted by a New York State Supreme Court and awaiting sentencing is Mark Swartz of Tyco International for grand larceny, conspiracy, securities fraud, and falsifying business records. Convicted by a federal court is Scott Sullivan of WorldCom, who pleaded guilty to fraud charges. Swartz and Sullivan each face a maximum sentence of twenty-five years. Swartz's sentence could by reduced to seven years with parole; there is no parole in the federal system, although Sullivan's sentence could be reduced by as much as 15 percent for good behavior.

Enron

The very symbol of corporate excess and abuse of stockholder trust is Enron, the Houston-based energy company.[3] In a high-profile case, Enron's top executives were indicted on numerous charges: using false accounting techniques to hide massive debt and committing securities fraud, money laundering, conspiracy, wire fraud, and lying under oath—all to inflate their stock price artificially and to enrich themselves. When Enron was exposed, it collapsed like a house of cards. Its 26,000 employees lost their jobs, retirees lost their pensions, and shareholders lost $64.2 billion when the company went bankrupt.[4] Some of Enron's executives have pleaded guilty, some are serving time, while others are on or await trial. Enron's CEO, Kenneth Lay, was indicted on 11 criminal counts, and Jeffrey Skilling, the COO, has a 30-count indictment.

TABLE 9.1
Federal and State Convictions of High-Profile Executives

Name	Company	Charges	Sentence
Bernard Ebers	WorldCom	Fraud, conspiracy, false filings	25 years
L. Dennis Kozlowski	Tyco International	Fraud, conspiracy, grand larceny	25 years
Jamie Olis	Dynegy	Fraud, conspiracy	24 years, 4 months
Timothy Rigas	Adelphia	Fraud, conspiracy	20 years
John Rigas	Adelphia	Fraud, conspiracy	15 years
Andrew Fastow	Enron	Pleaded guilty to commit securities fraud	10 years
Martin Grass	Rite Aid	Pleaded guilty to conspiracy	8 years
Sam Waksal	ImClone Systems	Pleaded guilty to insider trading	7 years
Frank Quattrone	Credit Suisse First Boston	Obstruction of justice, witness tampering	18 months vacated
Martha Stewart	Martha Stewart Living Omnimedia	Conspiracy, obstruction of justice	5 months prison, 5 months home confinement

According to federal prosecutors, as the criminal trial for Kenneth Lay and Jeffrey Skilling began in early 2006, the company had been run like a criminal conspiracy to enrich its top executives and defraud shareholders largely by engaging in "accounting hocus-pocus." At its inception, Enron was named Enteron Corporation—until its executives realized "enteron" refers to the intestines. An irate shareholder said, "We're trying to figure out which end of the enteron we are."[5]

Buying stock in America's corporations or taking a job and working for one of them should not be a matter of high risk. Individuals should expect responsible management practices and ethical behavior by their corporations' top leaders, which the great majority do provide. Good governance is the first line of defense in establishing and policing good behavior.

FORMAL SOURCES OF GOVERNANCE

A corporation's board of directors has the obligation on behalf of its shareholders to oversee the performance of the corporation's management. The roles of the board of directors, the officers, and the shareholders all stem from four formal sources of governance for U.S.-based corporations:

1. Federal laws, rules, and regulations and the legal system that adjudicates behavior
2. State laws, rules, and regulations and the legal system that adjudicates behavior
3. Regulations of the securities exchange on which the company's stock is listed
4. The articles of incorporation and the bylaws of the corporation itself

The legal system refers to federal and state regulators, prosecutors, and courts that oversee corporations' behavior and bring charges and try cases of improper behavior when it is found.

If a company is a multinational corporation (having businesses in a number of countries around the world), it must also conform to the laws and regulations of each of the countries in which it operates and must abide by those countries' legal systems. A problem for some multinationals is that laws in some countries are at variance with those in others. For example, the *whistle-blower* protections under U.S. law are not provided—indeed, are prohibited—under the laws of many European countries, creating a conflict if an employee discovers and reports improper behavior by an executive in a European subsidiary of an American company.

In addition to these *formal* sources, governance also stems from external market forces, and internal governance systems respond to these.[6] Market forces are pressures our capitalist system brings to bear on a corporation's directors and officers to sustain or alter their behavior by driving the value of the company's stock or other securities up or down, as the case may be. Let us now review each of the formal sources of governance.

Federal Laws, Rules, and Regulations

Companies must incorporate in states; there is no federal procedure for doing so. The state-by-state legal structure of corporations, however, is guided by the Revised Model Business Corporation Act, which is not a law but a suggested law.[7] Many states use it as the basis for their corporation codes, so that when a company incorporates in any state it can easily do business in other states.

After a company has incorporated, it must then abide by federal and state laws that govern its activities. For issuing stock, corporations follow the requirements of the Securities Act of 1933, a federal law that established procedures for initial public offerings (IPOs) and for proper disclosures and financial reports.

For trading its stock and other securities (such as corporate bonds), corporations must abide by the Securities Exchange Act of 1934, which also created the Securities and Exchange Commission (SEC). The SEC's role is to enact and enforce regulations regarding issuing securities and securities trading to protect the public's interest, which includes shareholders' interests.

These acts of Congress were a response to the stock market crash of 1929 and the Great Depression that followed. These historically important events focused the nation's attention on the trading of securities—stocks, which are certificates showing evidence of corporate ownership, and bonds, showing ownership of companies' debt. These two laws, and the establishment of the SEC to administer and enforce them, comprised Congress' initiative to prevent future manipulation of the nation's securities markets and to prevent unfair, deceptive, and harmful practices.

The SEC

The Securities and Exchange Commission is an independent agency of the federal government. It plays a vital role in overseeing the entire securities industry of the country, enacting regulations governing the ways securities are offered, purchased, sold, and liquidated. Its enforcement powers are administered through the U.S. Department of Justice and adjudicated in federal courts.

The SEC's specific activities follow:[8]

- Requires disclosure of facts regarding offerings of securities that will be traded (bought and sold) on the nation's stock exchanges (such as the New York Stock Exchange and Nasdaq) and the offering of securities traded over the counter (OTC)
- Regulates securities trading on national and regional securities exchanges and OTC markets
- Requires registration of securities brokers, dealers, and investment counselors and regulates their activities
- Regulates activities of mutual fund companies
- Investigates securities fraud
- Recommends to the criminal division of the U.S. Department of Justice sanctions, remedies, and criminal prosecution in instances involving violations of securities laws

Over the years since the SEC was founded, Congress has enacted numerous laws strengthening the SEC's hand in dealing with securities activities in different areas. Some of these include seeking sanctions against those who violate foreign securities laws, permitting the SEC to suspend trading in the event prices rise and fall excessively in a short period of time, and permitting the SEC's own administrative judges (as opposed to federal court judges) to hear a growing number of types of cases involving securities violations.

Securities and antitrust laws and regulations are closely linked to strengthen the government's effort to prevent fraud and restraint of trade by two or more companies. Many companies that have engaged in securities fraud have also sought monopolistic power in the marketplace. Both of these activities are illegal and can be prosecuted by federal authorities.

Table 9.2 summarizes major federal laws governing securities transactions and antitrust actions.[9] These laws and their implementation through the regulatory agencies they set up, especially the Federal Trade Commission and the SEC, established the "rules of the road" for corporations to issue stock, trade stock and other securities (such as bonds), engage in business practices that promote competition (not restrict it or create monopolies), and generally regulate the conduct of business. They were reactions to conditions and situations that came to light, with government attempting to erect a barrier to their reoccurrence. Yet, they did not prevent certain corporations from engaging in similar or new practices that proved harmful to their shareholders, employees, retirees, and the public. As a result, Congress enacted the Sarbanes-Oxley Act in 2002 in reaction to these abuses.

Sarbanes-Oxley Act, 2002

In the face of a host of corporate scandals, Congress enacted a sweeping new law to further strengthen the SEC's powers to oversee American publicly traded companies and the securities industry. This act, named for its Senate and House sponsors, went into effect in August 2002. Its purpose was to increase accountability of corporate officers by requiring greater disclosure requirements and harsher penalties for violations of securities laws and to set higher standards for the accounting/auditing industry.

The act requires chief executive officers (CEOs) and chief financial officers (CFOs) to take personal responsibility for the accuracy and completeness of financial statements and reports filed with the SEC. Falsified reports could result in criminal prosecution, possibly resulting in fines and imprisonment.

The following are some key provisions of the Sarbanes-Oxley Act (also known as SOX):

- For financial reports filed with the SEC, the corporation's CEO and CFO must certify that the reports "fully comply" with SEC regulations and that all information contained in them "fairly represents in all material respects, the financial conditions and results of operations of the issuer."

TABLE 9.2
Summary of Major Federal Antitrust and Securities Laws, 1890–2002

Name of Law/Date	Purpose/Effect of Law
Sherman Antitrust Act, 1890	Made "restraint of trade or commerce" illegal; made unlawful to "monopolize, or attempt to monopolize" trade through "unreasonable methods." Established criminal penalties and provided for civil damages.
Clayton Act, 1914	Made illegal a host of business practices that "may be to substantially lessen competition, or tend to create a monopoly," such as price discrimination, exclusive contracts, tie-in contracts, and interlocking boards of directors in the same industry; established law governing mergers.
Federal Trade Commission Act, 1914	Made it illegal to engage in "unfair methods of competition" or deceptive business practices, such as bait and switch, deceptive advertising, commercial bribery; established the Federal Trade Commission to enforce antitrust laws.
Robinson-Pattman Act, 1930	Made it illegal to engage in direct or indirect price discrimination in the sale of goods because it is an anticompetitive practice.
Securities Act, 1933	Established requirement that companies wishing to issue securities must follow certain procedures, make proper disclosure, and must register public offerings with the SEC.
Securities Exchange Act, 1934	Established the Securities and Exchange Commission (SEC) to regulate the trading of securities and establish requirements for financial reporting.
Celler-Kefauver Act, 1950	Amended Clayton Act to add regulations on asset and stock purchases.
Williams Act, 1968	Regulates tender offers and requires waiting period before completing transactions.
Hart-Scott-Rodino Act, 1976	Requires waiting period before completing IPO transactions and defines data requirements for submission.
Sarbanes-Oxley Act, 2002	See text.

- CEOs and CFOs filing reports with the SEC knowing that the reports do not fulfill all of the requirements of SOX will be subject to criminal penalties up to $1 million in fines, up to 10 years in prison, or both.
- If the CEO or CFO "willfully" certifies a report knowing it does not comply with all the act's requirements, the penalty can go up to $5 million in fines, 20 years in prison, or both.
- CEOs and CFOs must certify that they have established internal control systems designed to ensure discovery of material information that should be in the report and any significant deficiencies in the internal control system must be disclosed.

- Anyone who alters, destroys, or conceals documents or obstructs or impedes official proceedings will be subject to fines, imprisonment for up to 20 years, or both.
- Company loans to corporate directors and officers are prohibited, to prevent boards from later "forgiving" these loans, making them gifts. Certain housing exceptions are permitted.
- Whistle-blowers are protected. These are employees who report illegal activities by their employers. Under the law, they cannot be discharged, demoted, suspended, harassed, or threatened for providing information to the government regarding conduct of their employers they reasonably believe to be a violation of securities laws.

Accuracy of company information is viewed as essential, both to the government to perform its oversight duties and to the public, so that investors will have reliable information on which to make their decisions to buy or sell the company's stock.

In addition to the items listed here, SOX also established a new government entity: the Public Company Accounting Oversight Board (PCAOB). The purpose of this board is to set standards for accounting firms that audit the books of publicly traded companies and police them. The scandals associated with the once-respected accounting firm Arthur Andersen and its complicity in the fraud perpetrated by Enron stimulated the establishment of PCAOB. The board has five full-time members appointed by the SEC chairman in consultation with the secretary of the treasury and the chairman of the Federal Reserve System. The board may "compel" information from accounting firms and their client companies, and it has the power to impose sanctions on auditors and auditing firms.

STATE LAWS AND REGULATIONS

All fifty states and the District of Columbia have enacted laws that regulate the securities industry in their jurisdictions. These laws are enforced by state agencies that normally cooperate with federal authorities, such as the SEC and the Department of Justice.

State laws govern the issuance of corporate charters, also known as articles of incorporation. These instruments define the powers of the corporation, the rights and responsibilities of its board of directors, officers, and shareholders. States also have enacted antitakeover laws establishing conditions under which a change in corporate ownership can occur; these may differ from state to state, complicating takeover activities. Finally, states have antitrust laws that are similar to federal law; states can sue to prevent mergers even if the merger is not challenged by federal authorities. States may not pass laws that restrict or regulate interstate commerce; the Constitution grants this power exclusively to the federal government.

As of 2001, thirty-eight states had laws that allow corporations to consider stakeholder interests in major decisions, such as mergers and acquisitions. What are stakeholder interests? These are the interests of individuals and groups that have a stake in the success of the company. They include shareholders, employees, retirees, creditors, suppliers, and others that would be impacted by a major company decision, not just the top executives and managers of the firm.

Enforcement of securities laws is under the authority of states' attorneys-general, and it has greatly increased in many states. New York State's attorney-general, Eliot Spitzer, has been in the headlines for his aggressive prosecution of such major companies as Merrill Lynch and Citigroup's Smith Barney on various felony charges and the former head of the New York Stock Exchange, Richard Grasso, for receiving "excessive" pay.[10] Massachusetts' attorney-general prosecuted Morgan Stanley for making "false and misleading" statements, and in Oklahoma, the attorney-general filed criminal charges against MCI executives accused of fraud, saying, "I don't think this company has been punished. I intend to prosecute them criminally."[11]

SECURITY EXCHANGE REGULATIONS

Major American corporations have their stocks listed on the New York Stock Exchange (NYSE), Nasdaq, or the American Stock Exchange. Under a new rule they can be listed on both the NYSE and Nasdaq. These stock exchanges have their own regulations for companies listed on them and traded on their exchanges. Companies failing to obey these rules can be delisted, barring trading in their stock on that exchange.

In 2002 the NYSE and Nasdaq enacted the following requirements for the boards of directors of companies listed on these two largest exchanges:

- Companies must have a majority of independent (nonemployee, outside) directors who do not have present or previous close links with the company.
- Independent directors must have regular meetings at which the company's management is *not* present,
- Three key committees of the board—audit, compensation, and nominating—must be composed entirely of independent directors,
- Companies must publish their corporate governance guidelines, setting out provisions for annual evaluation of the board and the CEO.

Prior to the enactment of these rules, studies showed that 13 percent of NYSE-listed companies' boards did not have a majority of independent directors (that is, nonemployee outsiders), 20 percent of NYSE-listed companies' boards had no nominating committee at all (the CEO usually nominated individuals to join the board), and over 20 percent of two thousand companies studied had compensation committees that included relatives of people economically tied to the company or directly to the CEO. These practices enabled CEOs to have unbridled control over the decisions of their corporations, and these decisions may or may not have been in the best interests of shareholders and employees.[12]

Who is an *independent* director? The New York Stock Exchange and Nasdaq have the following rules to determine whether a person is independent: (1) A director or his or her relative may not receive $100,000 or more per year in certain types of nonsalary compensation, such as consulting; (2) a director may not be affiliated with another company that does more than $1 million or 2 percent of its revenue, whichever is greater, in business with the company; and (3) a director has not had *material* (that is, significant) outside dealings with the corporation in the prior three years.

Coca-Cola Company

Coca-Cola Company's fifteen-member board of directors provides a good test case of these rules. Looking at 2003, the first full year the rules were in place, four of Coca-Cola's directors were evaluated because their independent status was questionable:[13]

- Herbert Allen was not independent because he had a financial interest in a company that received $1 million in 2003 from Coca-Cola, plus his son is president of that company.
- Warren Buffet was and is chairman and CEO of Berkshire Hathaway, Inc., a company that did more than $100 million of business with Coca-Cola in 2003. Yet he was deemed independent because his company's sales to Coca-Cola were under the 2 percent rule—a fraction of Berkshire's 2003 revenue of more than $60 billion.
- Donald McHenry was not independent because his consulting firm did work for Coca-Cola until 2002, a violation of the three-year rule.
- Former Senator Sam Nunn retired from his Atlanta law firm to be independent; the law firm had been Coca-Cola's main outside counsel for decades.

These rules on independence, a response to the fraud scandals at Enron and other companies, were designed to increase the number of directors serving on boards who have no personal or financial interest in the companies they serve—beyond the duty of care of looking out for that company's shareholders. These rules have an underlying premise that significant financial ties to outside firms are a temptation to directors to allow their own financial interests to override those of shareholders, a violation of the duty of loyalty.

Many corporations had *interlocking directorships*; that is, CEOs or directors of companies sit on boards of other companies with whom they do business. The Corporate Library, a lobbying group for good governance, found that companies such as Pfizer (pharmaceuticals), Verizon (communications), Citigroup (financial services), and Bank of America have interlocking directorships, which is legal because these companies are not in the same industry. Interlocking occurs because large corporations do considerable business with each other and have a major impact on other companies' businesses.

Interlocking directorships was one of the ways J. P. Morgan's bank in the early 1900s gained such great influence on corporate decisions and thereby amassed great wealth. Morgan or top executives from his bank would sit on the boards of directors of companies to which he lent money or in which his bank bought major interests to keep track of their investments and to shape key decisions of those companies. In 1933, the J. P. Morgan Bank alone controlled directly or indirectly about one-fourth of the nation's total corporate assets, according to the Senate Banking Committee.[14]

Such concentrations of control stifle competition and are illegal as antitrust violations under the Clayton Act of 1914 and the Banking Act of 1933 for U.S. companies competing in the same industry. The fact that these activities are illegal does not mean they will be prosecuted.

ARTICLES OF INCORPORATION

The governing documents of corporations are also a source of their own governance regulations. The key documents are the corporation's articles of incorporation (also known as the corporate charter) and the bylaws of the corporation. The company's articles of incorporation must be written in conformity with the laws of the state in which the company is incorporated and must be approved by that state. Once approved, they can then be filed with the office of the secretary of state, establishing the corporation.

The approving and filing process is complex and must follow precise procedures prescribed by state law. To ensure compliance, attorneys specializing in this area of practice are usually required, and their fees and registration costs can be considerable.[15]

There are two types of corporations: C corporations and S corporations. C corporations are the most common type: they are established in accordance with state law, file their own corporate tax returns, and pay taxes on income. If a C corporation pays a dividend, shareholders receiving dividends pay taxes on them on their own individual tax returns.

S corporations are a special type. They are established by filing a form with the Internal Revenue Service of the U.S. Department of the Treasury, not with the secretary of state's office in a particular state. S corporations can have no more than seventy-five shareholders and all must be U.S. citizens. S corporations pay no federal income tax; their profits are passed through to the shareholders, who pay tax on them on their individual income tax returns. S corporations are popular when a company is formed for a particular project, such as producing a motion picture or drilling for oil, and is expected to incur major gains or losses that can be offset by other losses or profits by its shareholders on their individual tax returns.

ETHICAL ISSUES SPARKING REFORMS

Since 1999, dozens of corporations have been indicted by federal and state authorities for corruption, fraud, securities violations, embezzlement, stock manipulation, falsification of records, destruction of records, kickbacks, false testimony, and other criminal charges—costing their companies and shareholders hundreds of billions of dollars. Several top executives of famous companies have been indicted or convicted of these charges, many have been fined, and some are serving time in federal penitentiaries. Other major cases are still pending in the courts.

Bad governance is a major risk factor for all companies' stakeholders. The cost of bad governance can include indictment of top corporate executives and their criminal prosecution. It can also include loss of shareholder value because scandals erode the investing public's confidence in the firm. It can result in the loss of jobs; if the company's standing in its industry is hurt, its sales will diminish and its payroll will have to be downsized, costing jobs. With a loss of public trust, companies involved in these high-profile scandals will lose customers, market share, and income. All the company's stakeholders (investors, corporate officers, employees, retirees, suppliers, lenders, etc.) will be hurt.

The world's largest insurance company, American International Group (AIG), Inc., was sued by New York State authorities for illegal accounting manipulation to plus-up the company's financial reports over several years. The long-time chairman and CEO of the firm, Maurice R. "Hank" Greenberg, was fired; he denied the charges and is mounting a defense of his innocence. However, the company, under new leadership, agreed to a massive $1.6 billion settlement split between state regulators and the SEC, which had not yet filed a lawsuit, constituting one of the largest finance industry regulatory settlements with a single company in U.S. history. The settlement includes fines, penalties, compensation to investors and policyholders, restitution to several state workers' compensation funds, and structural reforms at AIG to prevent recurrence.[16]

The ultimate price paid for bad governance is the death of the corporation, bankruptcy. The following major companies having scandals of one type or another have gone bankrupt (chapter 11): Enron, Arthur Andersen, WorldCom, Global Crossing, and Kmart (which has reemerged from chapter 11 to acquire Sears). ImClone Systems stock lost 50 percent of its value in the year following the disclosure of its accounting irregularities, and the CEO went to jail for seven years and paid a multimillion-dollar fine for insider stock trading.

The other side of the coin is that good governance is so much appreciated that the investing public will pay a premium for it. Although good governance does not guarantee good performance, it at least reduces risk.

McKinsey and Company, a large management consulting firm, conducted a study in 2002 and found that institutional investors (major pension funds, mutual funds, etc.) were willing to pay on average a 14 percent premium for shares of well-governed U.S. companies. McKinsey defined good governance as a corporation having a board with a majority of outsiders who are truly independent of the company and its officers, who have significant holdings of the company's stock, and who are paid chiefly in company stock or its equivalent.[17]

Credit rating companies, such as Moody's Investors Services and Standard & Poor's, are beginning to factor corporate governance into their evaluations, having the effect of reducing the cost of borrowing by companies having good governance. And firms that sell liability insurance to corporate officers, called directors and officers policies, are adjusting premiums to reward companies with good governance and punish those with poor governance.

Reforms Follow Periods of Recession and Scandals

Pressures for reform of corporate governance typically follow periods of economic downturn or scandal. The stock market crash of 1929 and the ensuing Great Depression sparked the reforms of the 1930s: the Securities Act of 1933 and the Securities Exchange Act of 1934, which established the SEC to enforce regulations governing the securities industry.

The worldwide recession of 1990–1991 produced reforms in other countries, not in the United States.[18] In 1992 the Cadbury Commission in Britain developed a Code of Best Practices that was the first in the Western world. Its major recommendations were to separate the CEO position from the chairmanship, have a majority of outside directors on the board, and have only outsiders on the audit, nominating, and compensation committees.[19]

Later in the 1990s and in 2000, in the wake of economic crises in Asia, Russia, and Latin America, the Vienot Commission in France, the Dey Commission in Canada, the King Commission in South Africa, the Peters Commission in the Netherlands, and the Cromme Commission in Germany all recommended reforms in their countries' securities industries, largely based on the Cadbury Commission's report.

OECD Guidelines

In 1999, the Organization of Economic Cooperation and Development (OECD), an organization of twenty-nine nations constituting the rich countries of Western Europe, the United States, Canada, and Japan, attempted for the first time to develop transnational guidelines to improve corporate governance. Its five guidelines called for the following:

1. Protection of shareholder rights
2. Assurance of equitable treatment for all shareholders
3. Attention to concerns of other stakeholders
4. Strong disclosure requirements and transparency of financial reports
5. Board responsibility for monitoring management performance

These were only guidelines, not laws, and many nations only partially incorporated them into their national regulations, wheras other nations used them as blueprints for national regulations and stock exchange rules.

U.S. Reforms

In 1999 in the United States, a blue ribbon committee formed by the National Association of Securities Dealers and the New York Stock Exchange released a report establishing new audit committee standards for corporate boards. The SEC chairman, Arthur Levitt, endorsed the recommendations. The essence of the report was that members of audit committees must be financially savvy and meet new, tougher reporting requirements. The NYSE and Nasdaq made their own governance initiatives for reform during this time.

These pressures for reform were also strengthened by various institutional investor groups and public interest groups. Large pension funds, such as CalPERS (the California Public Employees' Retirement System); mutual funds, such as Fidelity and Vanguard; and public interest groups, such as the National Association of Corporate Directors, the Investor Responsibility Research Center, and the National Center for Nonprofit Boards, were especially vocal urging reform.

Some of the most famous scandals in the 1999–2003 period that stimulated these pressures for reform included Enron, Arthur Andersen, WorldCom, Adelphia, Rite Aid, HealthSouth, and Tyco. Accounting practices and leadership accountability were the core issues in most of these cases. Additional bad publicity for corporations resulted from Martha Stewart's conviction for false testimony and conspiracy in connection with the sale of her ImClone Systems stock; lawsuits against Richard Grasso (former head of the New York Stock Exchange) for his "excessive" pay and other perquisites; and the prosecution and conviction of Dennis Kozlowski, former CEO of Tyco International, for his lavish lifestyle at company expense.[20]

A crisis of confidence arose with the prosecution of so many company leaders and the fact that so many companies (nearly 10 percent) had to *restate* their earnings because of errors in prior reports, a practice permitted under accounting procedures if later information reveals errors in prior reports or if the company did not make as much money as it initially reported.

Under the more rigid accounting rules that went into effect in 2002, companies are more closely scrutinizing their financial reports and are catching more errors than previously; error-driven restatements were up 28 percent in 2004 over the prior year. Companies that had reported higher than actual earnings (typically to hype their stock price) also had to restate their earnings. This reason accounted for 16 percent of the 414 restatements filed with the SEC in 2004. Restatement of financial reports is required if errors of any major type are discovered in previous reports, saving the CEO and CFO from prosecution. A *Wall Street Journal* headline summed it up: "To Err Is Human, to Restate Financials, Divine."[21]

In 2002, President George W. Bush announced a plan for improved accuracy and accessibility of financial information, accountability of companies' management, and independence of auditors. He established a corporate fraud task force composed of enforcement officials from the Department of Justice, the SEC, and other U.S. government agencies to investigate allegations of fraud and malpractice.

That same year the Sarbanes-Oxley Act was passed, significantly strengthening accountability of management and directors, and it also authorized the establishment of the Public Company Accounting Oversight Board (PCAOB) to regulate auditing and accounting firms. These reforms were the most sweeping changes and additions to U.S. regulations for corporate governance since the early 1930s and the establishment of the SEC itself.

SUMMARY OF TODAY'S BOARD OF DIRECTORS REQUIREMENTS

In summary, today's requirements for boards of directors, taking into account regulations of the stock exchanges, the Sarbanes-Oxley Act, and recent SEC and other rules, are as follows:

- Boards of directors must have a majority of outside (independent) directors who have no close links to the company, now or in the recent past.
- CEOs and CFOs take personal responsibility for authenticating company financial reports and statements.
- Company financial reports must be reconciled with generally accepted accounting principles.
- Company reports must disclose transactions that are off the balance sheet.
- Companies must publish their corporate governance guidelines.
- Companies must provide for an annual performance evaluation of the board and the CEO.
- The board's audit committee is now required to have

    Only outside directors who have no material relationship with the company.

    At least one financial expert who will serve as chair of the committee.

    Compliance with Public Company Accounting Oversight Board rules and requirements for reporting and disclosure.

    Power to select the outside auditors and determine their compensation (the outside auditors may not provide any nonaudit services for the company).

- The board's compensation and nominating committees must be composed entirely of outside directors.
- The corporation's attorneys are required to report violations of law and breaches of duties to the firm's general counsel, to the CEO, or to the board's audit committee.

OTHER REFORMS: THEIR IMPACTS AND COSTS

Some corporations already having many of these admirable traits were also among those prosecuted for securities violations, fraud, and embezzlement, such as Enron, which had an elaborate code of ethics.[22] Other companies therefore have gone beyond what is required by law and by the stock exchanges to ensure company integrity. Some corporations have established a position called "chief compliance officer" to act as internal ethics police.[23]

With so many scandals in corporate America, one would think that the turnover of CEOs would be high and that new CEOs would largely come from outside the company. The fact is that of the *Fortune* 1,000 companies (the 1,000 largest U.S. firms measured by sales) the turnover of CEOs has accelerated in recent years. From 1999 to 2002, when so many scandals were revealed, turnover averaged 51 CEOs per year; from 2003 to 2004, it averaged 91 CEOs, a 56 percent jump. Yet, despite this relatively high rate of turnover, companies still looked to their own executive suites for replacements by 66 percent versus 34 percent from the outside.[24]

Some companies have separated the positions of CEO from chairperson of the board of directors to provide more independence in board discussions and decisions. This procedure is the general practice in Britain and is required by law in Germany.

In the United States, before 2002 when the Sarbanes-Oxley Act was passed, 75 percent of the boards of the nation's largest 500 companies (Standard & Poor's 500) had the roles of CEO and chairperson held by the same person.[25] Since then, about one-third have separated them, though they are not required by law or regulations to do so.

Microsoft Corporation

This is an example of a company that had separated these roles. Bill Gates, the richest man in the world, voluntarily gave up the CEO position to Steven Ballmer, who had been chief operating officer, while retaining the chairmanship position.

Walt Disney Company

This is an example filled with front page drama.[26] When chairman/CEO Michael Eisner received an unheard of 45 percent no confidence vote by Disney shareholders at the company's annual shareholders' meeting in 2004, the Disney board, instead of firing Eisner, merely separated the chairman and CEO positions, leaving Eisner as CEO. The board promoted an outside board member, George Mitchell, to be chairman of the board, even though Mitchell received a huge 24 percent no confidence vote. The board forced Mitchell to give up his Disney consulting fees.

"Giving the company's chairmanship to former U.S. Sen. George Mitchell, Eisner's lap dog," wrote an observer at the time, "is a fig leaf covering Eisner's continuing control of the company."[27] Separating the two positions is no guarantee of improved governance, of weakening the CEO's power, or of securing the new chairman's power, as subsequent events revealed.

The Delaware Chancery Court judge's indictment of Eisner's personality and CEO style, delivered in his opinion in the Michael Ovitz case the following year, is instructive. (Ovitz had been appointed Disney's president by Eisner, who soon fired him, providing a huge $140 million severance payment; shareholders sued the company for recovery.[28])

Judge William Chandler III stated, "His [Eisner's] lapses were many. He failed to keep the board as informed as he should have. He stretched the outer boundaries of his authority as CEO by acting without specific board direction or involvement." For good measure, the judge added, "By virtue of his Machiavellian (and imperial) nature as CEO, and his control over Ovitz's hiring in particular, Eisner to a large extent is responsible for the failings in process that infected and handicapped the board's decision-making abilities."[29] Such stunning rebukes from the bench are rare.

George Mitchell (D., Maine) had been a U.S. Senator and, until he retired in 1995, was the Senate majority leader. After retirement, he became a partner in a prominent Washington, D.C., law firm and accepted Michael Eisner's invitation to join Disney's board of directors and those of eight other companies. As a nonemployee director at Disney, he was paid $45,000 annually, plus $1,000 per meeting he attended. Disney also hired him as a $50,000-per-year consultant, and he became a consultant to six of the other companies on whose boards he served. Two of those firms, Federal Express (FedEx) and Staples, for which he was both director and consultant, also employed his law firm, as did Disney.

This is all pre-2002. In that year, with corporate governance reforms occurring, Disney dropped Mitchell's law firm, having paid it $2.6 million in fees over the previous seven years, and required Mitchell to give up all other board seats except three. He kept FedEx, Staples, and Starwood Hotels. He continued to take consulting fees, amounting to $175,000 annually from FedEx and Staples.[30] His consulting fees from Disney had brought him $300,000 over seven years.[31]

In March 2005, Disney's board of directors, following a search in which only one outsider was interviewed (in Eisner's presence), announced their choice of Robert Iger, then president of Disney and Eisner's handpicked insider choice, to succeed him as CEO later that year. Eisner announced he would retire from Disney's board in 2006.[32]

RECENT REFORMS

Some companies have established the position of presiding director or *lead* director in cases in which the CEO also holds the chairmanship position. Before 2002, few companies had lead directors, but this is becoming an increasingly popular concept for companies with combined CEO/chairperson positions. At Disney before George Mitchell was elected chairman of the board in 2004, he had been lead director.

By 2005 more than twenty-five companies had adopted amendments to their bylaws to add a provision that would make it easier for shareholders to force out directors in corporate governance disputes. Directors standing for reelection will be required to offer to resign if more than half of the shareholders withhold their votes, and the board will be required to accept the resignation unless there is a "compelling" reason. Corporations adopting these provisions include Walt Disney Company, General Electric, and Pfizer, Inc.[33]

Companies have also reduced the total number of directors to make boards more manageable.[34] Since the mid-1990s, the board size of the average large publicly held American corporation has declined from 15 to 11 directors, and the average small or medium-size company's board has about 7 or 8 members.[35] Microsoft has 10 directors and Walt Disney Company went to 12 in 2004, jettisoning individuals who had failed to qualify under the new ground rules for board membership put in place by that board in early 2004.

The number of directors sitting on companies' boards has declined for two reasons other than ease of management of a smaller number of members: increased liability for decisions and increased time commitment.[36] Liability is a major issue. In Britain, boards of directors have been sued for failure to properly police the company's management. One lawsuit against Equitable Life, an insurance company, was for $4.8 billion, and the company's insurance carrier claimed its coverage did not apply. Claims against directors of American companies for negligence and other lapses have been rising in number and dollar value, and insurance coverage is getting narrower and more expensive.

The time demand of directors has increased by at least 25 percent, according to one expert recruiter of board members, because meetings are now longer than the previous typical two- to four-hour sessions, and they are held at least eight or nine times per year. Board members who also sit on the audit or compensation committee often are at work a full day per month and frequently hold telephone conferences between regular monthly meetings.

Finally, many companies have reduced the number of insiders on boards, typically to two persons as of 2003: the CEO and either the chief operating officer or the CFO.

A number of companies *benchmark* their boards against other companies that are viewed as leaders in governance to find *best practices*. Intel, the computer chip maker, Pfizer, the largest pharmaceutical firm in the world, and Bank of America, the nation's second largest bank, regularly benchmark, seeking ways to improve their boards' management.

Certain *qualitative* reforms are also used to prevent loss of shareholder and employee wealth.[37] These include selecting the "right" directors, training them continuously, giving them the correct information, nurturing a culture of collegial questioning, gaining an adequate commitment of time from outside directors, and measuring and improving performance regularly.

COSTS

Governance reforms, especially Sarbanes-Oxley, have increased the cost of doing business in several ways.[38] Premiums for directors and officers liability insurance have dramatically increased; companies pay these premiums, adding to their overhead burden. The cost of outside auditors has increased; certified public accounting firms' fees have risen because the risks of failing to find problems and liabilities associated with such failures have increased the time and scrutiny of the CPA firms, adding costs. The cost for board members of lapses in oversight has turned what used to be business risks into possible grounds for criminal prosecution. More aggressive due diligence on the part of directors to ensure that they do not fail to find problems has created incentives for directors to micromanage their management. These costs are not inconsequential to large corporations, and they can be devastating to small ones.

Public companies in the United States spent approximately $5.5 billion in 2004 to comply with Sarbanes-Oxley requirements and were forecast to spend $5.8 billion in 2005. Most of this spending will go to auditors at large U.S. accounting firms, but more than a quarter of outlays will pay for new technology, software, and systems, some of which will be supplied from abroad, especially India, because their charges are one-third those of U.S. accounting firms. Large Indian firms such as Infosys Technologies Ltd. and Patni Computer Systems Ltd. are developing software and hardware to track internal transactions and approvals. Their business is growing by 50 percent per year.

Direct and indirect costs to U.S. firms from SOX are huge and growing, giving rise to two other costs: opportunity costs and loss of business to foreign competitors. Focusing on SOX compliance at all levels of public companies increases the cost of doing business because internal transactions are required to have careful documentation and approval. Opportunities for new ventures and products are therefore put on the back burner, taking a secondary position to regulatory compliance. Foreign competitors have no Sarbanes-Oxley-type requirements and therefore are unburdened by these costs borne by their American rivals.

Another cost is the reluctance of well-qualified individuals to serve on companies' boards. The time commitment is too great for many, there is an increasing workload to do a proper job, and the personal risks of failing to do a proper job are growing. CEOs, who used to represent a deep pool of board candidates, are increasingly unwilling or unable to serve on other companies' boards. Until recently, about one in four major companies had policies limiting the number of boards their CEOs could serve on; today, more than half of companies have such policies. In 1997, CEOs of S&P 500 companies served, on average, on two outside boards; by 2004 that number had fallen by half: the average is 0.9 outside board. This means that some of the most experienced board members are unavailable.

A stunning event that occurred in January 2005 sent shock waves throughout corporate boardrooms and further reduced the appeal of serving on boards. As part of a court agreement in the WorldCom and Enron cases, ten former directors from each company agreed to dig into their own pockets and pay out a total of $18 million and $13 million, respectively, to settle shareholder lawsuits. "The trade-offs of becoming a director of a corporation don't look nearly as attractive these days," said John Thain, CEO of the New York Stock Exchange. "The compensation hasn't gone up that much, the hours have gone up a lot and the liabilities have increased."[39] This is a remarkable understatement.

COMPENSATION

CEOs always sit on their own boards of directors, but they receive no extra pay for doing so. In 2003, reflecting improved earnings and the return of the bull stock market, the median CEO base salary for S&P 500 companies was $950,000, up 3.1 percent from 2002. Bonuses jumped 20.4 percent to $1,064,099 from $883,944. Thus, median cash pay for S&P 500 CEOs in 2003 was $2,029,500 (base salary plus bonus). Fewer CEOs received outright grants of stock (called restricted stock rights) and stock options (the right to purchase shares of the company's stock in the future at a previously fixed price) in favor of compensation more closely tied to the performance of the company.

For outside directors, the average annual retainer and per-meeting fees at the 1,000 largest U.S. companies rose 35 percent in 2005, to $76,707, according to a study by Korn/Ferry International.[40] For directors at S&P 500 companies, total cash pay grew by 22 percent in 2004 to a median of $67,556, and stock awards rose nearly 35 percent to a median of $69,616. Compensation for directors at smaller, non-blue-chip companies is of course much less. For nonprofit companies, directors serve pro bono (without pay).[41]

COMCAST CORPORATION

An example of executive compensation is Comcast Corporation, the cable communications company. Brian Roberts, Comcast's CEO, had his contract with the company renewed in 2005 for four years, according to company filings with the Security and Exchange Commission. The new contract was prepared by the compensation committee of Comcast's board and approved by the full board of directors. It added $2 million to his previous compensation package as follows: his base salary increased to $2.5 million from $2.2 million and his bonus remained at as much as 300 percent of base salary, depending on the company's stock performance. (He had been awarded a bonus of $6.6 million in 2004, the maximum possible.) He also was given a deferred-compensation account starting with a $2 million contribution in 2005 that will increase 5 percent per year thereafter. There was no signing bonus and no additional stock, Roberts having received $11 million in Comcast stock options up front in 1998 when he signed his last contract.[42]

Table 9.3 summarizes the profile of U.S. boards of directors after 2002. Thus, in 2004, the country's largest companies' boards (S&P 500) have an average of 11 members, 81 percent of whom are outsiders whose average age is 60, who serve on a board for an average of 8-plus years.

WHY SOME BOARDS STILL FAIL

Despite best efforts, some boards still fail in their duties to protect shareholder and employee interests. Why? Ralph Ward, a board expert, offers his Top Ten reasons in this order:[43]

1. Boards don't handle bad news well.
2. Boards have no idea how to evaluate, motivate, or pay directors.
3. Boards do a lousy job of handling their personal issues.
4. Poorly conducted board meetings are held with poor logistics (hard-to-get-to meeting places).
5. Directors are cut off from company staff, shareholders, and major decisions.

6. Directors have competing and sometimes conflicting governance agendas.

7. Audit committees have been a joke.

8. Directors have inadequate time, resources, and expertise for the job.

9. Boards chaired by the same person who is also the CEO cannot oversee the CEO.

10. Boards receive too little, too much, or just plain bad information from management.

Thus, boards need to have timely, accurate, and reliable information about the company's performance to properly perform their legally required oversight function. In the 1990s, boards had shown their clout by sacking a number of CEOs for various reasons: James Robinson of American Express, Rod Canion of Compaq, Ken Olsen of Digital Equipment, John Akers of IBM, and Robert Stempel of General Motors.[44]

A year of high-profile cases of boards firing CEOs was 2005. Hank Greenberg, the long-time CEO of American International Group insurance, the largest carrier in the world, was fired for suspicion of accounting irregularities in connection with a business deal with one of Warren Buffet's insurance companies.

HEWLETT-PACKARD

In February 2005, the 10-member board of Hewlett-Packard (H-P) fired the company's CEO, Carly Fiorina.[45] At the time she was hired from Lucent Technologies in 1999, Fiorina was the first woman ever to serve as the CEO of a *Fortune* 100 company (the 100 largest companies in the United States

TABLE 9.3
Board Basics in the United States after 2002

| | | S&P 500 Company Boards | |
Item	All Boards	2003[*]	2004[†]
Average board size	9.2 members	10.9	11
Largest board	31 members	N/A	N/A
Smallest board	3 members	N/A	N/A
Outsiders	66%	72%	81%
Average tenure	N/A	8.4 years	8.4 years
Average age of director	58.9 years	59.9 years	60 years
Percentage of men	90%	87%	84%
Percentage of women	10%	13%	16%
Number of directors	14,091		

[*]*Wall Street Journal*, October 27, 2003, R7.
[†]*Los Angeles Times*, January 12, 2005, C4.

measured by sales) and was the first outsider ever to be made CEO in H-P's 60-year history. A year later she was also made chairwoman. In 2004 H-P's sales were $80 billion, with its printer business accounting for only 30 percent of its sales but 85 percent of its profits.

When Fiorina took the job she stated that H-P's profit margins would significantly improve within three years. Even after she engineered H-P's bitterly contested $19 billion acquisition of Compaq Computer, the combined company continued to lose PC market share to Dell, Inc., with Dell becoming the number-one PC seller in the world at the end of 2004.[46] With its stock price down by 50 percent during her five-year tenure, while archrival Dell's rose 12 percent, the board developed a recovery plan, which Fiorina resisted. The plan would have delegated to other top executives many of the powers Fiorina had assembled in her own office to reduce the decision-making bottleneck.

BOEING

During this same time period, the board of the Boeing Company was also going through turmoil. In 2004 the company's CFO had been indicted for violating federal regulations by offering employment to a Department of Defense official who could influence key government decisions to benefit Boeing with billions of dollars of U.S. Air Force contracts. The CFO was fired, as was the CEO who had overseen this activity. In early 2005 Boeing's new temporary CEO, Harry Stonecipher, who had been called back from retirement, was also fired by Boeing's board for improper behavior with a female employee, based on a whistle-blower's tip. Louis Platt, Boeing's non–executive chairman and the retired CEO of H-P, immediately placed the new CFO in charge as acting CEO pending a search for a permanent CEO, which resulted three months later in James McNearney of 3M Company becoming Boeing's CEO.

Thus, armed with adequate and reliable information, boards can do their proper job of safeguarding stakeholders' interests by changing top management when necessary. The H-P example also shows that women executives will be treated the same as men in both hiring and firing. Fiorina was replaced as interim chairwoman by board member Patricia Dunn, while a search for a new CEO was undertaken.

THE ROLE OF TODAY'S DIRECTOR

How to prevent boards of directors from failing has a lot to do with the role directors play and their interactions with the company's top management. Whatever role directors play has a great deal to do with the directors themselves. Are they aggressive? Do they demand information from management about the company's performance? Or are they passive? Do they just go along with management in an effort to keep their seat on the board and the compensation and perquisites that come with it? Are they willing to do their homework? In other words, what is the personality of the board member?

Clearly, today, under new and more rigorous ground rules for board members' behavior, each director has to invest much more time and effort into the job of being a director. This means that each person will sit on fewer boards than in the past if for no other reason than each seat requires much more time and effort, with increased liability for failure to perform due diligence. The passive careerist board member is now largely a thing of the past.

Understanding what *not* to do is quite clear. Understanding exactly what *to do* is less clear. A consensus is emerging that directors have to be well informed, more skeptical, and more independent of management than ever before. Directors have to focus on legal and accounting issues, be available to investors to answer questions, and play a multiplicity of other roles.

"No one has thought enough about how doable this is, especially for directors who have other big jobs and responsibilities," said the head of McKinsey and Company's governance practice in North America. What does a CEO think directors' roles should be? Steve Reinemund, chairman and CEO of PepsiCo, Inc., believes "directors should be the CEO's sounding board. If they get so absorbed in operating details, then they are doing management's job and can't provide a check and balance to management."[47]

Reinemund wants directors to see the forest, but members of the audit committee must also see the trees and be willing to challenge management. This is perhaps the most important trait: willingness to challenge management. This also means being willing to do a lot of homework. The typical director devoted approximately 250 hours to board-related work in 2003, twice the amount from four years previously, according to the National Association of Corporate Directors.[48]

CORPORATE SOCIAL RESPONSIBILITY

Publicly traded corporations have a *fiduciary duty* to their shareholders. This means that corporations carry a legal responsibility to safeguard the investments of shareholders, the owners of the corporation, and to manage the affairs of the business responsibly in full compliance with legal requirements to promote the health and growth of the firm. On this fundamental point, the duty of care, there is no disagreement. Beyond this, however, views diverge as to whether corporate leaders have a responsibility only to the stockholders or whether they also have broader responsibilities to society.

The two schools of thought on the role corporations should play are the traditional view and the social responsibility view.

TRADITIONAL VIEW

This school of thought argues that corporations best perform their duties to society as a whole by managing the affairs of the company responsibly and ethically and by earning a profit. Another way of saying this is a corporation's responsibility is to produce the highest quality product to earn a profit while doing its best to conserve society's scarce resources and doing all of this honestly and within the bounds of the legal framework.[49] In this way corporations properly serve their investors, employees, customers, suppliers, lenders, and communities by being thriving businesses.

Milton Friedman, a Nobel Prize winner in economics, is the leading advocate of this traditional view. He argues that social responsibility is a "fundamentally subversive doctrine" that can undermine the efficiency of a business. "There is one and only one social responsibility of business—to use its resources and engage in activities designed to increase its profits so long as it stays within the rules of the game, which is to say, engages in open and free competition without deception or fraud."[50] This view argues for minimal governmental regulations and other restraints on the corporation's ability to conduct its business activities most efficiently. Spending resources on socially desirable activities is a decision for individuals to make; it should not be a company decision.

SOCIAL RESPONSIBILITY VIEW

The second school of thought argues that corporations must go beyond their minimal legal and economic responsibilities—simply making a profit and obeying the law—and should actively work to benefit society. To continue in existence, this view argues, corporations' responsibilities also include ethical and discretionary activities. These include doing things that are desirable for society but not yet required by society through law and regulation. These functions should be done voluntarily by companies, otherwise government will likely increase regulations and force companies to do them, reducing firms' efficiency.

Several writers subscribe to the *social responsibility* school of thought; among them is Archie Carroll. He and Friedman agree that corporations must be responsible economic entities: work to make a profit and obey the law. Beyond that, Carroll argues that companies should also perform discretionary activities that benefit society. Such activities include working with community leaders in advance of a layoff to soften the blow to the local economy, providing day care centers for employees with young children, and making philanthropic gifts to local charities. None of this is required by law or regulations, but Carroll argues that it is right for companies to do these things to sustain long-term profitability, before government requires them to do so.[51]

Other socially responsible activities include the following examples: Gap, Inc. and Nike, Inc. have collaborated with labor advocates to clean up sweatshops in Cambodia; Whirlpool Corporation switched to environmentally friendly insulation in its appliances; and Dell, Inc. and Hewlett-Packard are working with consumer groups to step up recycling of computers to cut down toxic waste.[52] These types of activities involve costs that may be passed on to customers in the form of higher prices, thus reducing these firms' competitive advantage against others that do not incur costs to achieve these socially desirable results. That is the key trade-off issue.

Mutual Funds

A number of mutual funds feature investments that are socially responsible according to criteria advertised by the fund. The Sierra Club mutual funds include only stocks that meet its environmental criteria. The Women's Equity fund buys stock in companies that advance the status of women in the workplace. The Timothy Plan fund avoids investing in companies whose practices are considered contrary to Judeo-Christian principles. The Amana funds invest according to Islamic principles. The MFS Union Standard Equity fund supports labor union issues. Many of these funds have fairly high fees and expenses.

Do these funds and others like them reward investors with good returns, as well as good feelings about their investments? The answer is they perform about as well as other funds. Over the decade 1995–2004, socially responsible funds averaged 9.1 percent per year returns, slightly under the 9.4 percent average return for all U.S. stock funds. The "feel good" index is, however, a lot higher for these investors, who are not in fact transforming the business world.[53]

CONCLUSION

This chapter has summarized corporate governance, beginning with the role of the board of directors, reasons why governance should be studied, laws and regulations that must be obeyed, internal company governing documents establishing governing procedures, some illegal and unethical behavior of major companies, the consequences of those activities, and a brief discussion of the issue of corporate social responsibility, both pro and con.

Good governance does not guarantee good behavior any more than good governance will guarantee profitability, but it clearly is the first line of defense against abuse and the first line of offense in managing the firm toward profitability and sustained health.

NOTES

1. Council of Economic Advisors, *Economic Report of the President, 2003* (Washington, D.C.: U.S. Government Printing Office, 2003), 73.

2. Adapted from *Wall Street Journal*, July 14, 2005, A8; *Los Angeles Times*, September 20, 2005, C1.

3. Bethany McLean, "Why Enron Went Bust," *Fortune*, December 24, 2001, 59–68.

4. *Wall Street Journal*, October 3, 2003, B1.

5. Ibid., February 4, 2006, A7.

6. Council of Economic Advisors, *Economic Report of the President, 2003,* 22–23.

7. For a discussion, see Wesley B. Truitt, *What Entrepreneurs Need to Know about Government: A Guide to Rules and Regulations* (Westport, CT: Praeger, 2004), 93–94, 146–147.

8. This and the following section are based on Frank B. Cross and Roger LeRoy Miller, *West's Legal Environment of Business*, 5th ed. (Mason, OH: Thomson South-Western, 2004), 632–633.

9. Wesley B. Truitt, *What Entrepreneurs Need to Know about Government*, 121, 130–31.

10. *Wall Street Journal*, February 3, 2005, C1.

11. Ibid., July 15, 2005, C1; July 25, 2005, C1; August 28, 2003, A4.

12. Data in this and the following paragraph are from "The Way We Govern," *The Economist,* January 11, 2003, 59–61.

13. *Wall Street Journal*, March 3, 2005, C1.

14. Samuel Eliot Morison and Henry Steele Commager, *The Growth of the American Republic,* 4th ed. (New York: Oxford University Press, 1958), Vol. II, 137–138.

15. Mark Diener, "Seeking Counsel," *Entrepreneur*, January 2003, 69.

16. *Wall Street Journal*, February 9, 2006, C8.

17. Ibid., October 27, 2003, R6.

18. "The Way We Govern," *The Economist*, 59.

19. For a discussion of the Cadbury Commission report, see Murray L. Weidenbaum, *Business and Government in the Global Marketplace,* 6th ed. (Upper Saddle River, NJ: Prentice Hall, 1999), 360.

20. *Wall Street Journal*, January 6, 2004, C13; February 4, 2005, C3.

21. Ibid., January 20, 2005, C3.

22. *Business Week*, February 13, 2006, 77.

23. Ibid., 76–77.

24. *Fortune*, February 21, 2005, 26.

25. "The Way We Govern," *The Economist*, 59.

26. James B. Stewart, *Disney War* (New York: Simon & Schuster, 2005).

27. *Los Angeles Times*, March 4, 2004 C1; March 8, 2004, B10.

28. *Wall Street Journal*, January 12, 2006, B2.

29. *Los Angeles Times*, August 10, 2005, A11. See also *Wall Street Journal*, August 10, 2005, A1.

30. *Wall Street Journal*, July 22, 2003, B1.

31. *Los Angeles Times*, March 29, 2004, C132.

32. *Wall Street Journal*, March 14, 2005, A1.

33. *Los Angeles Times*, November 5, 2005, C2.

34. *Wall Street Journal*, January 7, 2004, C2.

35. J. David Hunger and Thomas L. Wheelen, *Essentials of Strategic Management*, 3rd ed. (Upper Saddle River, NJ: Prentice Hall, 2003), 22.

36. "The Way We Govern," *The Economist*, 61.

37. Paul F. Kocourek, Christian Burger, and Bill Birchard, "Corporate Governance: Hard Facts about Soft Behaviors," *Strategy+Business*, Spring 2003, 1–12.

38. Professor Walter Williams suggested these points in private correspondence, December 2004. See also Deborah Solomon, "At What Price?" *Wall Street Journal*, October 17, 2005, R3.

39. *Wall Street Journal*, January 28, 2005, B1.

40. Ibid., January 30, 2006, B3.

41. *Los Angeles Times*, April 7, 2004, C3; January 12, 2005, C4.

42. *Wall Street Journal*, August 8, 2005, B3.

43. Ralph D. Ward, *Saving the Corporate Board: Why Boards Fail and How to Fix Them* (New York: Wiley, 2003). See also Ralph D. Ward, *Improving Corporate Boards* (New York: Wiley, 2000).

44. Jay A. Conger and Edward E. Lawler III, "Corporate Governance," *Strategy + Business,* fourth quarter 2001, 94.

45. The H-P discussion is based on *Wall Street Journal*, February 10, 2005, A1, A8–A9; *New York Times* February 10, 2005 A1, C1; *Los Angeles Times*, February 10, 2005, C1; *Fortune*, March 7, 2005, 99–102.

46. *Wall Street Journal*, January 19, 2005, B3; in the fourth quarter 2004, Dell gained 15.9 percent and H-P lost 15 percent of PC market share worldwide. Dell had been number one in worldwide PC sales before H-P and Compaq merged. *Fortune*, March 7, 2005, 73–82.

47. *Wall Street Journal*, October 27, 2003, R1, R4.

48. Ibid., R4.

49. Professor Walter Williams, private correspondence, December 2004.

50. Milton Friedman, "The Social Responsibility of Business Is to Increase Its Profits," *New York Times Magazine,* September 30, 1970, 30, 126–127.

51. A. B. Carroll, "A Three-Dimensional Conceptual Model of Corporate Performance," *Academy of Management Review,* October 1979, 499; cited in J. David Hunger and Thomas L. Wheelen, *Essentials of Strategic Management,* 3rd ed. (Upper Saddle River, NJ: Prentice Hall, 2003), 25–26.

52. *Los Angeles Times,* February 20, 2005, C1.

53. *Wall Street Journal,* August 3, 2005, D1.

RECOMMENDED READINGS

Alsop, Ronald, "Corporate Scandals Hit Home," *Wall Street Journal,* February 19, 2004.

Bakan, Joel, *The Corporation: The Pathological Pursuit of Profit and Power* (New York: Free Press, 2004).

Carroll, A. B., "A Three-Dimensional Conceptual Model of Corporate Performance," *Academy of Management Review,* October 1979.

Charan, Ram, "Boardroom Supports," *Strategy + Business,* winter 2003.

Denis, Diane K., and John J. McConnell, eds., *Governance: An International Perspective* (Northampton, MA: Elgar Publishing, 2005).

Friedman, Milton, *Capitalism and Freedom* (Chicago: University of Chicago Press, 1963).

Gunther, Marc, "Disney's Board Game," *Fortune,* March 22, 2004.

Kocourek, Paul F., Christian Burger, and Bill Birchard, "Corporate Governance: Hard Facts about Soft Behaviors," *Strategy + Business,* Spring, 2003.

Lavelle, Louis, and Amy Borrus, "Ethics 101 for CEOs," *Business Week,* January 26, 2004.

MacMurray, Worth D., "Applied Governance: Beyond Compliance," *Strategy + Business,* winter 2003.

Millstein, Ira M., and Paul W. MacAvoy, "The Active Board of Directors and Improved Performance of the Large Publicly Traded Corporation," *Columbia Law Review,* Vol. 98, 1998.

Ward, Ralph D., *Saving the Corporate Board: Why Boards Fail and How to Fix Them* (New York: Wiley, 2003).

Zadek, Simon, "The Path to Corporate Responsibility," *Harvard Business Review,* December 2004.

Ten

The Future of the Corporation

Corporations have existed for nearly a millennium. Through the centuries they have grown in strength, transformed themselves several times to meet the needs of each era, and have become the dominant form of business organization on Earth, accounting for the vast majority of wealth generated in the world today.

Indeed, except for the state, corporations have become the most powerful social force in modern society. The corporation's future appears to be as bright as ever, partly due to its ability to adjust and adapt to changing circumstances.

This chapter summarizes the power of the corporation to weather the problems it has faced, identifies its most challenging opponents in the future along with some previous challengers that have been defeated, and offers some concluding thoughts. Let us begin with a summary of why corporations exist.

THE PURPOSE OF THE CORPORATION

At the heart of its success is the single-minded purpose of the corporation: to make money for its shareholders. This is the core concept of capitalism, the sine qua non of the corporation's reason for being. Today this is usually described as maximizing shareholder value. When leaders of corporations keep this purpose firmly in mind—such as at Microsoft today, General Motors in the 1920s, the Pennsylvania Railroad in the 1890s, and the British East India Company in the eighteenth century—the corporation thrives, performs its mission, and creates wealth for its shareholders and other stakeholders including society at large.

When leaders of corporations forget this fundamental mandate or put other criteria ahead of it, such as failing to perform their jobs properly, doing good in the community, or feeding personal greed, corporations decline and in most cases fail—like the Pennsylvania Railroad in the 1960s, TWA and Polaroid the 1990s, and Enron in 2002.

In the politically correct culture of the early twenty-first century, it may sound crass to say that making money, that is, profits, is a desirable thing. It is not desirable; it is crucial, crass sounding or not. When corporate leaders or political leaders impose other criteria on corporations, they blur and subvert the core purpose of the firm, no matter how lofty and well intended the other purposes may be.

This is not to say that a company, such as Wal-Mart, should not provide aid to hurricane disaster victims or contribute to other socially beneficial activities. These may be responsible things to do, not only to help victims recover but also to improve the company's image as a caring organization, in the face of relentless negative press from pro-union groups, in Wal-Mart's case.

When a pharmaceutical company such as Pfizer or Merck invests its shareholders' funds to develop a new drug that cures a dreaded disease, thus doing something socially responsible, it should reap the financial rewards of having made that investment and incurred that risk. When its profit stream from that drug is diminished by government action by making the drug's formula available to rivals to produce a generic version of it, Pfizer and Merck's shareholders are punished—by government. Their resources and their incentive to invest to find the next miracle cure are diminished.

Avon Products is one of the world's largest contributors to breast cancer research. Does this help sell its cosmetics, to make a return on investment for its shareholders? Perhaps it does by generating goodwill among its target market, women. Would its returns to shareholders be greater if it invested those resources into new products or improved processes for making them? Only Avon and its female CEO can answer that question.

If a company fails to make a return for its investors, either through growth in the price of its stock or through the payout of dividends, investors will desert the corporation and find more fertile ground elsewhere for their capital. This trend, left unchecked by companies' leaders, is the death knell of the company. Bethlehem Steel, AT&T, and Kmart all died as independent corporations following prolonged declines in their stock price, a reliable symptom of a decline in their managements' attention to the core purpose of making money. GM and Ford Motor Company are experiencing this same trend in the first half of the 2000s.

This is not to say that a corporation should make money any way it wants, ignoring society's rules and regulations and the canons of morality and ethics. Companies must obey society's rules, just as individuals must. Otherwise they will be disciplined by the state, and their leaders will serve prison terms (like the leaders of WorldCom, Adelphia Communications, and Martha Stewart Living Omnimedia).

The corporation will also be disciplined by the market, possibly losing its entire value through bankruptcy, such as Enron, Arthur Andersen, and Global Crossings. Violations of law and sharp practices are not consistent with the purpose of the corporation; they are an aberration of that purpose and they and their leaders will suffer the consequences.

Capitalism disciplines performance very well, rewarding good performance and punishing poor performance. Market mechanisms provide the discipline if left to perform without interference. Apple Computer was slowly digging its way out of a decade of poor performance when Steve Jobs introduced a hot new product, the iPod, which sold like hotcakes. Apple's revenue and its stock price shot up. This is the market's way of rewarding good performance. Steve Jobs never took his eye off the purpose of the corporation—to make money for his shareholders by making good products that attract customers.

At the dawn of the twenty-first century, there appear to be three major challengers to the corporation's fulfilling its core purpose: government, globalization, and the media.

THE GOVERNMENT CHALLENGE

What challenge to companies does government represent? At the beginning of the Progressive Era it was feared in corporate boardrooms that government would regulate big business out of business. Theodore Roosevelt, the first president to use the government's new regulatory authority and antitrust powers, said, "I believe in corporations. They are indispensable instruments of our modern civilization; but I believe that they should be so supervised and so regulated that they shall act for the interests of the community as a whole."[1]

Note he did *not* say corporations should act for the interests of their shareholders! Roosevelt's view is close to that of German and Japanese corporate law, putting the community (or society) ahead of all else. And Teddy Roosevelt was a Republican, supposed to have been business friendly. Woodrow Wilson, a Democrat whose presidency was after Roosevelt's, took an even sterner position against corporations, establishing numerous regulatory agencies and boards to police them.

Thus, from the beginning of the regulatory regime in the United States, there has been an adversarial relationship between government and business, especially big corporations.[2] New Deal legislation in the 1930s deepened government's regulatory role, especially with respect to financial matters: banking and stock issuance and trading.

In the 1970s Congress enacted legislation that further regulated corporations' behavior regarding a host of activities such as environmental impacts (Environmental Protection Agency), workers' safety and health (OSHA), consumer protection, hiring and firing practices (nondiscrimination), and so forth.

Legislation in the 1970s also restricted corporations' freedom of action in international commerce. The Foreign Corrupt Practices Act and the Arms Export Control Act limited companies' ability to do business competitively outside the United States by imposing our nation's code of conduct on American corporations doing business abroad, particularly with respect to paying bribes.

The prevailing norm of behavior in certain parts of the world is quite different from ours. Some of those cultures accept a level of bribery for government officials who make purchasing decisions for their governments, whether it be for pharmaceuticals for state-run hospitals or jet fighters for their air forces. Foreign-based companies have no laws like these restricting their companies' ability to do business in these cultures, thus creating a competitive disadvantage for American firms in those markets.

Despite the deepening of government's regulatory control over the activities of American business over the last hundred years, it has survived and prospered, finding ways and means to accept these new controls, work through them, and still manage to produce products and services beneficial to consumers here and abroad, while still making a reasonable return for its shareholders.

CHRYSLER CORPORATION BAILOUT

Let us turn to a modern example of how government *helped* one corporation and in so doing harmed others. When Chrysler Corporation nearly went under in the late 1970s due to poor performance—producing ugly, overpriced cars built with poor quality—the market was disciplining the company (customers not buying these cars) for failing to meet the preconditions of its core purpose: designing and building quality products that customers would want to buy at a competitive price. Such cars, if they had been built, would sell, the company would then make money, and the corporation's investors would receive their reward.

To forestall bankruptcy, Chrysler lobbied the federal government for a $2.5 billion bailout to rescue it at the last possible moment. (A few years earlier, in1971, Lockheed also faced bankruptcy, having overextended itself with a nonselling airliner, and lobbied for and received a federal government bailout of $250 million.) After receiving the bailout, new leadership at Chrysler wisely used this time and money to reinvent the company and make new-car models that customers bought. Chrysler paid off $600 million in prior debt at 30 cents on the dollar and laid off 40 percent of its workers.[3]

This "interference" by government in the market mechanism saved one auto company and along with it 60 percent of its jobs and returned something to its creditors. Yet, the world had overcapacity of auto manufacturing and the correction of this imbalance by the market was prevented by government. GM and Ford, Chrysler's domestic rivals, at that time were performing well and were being rewarded by the market, selling cars and paying their investors dividends. Their success in the marketplace was harmed by the government's favoritism of Chrysler, allowing a weak domestic rival to be revitalized at the same time foreign rivals, especially Toyota and Honda, were gaining U.S. market share. Chrysler later disappeared anyway, being acquired by Daimler-Benz to form DaimlerChrysler. When government helps one company, it usually harms others.

GOVERNMENT "HELP" HARMS OTHERS

The Chrysler example illustrates one of the key relationships corporations have—with government. In this instance, government helped save Chrysler Corporation, indirectly harming its rivals. Other corporations have been allowed by government to die, such as TWA, and still others have been put to death by government, such as the British East India Company, the New York Central Railroad, and Pan American World Airways.

Government has helped other companies and whole industries. Import quotas on autos and high tariffs on steel imports, for example, enable marginally performing companies and whole industries to continue performing inefficiently, when in fact the market would let them go under and permit other more efficient users of those resources to take them over. "Government 'help' enables failing companies to continue squandering resources" writes Walter Williams. "In this context it is important to remember that a business going bankrupt doesn't mean that its productive resources will vanish into thin air. It means someone else will own them."[4] And someone else will presumably use them more wisely.

As we have seen, corporations are creatures of the state. No corporation comes into existence without having been granted the authority to do so by a government. More than that, once the corporation is established government regulates not only its products but also its behavior and performance, setting operating rules for hiring and firing employees, requiring workplace health and safety compliance, regulating pension funds, setting requirements for issuing stock and making financial reports and audits, and so on. Virtually every aspect of every activity performed by and within a corporation has some governmental regulation associated with it.[5]

GOVERNMENT POWER VERSUS CORPORATE POWER

Does this mean that government is more powerful than a corporation, including the gigantic multinational corporations, some of which are larger than entire nations? The short answer is yes; government power can trump corporate power if it has the will to do so. For example, Wal-Mart, the world's largest corporation, has been barred by some medium-size cities from locating its super centers in their communities. Wal-Mart's annual sales exceed many times over the gross domestic product of these communities, but it still has to get city planning department permits to build stores.

Several of the world's largest oil companies were helpless in the face of the decision by Saudi Arabia's government to buy them out of their portions of ownership in the world's largest oil producer, Aramco, the Arabian-American Oil Company, when the state wanted to make it a wholly owned government corporation, which it did.

Yet, in some instances, corporations have the power to resist government and are often successful in doing so. The largest antitrust suit brought against an American company in the 1970s was against IBM, and IBM prevailed when the government, after years of expensive litigation, dropped the case. A similar Department of Justice antitrust attack against Microsoft Corporation, beginning in the 1990s, resulted in a series of financial settlements by Microsoft, the dollar value of which was a few days' profits for the company and some adjustments in how its software is built into PCs and laptops.

German Experience

Another threat to the profit motive of corporations is state regulations requiring the corporation to have other or additional purposes than making profits. The home of this stakeholder model of corporate governance is Germany. The law in that country, as discussed in chapter 7, requires corporate management to take into account not only making money for shareholders but also the needs of other stakeholders, such as workers, suppliers, the community, and indeed "the common weal." Japan adopted this stake-holder model when it formed its commercial law in the nineteenth century. Today, companies and the government in Germany are attempting to loosen the grip of this concept on corporations, these companies having lost ground to their more profit-focused foreign competitors.

Germany has seen more initial public offerings in the first few years of the 2000s than in the preceding fifty years, making more Germans shareholders than trade union members. Giant companies such as DaimlerChrysler and Vodafone Mannesmann are working to break "jobs for life" labor agreements with their trade unions to increase management's flexibility with their labor force and reduce costs—in an effort to make money for shareholders.[6] This is the route Prime Minister Margaret Thatcher took in the 1970s and 1980s when she privatized much of British industry and then broke the stranglehold of labor unions on those industries, enabling Britain's economy to thrive.

Nissan Motor Company, Ltd.

Japan's ironclad system of stakeholder benefits was successfully challenged by Nissan Motor Company's chief executive, Carlos Ghosn. Within two years of taking leadership in 1999, Ghosn transformed this money-losing company from the verge of collapse to profitability, catapulting himself in 2005 to the leadership of Nissan's parent company, Renault Motors in France. Nissan's sales in 2005 were $80 billion, with net income of $4.6 billion.[7]

Ghosn's fame is now legendary in Japan because he broke with the past, executed a bold new strategy of cost cutting and factory consolidation, and introduced sharp leading-edge car designs that immediately caught on with the public. Nissan was going under when private enterprise saved it by applying solid capitalist principles, not the government with a bailout.

Sarbanes-Oxley

The Sarbanes-Oxley Act is the latest attempt by the U.S. government to solve a set of problems after the fact that surfaced in corporations in the late 1990s and early 2000s. These problems were caused by corporate leaders who, in some cases, pursued personal greed, performed illegal activities, promoted conspiracies with auditing firms to cover up their activities, and personally made tens of millions of dollars for themselves, while their corporations and their shareholders were left holding the bag—which by the time this surfaced was often empty. Adelphia and WorldCom are classic examples of grand larceny, for which their leaders have been convicted and are serving long sentences in federal prison. Tyco International's CEO's conviction is on appeal, and Enron's CEO is on trial.

Was a new law, the Sarbanes-Oxley Act, needed to correct these abuses? The answer is somewhat open because preexisting law was adequate to punish securities violations, fraud, and conspiracy, which were already felonies on the law books. Some politicians believed that new, tougher legislation was needed to make it more difficult to commit these offenses in the future, to require harsher punishment for those who did, and to provide a deterrent even to think about committing such crimes. Also, politicians wanted to show the public that they were "doing" something about corporate corruption. The resulting cost to corporations for Sarbanes-Oxley compliance is enormous.

With respect to the challenge by government, corporations are for the most part holding their own, and in some major instances are prevailing. Why? Because corporations have resources of their own to influence governments' behavior: making campaign contributions, lobbying, engaging in public affairs activities, and so forth.[8] In a free society corporations, being "persons" with First Amendment rights, can exercise their rights to influence the political process and most of them do, just as individual citizens, labor unions, public policy institutions, and other organizations do.

Moreover, government cannot possibly do without corporations. They supply it with virtually all the products and services required to perform its duties as well as being a source of tax revenue.

THE GLOBAL CHALLENGE

The second great challenge facing corporations today stems from the fact of globalization. This is a challenge for corporations in one country emanating from those in other countries. Thus, the corporation itself is not threatened, but particular companies in particular countries are challenged by foreign-based rivals.

At the opening of the twenty-first century, a company's most serious competitor may not be another company based within its own country. Foreign-based corporations, mostly multinational corporations, likely represent their greatest challenge. This is a stark fact of globalization that labor unions and activists rail against at meetings of international bodies, such as the World Bank and G8 summits.

Sara Lee Corporation is the largest U.S.-based general packaged food company with 2004 sales of $19.5 billion. Its principal competitors are Nestlé and Unilever, multinationals based in Switzerland and Britain/Holland, respectively, with sales for the same year of $70 billion and $50 billion, respectively.[9] Anheuser-Busch, the world's largest brewery, based in St. Louis, has as its major competitor in the United States market Miller Brewing Company, based in Milwaukee. Miller Beer was acquired by South African Brewery, which then changed its name to SABMiller PLC, and is based in London.

Pfizer is the world's largest pharmaceutical company, based in New York; its major competitor, number two in the world, is GlaxoSmithKline, based in London. General Motors' greatest rival in the American vehicle market is Toyota, not Ford. Motorola, the American inventor of the cell phone, has as its major rivals Eriksson of Sweden and Nokia of Finland.[10] These are examples of American-based companies having foreign-based competitors.

There are whole industries in which there are no American-based firms, all being foreign based. For example, not one electronics company left in the United States builds television sets. All are foreign owned: Philips in the Netherlands; Sony, Toshiba, and Panasonic in Japan; Samsung and LG in Korea; and RCA, a brand name owned by Thomson of France.

Another industry that has disappeared is shipbuilding. Only ships of war are produced in the United States, and that is because of a law that requires the Department of Defense to buy only U.S.-made warships. Textile manufacturing moved from New England to the South, to Mexico, and now to Central America and China; there is almost no textile manufacturing in the United States today. Shirt and dressmaking firms may be owned by American companies, but the work is performed offshore.

To remain competitive against foreign rivals, American companies must do what they judge best for their own needs. Today this may mean outsourcing manufacturing to foreign, low-cost operations, such as Levi Strauss's belated decision to close its manufacturing facilities in the United States and to transfer its production offshore. Competing in a global economy, national-based decision-making has become inappropriate for corporate leaders whose first obligation is to their shareholders, painful as the consequences may be.

THE MEDIA CHALLENGE

The third major twenty-first-century challenge to corporations is from the media. This includes traditional print media, broadcast media, cable and satellite television, and a new form of media—Internet blogs. Who knows what new types of media will emerge over time with constant innovations in technology.

The media are a watchdog of corporations' activities. When corporations do a "good" thing, such as Johnson & Johnson's 1982 withdrawal of Tylenol from stores in reaction to cyanide poisoning, they get "good" press.

Indeed, the Tylenol recall, undertaken at great cost to J&J, has become a classic case study in ethical performance by a corporation, illustrating that the cost of a product recall can generate far more value in goodwill for the company as a result of taking a highly responsible though costly action.

Southwest Airlines received excellent press when it became known that it was the only major U.S.-based airline that did not lay off any of its employees during the downturn in airline revenue following September 11, 2001; it later received 120,000 applications for 3,000 job openings. Starbucks is viewed as a pleasant place to work. This attitude has helped with the bottom line, reducing costs from employee turnover; Starbucks has 50 percent annual turnover versus the norm in the fast food industry of 250 percent. These are all good things that have financially benefited these companies because of the positive notoriety of their actions or policies.

When a company does a "bad" thing, such as when the press reported General Electric's dumping toxic waste into the Hudson River, polluting the environment, it gets hammered in the press and consequently loses public trust and respect. GE spent millions cleaning up the Hudson and has spent untold additional millions trying to erase the public's memory of what the press dubbed as a corporate attack on the environment.[11]

When it was reported that Ford Motor Company deliberately left unchanged the design and location of the fuel tank in the Pinto, which exploded on rear impact, killing a number of people, Ford's reputation was sullied. In a trial it came out that Ford had calculated the cost of future lawsuits as being lower than the cost of a design change. The Pinto died in the showrooms and had to be discontinued, and Ford's reputation was severely damaged as being heartless. In the early 2000s the Ford Crown Victoria sedan, a favorite of state police, was found to have an exploding gas tank under certain conditions. Today, Ford publicizes itself as an environmentally friendly company.

With the twenty-four-hour news cycle and red hot competition for ratings between cable and noncable networks' news departments, broadcasters are ever vigilant for new stories of corporate "waste, fraud, and abuse." The truth of the matter is that, as a former publisher of the *New York Times* titled his memoir, *Bad News Sells*. Bad news gets banner headlines and the lead story on the 6 o'clock news. Broadcast journalists subscribe to the maxim "if it bleeds, it leads." Good news, if reported at all, is relegated to the back pages in the belief that it does not sell newspapers or airtime.

With this constant scrutiny by news organizations and instant real-time global communications, corporations can expect more, not less, exposure and scrutiny of their activities, product performance, and corporate behavior. This is a serious check on management abuse and poor company performance because no company can long weather a sustained campaign against it by the media.

These media companies are also corporations, whether stand-alone corporations, such as The New York Times Company and The Washington Post Company, or as part of a larger corporation such as ABC News being part of the Walt Disney Company, CNN being part of Time Warner, and the *Los Angeles Times* and the *Baltimore Sun* being part of The Tribune Company, which also owns other newspapers and TV and radio stations. The purpose of these corporations is to reward their own shareholders; sometimes they achieve this objective by preying on other corporations, reporting the "news" about them.

FORMER CHALLENGERS TO THE CORPORATION

What does *not* pose a serious challenge to the corporation? In the twenty-first century corporations *are* challenged by government, global companies, and the media, with the latter two seeking their own profits. But today in the United States the corporation is no longer seriously threatened by two of its previous traditional challengers: farmers and labor unions.

FARMERS

In the latter part of the nineteenth and early twentieth century, the farm block hated corporations and sought to rein them in. Agricultural producing areas, especially in the Midwest, organized against the railroad robber barons and Wall Street bankers for disadvantaging small family farms by favoring large growers with respect to railroad rates, shipping schedules, grain storage availability, and so forth. The Granger movement sprang from this discontent and became the focus of political action, especially against the large Eastern-controlled railroads.

In 1887 the Interstate Commerce Act and the establishment of the Interstate Commerce Commission, which soon regulated railroad rates, helped ease this concern somewhat. Farmers versus corporate power continued as a major political struggle throughout the Progressive Era, 1885–1914, with the federal government enacting a plethora of legislation to level the playing field for farmers and consumers alike.

Today, the family farm is largely a memory. The overwhelming bulk of agricultural production in the United States is owned and managed by agribusinesses, large corporations that are highly efficient at producing enormous crop yields per acre. Less than 2 percent of America's workforce is employed in agriculture as of the twenty-first century, down from over 90 percent at the time of the nation's founding. Thus, farmers no longer challenge corporations; they are corporations.

LABOR UNIONS

Management and labor have a storied history. At the dawn of the Industrial Revolution in the United States, workers had no rights, only wages. After a while, workers sought improvement in their working conditions, long hours, and low wages. Management first met these grievances with indifference and later with contempt and in some instances with force, bringing in police and hired security guards to break up rallies and picket lines.

Early Period

The indifference for workers in that era is well illustrated by J. P. Morgan's reply to a question posed by the chairman of President Wilson's Commission on Industrial Relations: "To what extent are the directors of corporations responsible for the labor conditions existing in the industries in which they are the directing power?" Mr. Morgan: "Not at all I should say."[12]

One example of the use of force was the bloody Homestead Steel Works incident near Pittsburgh in 1883 when Pinkerton detectives, employed by Andrew Carnegie, openly battled members of the Amalgamated Association of Iron and Steel Workers.[13] Another example was Henry Ford's hiring Pinkerton detectives to battle his own workers in Dearborn, Michigan. Many people on both sides died in these skirmishes.

Tensions between workers and management continued, even though workers were organizing into unions, first based on their craft or trade, such as carpenters and welders, and later based on an entire industry, such as autos or steel. Unions had some success improving conditions in the early part of the twentieth century largely by lobbying for new legislation and regulations, rarely through negotiation with management.

Wagner Act

It was not until Franklin Roosevelt's New Deal and the passage in 1935 of the Wagner Act, also known as the National Labor Relations Act, that labor unions were recognized under the law as having a legitimate right to attempt to organize workers without interference, represent them, and to "collectively bargain" with management on the workers' behalf.[14]

In 1935, following passage of the Wagner Act, workers joined unions in large numbers, and union membership reached 13 percent of nonagricultural employment that year. During World War II, the government encouraged union membership as a condition for winning government contracts. The high point of union membership was reached in 1954 when 35 percent of private sector workers were organized in unions. Very few public sector workers were organized at that time.[15]

AFL-CIO

The following year, 1955, the two major confederations of labor unions merged, forming the AFL-CIO. American Federation of Labor unions are the traditional craft-type unions, representing carpenters, electricians, painters, and so forth. Congress of Industrial Organizations unions are organized around whole industries, such as the United Steel Workers, the United Auto Workers, and United Mine Workers. The Teamsters also joined the AFL-CIO. Later, newer unions, such as the Service Employees International Union, which represents janitors, maids, grocery store clerks, and so forth, joined the AFL-CIO, becoming its largest member organization.

Erosion of Unions

As the American economy changed, so did the need for unions. During the latter decades of the twentieth century, union membership declined as employers offered nonunion workers many of the same benefits and levels of compensation as union members, including health insurance, retirement programs, and better working conditions. Beginning in the 1970s, numerous federal laws (such as OSHA) were passed that regulated conditions in the workplace, eliminating the need for unions to press for these types of reforms; they were now mandated by law. For a host of reasons, union membership declined to approximately 13 percent of American workers by 2004.

These membership numbers conceal an even deeper problem for organized labor. Over the years public sector employees, such as schoolteachers, firefighters, county workers, and so forth have joined unions. These public sector unions grew during the time private sector membership declined. By 2004, only 8 percent of union members were from the private sector, whereas 5 percent were public service workers. Also, over the preceding 20 years, union membership declined in 36 of the 50 states.[16]

The old labor–management adversarial relationship of one hundred years ago has now largely eroded, with many union members realizing that not only the workplace environment has changed but also management has changed, providing workers with incentives to join their firms and stay on the job. Moreover, the attitude of workers has changed, many not feeling the need to be represented; this is especially true among independent-minded professionals in high-tech industries, a major growth sector of the economy.

A further erosion of private sector union strength results from certain large and growing companies not having unions: Wal-Mart, the world's largest private employer, Honda Motor Company, Target, Lowe's, Home Depot, Hewlett-Packard, Microsoft, Yahoo!, and FedEx (pilots are unionized) are examples. Under the Wagner Act, these companies could become unionized if their workers voted to have it, but they have not.

Tectonic Shift at AFL-CIO

In 2005, exactly a half century after it was formed, the AFL-CIO was struck a major blow, not from management but from its own member unions. Its two largest unions, the Teamsters and the Service Employees International Union, and one other union voted to split off and form their own new organization, the Change to Win Coalition.[17] This new group plans to focus on recruiting new union members and to reverse organized labor's steady decline by having focused so much on politics.

"If the Change to Win Coalition is correct," as Michael Barone put it, "in charging that the AFL-CIO under [President] John Sweeney has become little more than an ATM machine for the Democratic Party, its breakup will not be so much of a tragedy ... " for union members.[18] Labor union political action committees have lopsidedly supported Democratic candidates for federal office, giving over $40 million per year to them in 1992, 1996, 2000, and 2004, which respectively represented 94 percent, 92 percent, 91 percent, and 86 percent of total campaign contributions for those years.

Yet, union member households are not so unanimous in their political support for Democrats: only 59 percent of union households voted for the Democratic presidential nominees in 1996, 2000, and 2004, and just 55 percent of them supported the Democrat in 1992.[19]

Are Unions a Threat?

Today unions are not a threat to corporations provided management treats workers with fairness and respect and provided workers and their union representatives treat management and the company's welfare the same way. This partnership attitude is nonthreatening to both. Many workers, having not only their wages but also their health and retirement benefits linked to their company's success, have come to the realization the company's health, the union's health, and their own fortunes are inextricably linked.

Despite this, there are still occasions when the old adversarial attitude surfaces and a confrontation results. An example is the seven-month-long supermarket strike/lockout in California in 2004.[20] This harmed workers, with many permanently losing their jobs, it cost unions by having to settle for less attractive benefits for new-hire workers, and it dealt the companies a mighty blow from which Safeway and Albertsons had not recovered a year later. Indeed, Albertsons, Inc., the nation's second largest super market chain, put itself up for sale.

AFL-CIO leaders increasingly see the role of unions as a lobbying force that seeks legislation favorable to American jobs and opposes anything and anyone that they believe might shift work offshore, such as NAFTA and CAFTA. The target of their focus is, therefore, less on corporations and more on Capitol Hill.

CONCLUSION

Corporations are among the most durable social organizations in history, second oldest in continuous existence to the Roman Catholic Church. They have survived in harsh times, grown and prospered in good times, and despite everything they are still with us, stronger than ever after nearly a thousand years.

They have nullified their greatest challengers in the past, made peace with government from which they spring, and today generate for the world wealth beyond imagining. Corporations and capitalism have become virtually synonymous.

Their greatest future challenges appear to lie in continuing to keep peace with government, gain global reach to compete against other global giants, and keep their own houses in order—or government, the media, and the marketplace will do it for them. As long as their leaders keep their fundamental purpose clearly in mind, they will continue to be magnificent engines of wealth creation.

NOTES

1. Quoted in John Micklethwait and Adrian Wooldridge, *The Company: A Short History of a Revolutionary Idea* (New York: Modern Library, 2003), 182.

2. For a discussion of the adversarial relationship, see Alfred Chandler, Jr. "Government vs. Business: An American Phenomenon," *Harvard Business Review,* March 1982.

3. Lee Iacocca, *Iacocca: An Autobiography* (New York: Bantam Books, 1984).

4. Walter E. Williams, "The Entrepreneur as American Hero," address at Hillsdale College, February 6, 2005, reprint, 4.

5. For a discussion, see Wesley B. Truitt, *What Entrepreneurs Need to Know about Government: A Guide to Rules and Regulations* (Westport, CT: Praeger, 2004).

6. John Micklethwait and Adrian Wooldridge, *The Company*, 187–188.

7. *Los Angeles Times*, July 27, 2005, C3.

8. For a discussion of corporations' government relations activities, see Wesley B. Truitt, *What Entrepreneurs Need to Know about Government*, Chapter 13. For an example of one company's lobbying program, Motorola, see James E. Post, Lee E. Preston, and Sybille Sachs, *Redefining the Corporation: Stakeholder Management and Organizational Wealth* (Stanford, CA: Stanford Business Books, 2002), 113–122.

9. *Fortune*, April 18, 2005, F52; July 25, 2005, 119.

10. James E. Post, Lee E. Preston, and Sybille Sachs, *Redefining the Corporation*, 115, 127–130.

11. The preceding examples are from John Micklethwait and Adrian Wooldridge, *The Company*, 188–190.

12. Jack Beatty, "Organize or Perish!" in Jack Beatty, ed., *Colossus: How the Corporation Changed America* (New York: Broadway Books, 2001), 176.

13. Ibid., 168–176.

14. For a discussion of the Wagner Act and the National Labor Relations Board, see Wesley B. Truitt, *What Entrepreneurs Need to Know about Government*, 109–110.

15. Union membership data are from *Wall Street Journal*, July 27, 2005, B1, B2.

16. Michael Barone, "Big Labor, RIP," *Wall Street Journal*, July 28, 2005, A10.

17. *Wall Street Journal*, July 27, 2005, B1, B2.

18. Michael Barone, "Big Labor, RIP," A10.

19. *Wall Street Journal*, July 27, 2005, A4.

20. *Los Angeles Times*, December 15, 2004, A1.

RECOMMENDED READINGS

DiMaggio, Paul, ed., *The Twenty-first Century Firm: Changing Economic Organization in International Perspective* (Princeton, NJ: Princeton University Press, 2001).

Doremus, Paul, et al., *The Myth of the Global Corporation* (Princeton, NJ: Princeton University Press, 1998).

Epstein, Marc, and Kirk Hanson, eds., *The Accountable Corporation,* 3 vols. (Westport, CT: Praeger, 2005).

Novak, Michael, *The Future of the Corporation* (Washington, DC: American Enterprise Institute Press, 1996).

Yergin, Daniel, and Joseph Stanislaw, *The Commanding Heights: The Battle between Government and the Marketplace That Is Remaking the Modern World* (New York: Simon & Schuster, 1998).

Glossary

Acquisition. Contractual process by which one corporation (the surviving corporation) purchases all the assets and assumes the liabilities of another corporation (the target corporation). Shareholders of the target corporation receive cash payment for their shares or shares in the surviving corporation.

Adjudication. The process of making a judicial decision.

After tax profit. Profit (or financial gain) a business attains after paying costs and taxes.

Agent. A person who represents or acts for another, known as the principal.

Agreement. The result of one party making an offer and another party accepting the offer.

Aktiengesellschat. German word for stock corporation, abbreviated AG.

Alien corporation. Term used in the United States for a corporation formed in another nation that does business in the United States.

Antitrust law. The body of federal and state laws and administrative rulings protecting trade and commerce from unlawful restraints, price discrimination, price-fixing, and monopolies with a goal of maximizing competition to benefit consumers.

Appeal. Resort to a higher court, such as an appellate court, to review the decision of a lower court or administrative agency.

Arbitration. The settlement of a dispute by asking a third, disinterested party (other than a court) to render a decision, which may or may not be binding based on prior agreement by the submitting parties.

Articles of association. In England, one of two documents (plus memorandum of association) that must be filed with the registrar of companies to form a corporation.

Articles of incorporation. The principal internal governing document of a corporation, also known as a corporate charter, that is filed with a government agency to establish a corporation.

Articles of organization. The document filed with a state office by which a limited liability company is formed.

Articles of partnership. The written agreement among the parties forming a partnership setting forth the partners' rights and duties with respect to the partnership.

Bankruptcy. The state of being bankrupt, as defined in federal law, usually administered under chapter 11 of the Internal Revenue Code.

Bearer instrument. A negotiable certificate that has the monetary value shown on its face.

Blue-chip companies. Firms that are judged as having high value as determined by large annual sales, outstanding financial returns, and have the respect of the investing public; often they are synonymous for companies listed on the Dow Jones Industrial Average or a comparable stock market index in other countries.

Blue-collar workers. Wage-earning employees who are usually non–college graduates and paid on an hourly basis.

Board of directors. The individuals elected by stockholders or members to represent them to appoint and oversee the officers who manage the business affairs of a corporation.

Bonds. A long-term debt security of a corporation that is secured by the collateral of the corporation.

Bonus. Compensation paid once per year in cash, usually for exemplary job performance.

Boycott. The action by individuals, groups, or a government not to purchase goods or services of another.

Breach of contract. The failure, without legal excuse, of a party to an agreement to perform the obligations of the agreement.

Breach of fiduciary duty. Violation of a duty of care, of a duty of loyalty, or of criminal or securities laws by a director or officer of a corporation involving financial matters.

Bretton Woods Agreement. An international agreement in 1944, named for the town in New Hampshire where it was negotiated, by the allies near the close of World War II that established the postwar international financial system, including the establishment of the World Bank and the International Monetary Fund. The system ended in 1971 though the two institutions remained.

Bribery. The offering, giving, receiving, or soliciting of anything of value with the goal of influencing a government official to take an action illegally benefiting the party making the offer or making the solicitation.

Bureaucracy. A large organization structured hierarchically to perform specific functions.

Business model. The fundamental approach a firm's management adopts for the basic operation of the business.

Business plan. A forward-looking document describing a company's vision, mission, goals, structure, finances, products, and services and how the firm intends to operate to achieve its stated objectives.

BV. Abbreviation used in the Netherlands to refer to a privately held, limited liability company.

Bylaws. A set of governing rules and procedures adopted by a corporation's board of directors.

Capital. Financial assets, goods, and possessions having market value that are used for the production of profits and generation of wealth; often used as a synonym for money.

Capital gain. The increase in the price of an asset.

Capitalism. Term used to describe an economic system based on private property ownership and characterized by free markets wherein individuals buy and sell.

Cartel. An association that controls supply and prices of a particular commodity, such as OPEC in oil, or a company that holds a monopoly in a particular industry, such as the Standard Oil Trust.

Case law. The body of law announced in court decisions; includes the aggregate of cases that interpret judicial procedures, statutes, regulations, and constitutional provisions. A key feature of the English common law system.

C corporation. A private corporation formed under state law to conduct business that pays tax on its earnings; the formal name for typical American corporations.

Certificate of authority. A certificate that foreign and alien corporations must obtain from a state to do business in that state.

Certificate of incorporation. The document issued by a state authority, usually the secretary of state, that declares a corporation exists and may conduct business.

Chapter 11. A synonym for *bankruptcy*. Term is taken from the Internal Revenue Code's chapter 11, which permits a firm that has more liabilities than income or assets to protect itself against creditors while attempting to reorganize its business to profitability.

Chartered company. A company granted a royal charter authorizing it to engage in commerce for a limited period of time and for specific purposes; a forerunner to the corporation.

Civil law. The branch of law that deals with private or public rights, as opposed to criminal matters.

Civil law system. A system of law, also known as codified law, based on a code rather than case law; the predominant system of law found on the continent of Europe and in the countries once controlled by those nations elsewhere in the world.

Close corporation. A corporation whose shareholders are limited to a small group of persons, often only family members, and whose rights regarding the transfer of shares to others are restricted.

Closely held corporation. See *close corporation.*

Collective bargaining. The process prescribed by the Wagner Act in which labor unions and management negotiate the terms and conditions of employment.

Commerce clause. A provision in Article I, Section 8 of the U.S. Constitution that gives Congress the power to regulate interstate and foreign commerce.

Common law. A body of law, also known as English common law, that is derived from customs, statutes, and judicial decisions; type of law used in the United States.

Common stock. Shares of ownership in a corporation that give the owner of the stock a proportionate interest in the corporation with respect to control, earnings, and net assets. Shares of common stock are lowest in priority in payment of dividends and distribution of corporate assets on dissolution of the corporation.

Commonwealth. The name of a governmental unit, such as a state.

Communism. A theory of government and a type of government in which all property is held in common by the citizenry (no private property) and all revenues derived from productive assets are distributed "in common"; that is, to each person equally or according to need. Today, a repressive system of state control.

Communist law. A system of law based on the philosophy of communism and the writings of Karl Marx, Friedrich Engels, and V. I. Lenin. Principal features are the rejection of the concept of private property and the role of the state as the embodiment of the leadership of the proletariat, the working class. The basis of law in Cuba and North Korea. No longer practiced in Russia after the collapse of the Soviet Union.

Concentrated industry. An industry having a large percentage of market share controlled by either a single firm or a small number of firms; term used in antitrust analysis.

Confiscation. The action of a government taking privately owned property, such as a business, without a proper public purpose, without just compensation, or on a discriminatory basis.

Conglomerate. A corporation that owns and operates numerous businesses in different industries.

Constitutional law. Law that is based on the U.S. Constitution and the constitutions of the fifty states.

Consumer goods. Commodities that are intended for personal or household use.

Contract. An agreement that is formed by two or more parties to undertake a particular activity that is enforceable in court.

Copyright. An exclusive right granted by government to authors to publish, print, or sell their intellectual property for a statutory period to time. It includes works of art, literature, and software.

Corporate charter. See *articles of incorporation.*

Corporate person. A term used in the Middle Ages to describe loose associations of people wishing to be treated as a collective entity; forerunner to a corporation.

Corporate raiders. Wealthy individuals who seek to gain controlling interest in the stock of a corporation for personal gain by improving the company's performance, selling off portions of the company, or laying off employees to increase the stock price.

Corporation. A public or private legal entity formed in compliance with statutory requirements and granted existence by a government.

Court of law. The governmental judicial entity in which remedies granted are things of value, such as money damages.

Creditor. A party to whom a debt is owed by another person, known as the debtor.

Crime. A wrongful act against society proclaimed in a statute and, if committed and proved, punishable by society through fines and/or imprisonment or death.

Criminal law. Statutes and precedent that define and govern actions that constitute wrongful actions committed against society for which society demands redress.

Crown. *The Crown* is a term used to describe the monarch of a country, such as a king or queen; it can also refer to the power of a parliamentary government in a monarchy.

Debenture. A bond that has no specific assets of the corporation pledged as backing. The bond is backed by the general credit rating of the corporation, plus assets that can be seized if the corporation defaults on the debenture.

Deed. A document showing legal title to property, usually real estate, which can be used to pass title of ownership to another person.

Default. The failure to live up to a promise or perform an obligation. Typically the term applies to the failure to pay a debt when it is due.

Defendant. The person being sued by a plaintiff or the person accused of a crime by a government authority.

Defined benefit pension plan. The traditional type of pension plan paid solely by the company with no employee contribution and is not portable to another firm should the employee change jobs before retirement. Employer contributions to the plan represent tax deductions for the employer.

Defined contribution pension plan. A type of pension plan in which the employee and typically the employer contribute toward the pension during the employee's working years and is portable should the employee change jobs before retirement. Employer contributions are not tax deductions.

Deflation. A condition in an economy in which overall prices fall.

Deregulation. Action by government to remove rules and regulations on an industry.

Developing countries. Nations on a United Nations' list that have per capita GDPs below a certain level.

Directors. Members of a board of directors of a corporation. Two types: inside directors, those who are employees of the corporation or who have a substantial business interest in the corporation; and outside directors, those who are independent of the corporation for their employment and livelihood.

Dissolution. The formal disbanding of a legal relationship, such as a partnership or corporation.

Distributorship. A business arrangement established between a manufacturer and a dealer that licenses the dealer to sell its product.

Diversification. A business strategy by which a company seeks to have products or business activities in several different markets or industries.

Divestiture. The act of selling one or more of a company's parts. Courts or regulatory agencies often mandate the sale of parts of companies in a merger to avoid antitrust implications.

Dividend. Distribution to shareholders of a corporation of corporate profits or income, disbursed in proportion to the number of shares held.

Divine right. The concept that monarchs derive their just powers from God and rule by divine right; a grant of power from God, not from the people they govern.

Domestic corporation. A corporation that is organized under the laws of a particular state and does business in that state.

Double taxation. A drawback of the corporate form of business: the corporation's profits are taxed by federal and state governments, and corporate dividends paid to shareholders are taxable again as ordinary income on their individual income tax returns.

Due process. Provisions in the Fifth and Fourteenth Amendments to the U.S. Constitution guarantee that no person shall be deprived of life, liberty, or property without "due process of law."

Dumping. Selling goods in a foreign country at a price below that charged for the same goods in the domestic market.

Duty of care. The obligation of all persons to exercise a reasonable amount of care in their dealings with others, particularly as applied to members of a board of directors in the discharge of their duties as elected representatives of shareholders of a corporation. The *reasonable person standard* as defined in tort law is used to define negligence in the performance of this duty.

Duty of loyalty. Similar to duty of care, the duty of loyalty requires members of a board of directors and officers of a corporation to put their obligations to the corporation ahead of any personal or other benefit in the performance of their official duties.

Economies of scale. Term used to describe decreases in the average cost of production resulting from increases in the size of the production facility.

Embezzlement. The fraudulent taking of money or other valuable property by a person to whom the money or property has been entrusted.

Eminent domain. A government's power to take private property for public use or to benefit a public purpose without the owner's consent by paying compensation.

Employee. A person who works for another for salary or wages.

Employer. A person or business that hires employees, pays them salary or wages, and exercises control over their work.

Entrepreneur. An individual who seizes opportunities and undertakes actions to establish and build a business for the purpose of making a profit.

Environmental law. A body of statutes, regulations, and precedent relating to the protection of the natural environment.

Equity security. Term relating to ownership of an interest in a corporation, such as preferred or common stock; an ownership right in the assets of a corporation.

Ethics. Moral principles and values applied to social behavior.

Export. The action of selling and shipping products to another country.

Express payments. Payment of small amounts of money, also called facilitation payments, that speed an individual or goods through customs or immigration procedures in another country. Under U.S. law, these are legal and permissible.

Expropriation. The act of seizure by a government of privately owned property, such as a business, for a proper public purpose, with just compensation, and on a nondiscriminatory basis.

Extraterritoriality. Term that refers to the extension of one country's law or regulations into another country's territory.

Family corporation. See *close corporation*.

Father of the modern corporation. Generally attributed to Alfred P. Sloan, president of General Motors.

Felony. A serious crime that carries severe penalties including monetary payments, time in prison, or ultimately death.

Fiduciary duty. The legal obligation of an officeholder, such as a member of a board of directors or a corporate officer, to act ethically and properly in the performance of those duties.

Fines. The requirement to pay monetary damages, based on statute or court order.

Foreclosure. A legal proceeding in which a mortgagee takes title to or forces the sale of the mortgagor's property to satisfy a debt.

Foreign corporation. A corporation that does business in a state but is incorporated in another state.

Foreign direct investment (FDI). Equity holdings of a company in other country.

401(k) plans. Savings plans authorized by the Internal Revenue Code's subsection 401(k) instituted by companies to enable salaried employees to undertake savings of their pay by purchasing stock, usually with a company matching amount.

Franchise. An arrangement whereby the owner of a trademark or trade name licenses another to use that trademark or trade name under terms and conditions delineated in an agreement to sell goods and services under that trademark or trade name.

Fraud. A misrepresentation knowingly made with the intent of deceiving another and on which any reasonable person would rely to his or her detriment; a crime.

Fringe benefits. Nonsalary or nonwage compensation paid by an employer.

Gesellschaft. German word for company.

Gesellschaft mit bushranger Haftung. German term for limited liability company, abbreviated as GmbH.

Gilded Age. The period, 1880s–1890s, in the United States when leading rich industrialists exhibited their wealth and built for themselves fabulous palace-like homes.

Global companies. Firms that regularly deal in international business on a worldwide basis but are not viewed as multinational corporations.

Global industries. Categories of industries (e.g., automobiles) that have worldwide activities in their purchasing, manufacturing, distribution, and selling of products.

Globalization. A term that refers to the extensive network of business and economic interaction between companies based in different countries; synonym for worldwide economic interdependence of companies and national economies.

Golden parachute. A popular term referring to a lucrative severance package paid to an executive when the executive terminates employment with a firm.

Good. Generic name for a product.

Good faith. Under the Uniform Commercial Code, this means honesty in fact. With respect to merchants, it means honesty in fact plus the observance of reasonable commercial standards of fair dealing in the trade.

Governance. Term relating to how a corporation is run based on a body of rules and procedures that directs its decision-making processes and operations.

Government corporation. A public corporation formed by a government for the purpose of undertaking a task to benefit society as a whole.

Gross domestic product (GDP). The sum of the market value of all goods and services produced in an economy in a given year.

Gross profit. The amount of money remaining to a business from revenue after paying costs. Net profit is revenue remaining after paying costs and taxes.

Guilds. Beginning in the Middle Ages in Europe, a term used to describe associations of individuals working in the same industry, trade, or branch of commerce; usually merchants or artisans formed these to establish best practices in their professions.

Holding company. A corporation that includes subsidiary corporations that actually operate businesses.

Home country. A term that refers to the nation in which a corporation is incorporated.

Horizontal integration. The result of acquisition or merger of companies who are competitors; that is, on the same level in the supply chain.

Horizontal merger. A merger between firms that are competitors in the same market.

Host country. A term that refers to a nation in which a corporation does business that is not its home country; that is, where it was not initially incorporated.

Hostile takeover. The attempt by one corporation to acquire the assets and liabilities of another corporation against the wishes of the target corporation's board.

Immunity. The status of being exempt or free from certain duties or requirements and their consequences.

Indemnify. To compensate or reimburse another for losses or expenses incurred.

Indictment. A charge by a grand jury that a person has committed a crime.

Individual retirement account. Known as an IRA; a type of savings program in which an individual can invest funds to gain a tax deduction in the year of investment to save for retirement, when the funds can be withdrawn and taxes can then be paid, presumably at a lower rate.

Industrial Revolution. The term used to describe the events during a period of time when an agrarian economy is transformed into an industrial economy, such as the 1860s to 1890s in the United States.

Inflation. Percentage change in overall prices in an economy year over year.

Infringement. A violation of another's legal rights, usually with reference to patents or copyrights.

Initial public offering (IPO). The procedure used when a corporation is authorized by the SEC to issue stock to the public for the first time.

Insider. A corporate director, officer, knowledgeable employee, or outside agent having confidential information regarding the corporation and having a duty not to use or disclose that information for personal gain or for others.

Insider trading. The purchase or sale of stock or other securities by a person having non public information regarding the corporation in violation of securities laws and regulations.

Integrated product development teams. Usually referred to as integrated product teams (or IPTs). This management technique assembles into one group all the functional disciplines (engineering, manufacturing, finance, marketing, and key suppliers) needed to develop a product so that when the product goes into production it will have a maximum probability of successful production and reliable quality.

Intellectual property. Property that is generated by creative work, such as works of art, literature, music, and software. Patents, copyrights, and trademarks are intended to protect it against unauthorized use or infringement.

Interlocking directorships. Members of one corporation's board sit on several other corporations' boards of directors to influence business decisions of those boards.

International company. A company that exports and imports.

International law. The body of law that governs relations among nations, derived from customs, treaties, and international courts' judicial opinions.

International organization. A body composed of nation-states, usually established by treaty. The United Nations is an example.

Investment company. A firm that acts on behalf of numerous shareholders by buying a portfolio of securities and professionally managing that portfolio.

Islamic law. A body of law called Sharia, based on the Koran practiced in certain Muslim countries primarily in the Middle East.

Joint and several liability. A doctrine under the law of partnerships wherein a plaintiff can sue an individual partner or all the partners and collect a judgment.

Joint liability. In partnership law all the partners share the liability for partnership debts and other obligations.

Joint stock company. A hybrid form of business organization combining characteristics of a corporation (shareholder owners, management by directors and officers, and perpetual existence) and a partnership (formed by agreement among the parties and shareholders have personal liability for debts). Also early name for a corporation.

Joint venture. A business arrangement formed by two or more companies for a specific commercial enterprise in which each party holds a percentage of interest.

Judgment. A term in law representing the final order or decision resulting from a legal action.

Judicial process. The procedures associated with the administration of justice through the judicial system.

"Junk" bonds. Certificates of corporate indebtedness that have low value (non-investment grade) as judged by one or more bond rating service, such as Moody's or Standard & Poor's.

Juridical entity. A business entity, such as a corporation, that has a legal identity of its own and is treated as a person before courts of law.

Laissez-faire capitalism. French term for a free-market economy characterized by no governmental restraints on the actions of corporations.

Law. A body of enforceable statutes and rules governing relationships among individuals and between them and their society.

Lead director. A nonemployee member of a corporation's board of directors who can act as presiding officer at board meetings and who chairs meetings of outside directors.

Legislature. The governmental body, the members of which are elected by the citizens, that enacts laws; for example, the U.S. Congress.

Leverage buyout. The activity of acquiring a corporation by borrowing heavily (leveraging) to acquire a controlling interest in its stock. Firms that engaged in this practice are termed leverage buyout companies (LBOs).

Liability. In law: an actual or potential legal obligation, responsibility, duty, or debt; in accounting: debts or obligations on a balance sheet.

Lien. An encumbrance on a property to satisfy a debt or to protect a claim for payment of a debt.

Limited liability. The situation in a business in which the obligations and responsibilities of the owners are confined to the amount of their investment in the firm.

Limited liability company (LLC). A hybrid form of business organization offering the limited liability protection of a corporation and the tax advantage of a partnership.

Limited liability limited partnership (LLLP). A type of limited partnership in which the liability of the general partner is the same as the liability of the limited partners, that is, the liability for all partners is limited to the amount of their investment.

Limited liability partnership (LLP). A form of partnership that allows a group of professionals to work together enjoying the tax advantages of a partnership while limiting their personal liability.

Limited partner. Partners in a partnership who contribute capital to the partnership but have no right to participate in the management of the business. Limited partners assume no liability for the debts of the partnership beyond the capital contributed.

Limited partnership (LP). A partnership consisting of one or more general partners (who manage the business and have liability to the full extent of their personal assets for the debts of the partnership) and one or more limited partners (who contribute only capital and whose liability carries to the extent of that contribution).

Line positions. Jobs in a company that perform the principal operating activities of the firm, as opposed to staff positions, which support line jobs.

Liquidation. Regarding corporations, the process by which corporate assets are converted into cash and distributed among creditors and shareholders according to rules of precedence.

Litigation. The process of suing and defending against a lawsuit in a court of law.

Margin. Another word for profit.

Market capitalization. Also known as market cap and market value. Determined by multiplying the price of a corporation's stock by the number of outstanding shares.

Market concentration. A situation that exists when a small number of firms in an industry share an overwhelming percentage of the market for a particular good or service.

Market mechanisms. Factors at work in a capitalist economy, such as supply and demand influencing prices, that affect behavior in a free market.

Market power. A situation that exists when a firm controls the market price of its product, such as in the case of a monopoly.

Market segmentation. A business strategy by which a company produces a range of products for different portions of a market.

Market share. The percentage of a given market supplied by a particular company.

Mediation. A procedure for settling disputes outside of court by using the services of a neutral third party, called a mediator. The results of the mediation can be binding or nonbinding, depending on the prior decision of the disputing parties.

Memorandum of association. In England, a document that must be filed, along with articles of association, with the registrar of companies to establish a public corporation.

Merger. A contractual process by which two or more companies agree to combine their businesses (including all assets and liabilities) into one of the companies or by forming a new, combined company. Each merging company's shareholders either receive payment for their percent of ownership, or they receive proportional numbers of shares in the surviving company.

Meritocracy. A social setting, such as in a business, in which merit is the sole criterion for success and reward, not family, social connections, or other nonachievement factors.

Minimum wage. The lowest wage determined by either government or union contract that an employer may pay an hourly worker.

Monopoly. The situation that exists when a single seller or a very limited number of sellers controls a market; illegal under the Sherman Antitrust Act.

Monopoly power. The ability of a monopoly to determine what takes place in a given market, usually charging higher than competitive prices.

Morals clause. A provision in an employment contract that provides if the employee violates reasonable standards of morality or a law the employment contract is vitiated.

Multinational corporation. A large corporation based in one country that owns and directs business operations in at least three other countries and treats the world as a single market.

Mutual fund. A type of investment company that continually buys and sells to investors shares of ownership in a portfolio of investments.

National law. The law that pertains to a specific country, versus international law.

Nation-state system. Current worldwide governmental arrangement of independent countries.

Negligence. The failure to exercise the standard of care that a reasonable person would exercise in similar circumstances.

Net profit. Amount of money remaining from revenue after paying costs and taxes.

Networked corporation. A company based on a business model in which the firm owns no tangible assets, outsources virtually all noncore activities, and manages a network of suppliers.

No liability corporation. Under common law practiced in England, this is a corporation whose shareholders are not required to pay any of the firm's debts but they do not receive dividends if the debts are unpaid.

Nonprofit corporation. A type of corporation authorized by a government whose purpose is to perform a service for society, such as education, and not to seek profit; also called not-for-profit corporation.

No-par-value shares. Shares of stock in a corporation that have no face value; that is, they have no dollar amount printed on the shares.

Note. A short-term (up to five years) debt security that is or is not secured by collateral; usually issued by a bank.

Not-for-profit corporation. See *nonprofit corporation.*

Ordinance. A law enacted by a municipal governmental unit, such as a city or county.

Outsource. A business strategy in which tasks that could be performed within the company are contracted out to other firms, known as suppliers or vendors.

Par shares. In England and most common law countries, only this type of stock may be issued, having a specified face value per share.

Partnership. A legal arrangement whereby two or more persons agree to carry on a business for profit as co-owners.

Par value shares. Shares in a corporation that have a specific monetary value written on their face, such as $1.00.

Patent. A monopoly right granted by a government for a limited time to an inventor to make, use, or sell the invention.

Pension. Monthly payments made by a company to an employee after retirement.

Perquisites. Usually abbreviated to *perks*, these are noncash forms of compensation.

Person. An individual human being or any other entity, such as a corporation, that has standing before a court of law.

Personal property. Property that is movable; not real property.

Pierce the corporate veil. To disregard the corporate entity that limits the liability of directors, officers, and shareholders by holding one or more of them personally liable for a corporate obligation or breach of obligation.

Plaintiff. A person who initiates a lawsuit.

Populist movement. A politically oriented activity by farmers, small business owners, blue-collar workers, and liberal thinkers in the United States during the 1880s–1910s that pressured the federal government to establish rules and regulations protecting these groups against the power of big business.

Precedent. A decision by a court or administrative body that provides an example or authority for deciding subsequent cases involving identical or similar facts. This is a critical basis of law in common law countries.

Predatory pricing. The act of setting a price for a good below cost with the intent of driving competitors out of a market.

Preferred stock. Classes of stock that have precedence over common stock in payment of dividends by a corporation or the distribution of assets at the time of dissolution of the corporation.

Price discrimination. The act of setting prices for goods or services so that different buyers pay different prices for the same item.

Price-fixing. An agreement between two or more competitors in which they set the prices of goods or services at a certain level; prohibited by the Clayton Antitrust Act.

Private corporation. A business entity formed by individuals for the purpose of seeking profit and granted authority to undertake business by a government entity. In England, it refers to a business corporation that is not required to have many of the formalities of a public corporation because it issues no shares or bonds.

Privately held corporation. See *close corporation*.

Private property. A term that refers primarily to real estate but could be anything of value that is owned by an individual or a business, not by a government.

Privatization. A government policy by which the government sells assets of government-owned businesses to private owners.

Productivity. Output per unit of inputs.

Product liability. The legal liability of manufacturers, distributors, and sellers of goods to consumers or other users for injuries caused by the goods.

Professional corporation. Found only in the United States; a type of close corporation composed of members of the same profession, like lawyers.

Profit. Amount of money remaining from revenue after paying costs; gross profit.

Profit and loss centers. Known as P&L centers, these are subunits of a company in which their managers have responsibility for the profit and loss of that particular activity.

Property. Anything of value subject to ownership that is legally protected as to rights and interests; real property and intellectual property are included.

Prospectus. A document required by federal law and state securities laws that describes the business and financial operations of a corporation, allowing potential investors to make informed decisions at the initial public offering.

Proxy. A written agreement between a stockholder and another in which the stockholder authorizes the other to vote the stockholder's shares in a particular way.

Public benefit nonprofit corporation. See *nonprofit corporation*.

Public companies. Another name for private corporations; the term is derived from the fact that the stock of such companies is traded on a public exchange.

Public corporation. In the United States, this is a corporation, sometimes called a government corporation, formed by act of a government to undertake a public purpose and not to make a profit. In England, a public corporation is the same as a U.S. private corporation.

Public limited corporation (PLC). A term used in England and Canada to describe a public corporation; also known as a limited corporation (Ltd.).

Punitive damages. Monetary award to a plaintiff to punish the defendant and deter future similar conduct; an amount over and beyond economic damages.

Quality circles. A technique used by Japanese management to improve the quality of manufactured products by having all the workers who are engaged in a particular activity in the manufacturing process gather periodically to discuss ways to improve their work to reduce cost and rework and to speed up the process.

Quorum. The number of members of a body that must be present to enable business to be transacted.

Quota. A limit assigned on imported goods.

Real property. Land and everything on it and attached to it, such as buildings.

Reasonable care. The degree of care a person of ordinary prudence would exercise in similar circumstances.

Restraint of trade. An agreement or combination that tends to reduce or eliminate competition or create a monopoly to restrict the free flow of goods and the market's determination of prices; illegal under various federal laws.

Restricted stock rights. Grants of a corporation's stock made to an employee for which the employee makes no payment but is not permitted to sell the stock for a period of years.

Retained earnings. The portion of a corporation's profits that is not paid out as dividends to shareholders.

Retention. Human resources techniques used to keep employees in a company.

Rivals. Competitors in the same industry.

Robber barons. A term used to describe railroad magnates in the 1880s–1890s in the United States whose pursuit of maximum profits produced excesses and harmed individuals, especially small farmers in the Midwest.

Royal charter. A document issued by a monarch authorizing a group of individuals to form a company to engage in business for a limited time in a specific location.

S corporation. A corporation that is a form of close corporation under the Internal Revenue Code that is taxed like a partnership but enjoys the limited liability protection of a corporation.

Securities. The usual reference of the term is to stocks and bonds; however, it may also include a note, debenture, stock warrant or any document given as evidence of ownership of an interest in a corporation or as a promise of repayment by a corporation.

Securities and Exchange Commission (SEC). Independent federal agency established by the Securities Exchange Act of 1934 that regulates the U.S. securities industry.

Share. A unit of stock; evidence of fractional ownership in a corporation.

Shareholder. One who owns shares of a corporation's stock.

Shareholder value. Generally refers to actions taken by a corporation to increase the price of its stock; stock price of a corporation.

Sharp practices. A term that refers to quasi-legal or even illegal business activities engaged in by an individual or a firm.

Social responsibility. A term referring to actions voluntarily taken by a firm to benefit society.

Sociedad anonyme. Spanish term for corporation, abbreviated S.A.

Societa per Azioni. Italian term for corporation, abbreviated SpA.

Société. French word for company.

Société anonyme. French term for stock corporation, abbreviated S.A.

Société á résponsabilité limitée. French term for limited liability company, abbreviated SARL.

Sole proprietorship. The simplest business form, in which the owner is the business and is personally responsible for all the business' debts and obligations and reports business income on his or her individual income tax return.

Staff positions. Jobs in a company that support the line activities.

Statutory law. A body of law enacted by a legislature, as opposed to constitutional law, administrative law, or case law.

Stock. An equity interest in a corporation.

Stock certificate. A document showing an equity interest (ownership) in a corporation, measured in units of shares.

Stock corporation. A type of corporation in civil law countries.

Stock exchange. A public place where stocks are traded (bought and sold), such as the New York Stock Exchange.

Stockholder. Same as shareholder.

Stock option. A certificate that grants an employee the right to buy a stated number of shares of stock in the issuing corporation within a set time period at a set price.

Stock warrant. Same as a stock option.

Strict liability. Liability regardless of fault.

Strike. An activity voted to be undertaken by union employees against their employer following the breakdown of collective bargaining involving employees leaving their jobs, refusing to work, and usually picketing the employer's place(s) of business.

Subscriber. An investor who purchases stock in a corporation through a subscription agreement.

Supplier. A company that sells to another company; same as vendor.

Supply chain. The link of companies and/or activities involved in the process of production and distribution of a good.

Syndicate. A group of investors or firms brought together to finance a project or launch a corporation that they would not or could not undertake independently.

Tariff. A tax on imported goods.

Tender. An unconditional offer to perform an obligation by a person who is ready, willing, and able to do so; usually refers to an offer to purchase.

Tender offer. An offer to purchase a corporation made by one corporation directly to the shareholders of another; often referred to as a takeover bid.

Tombstone. In business, an advertisement—historically in the format of a cemetery headstone—of a securities offering. The ad informs potential investors where, from whom, and how they may obtain a prospectus.

Trademark. A distinctive mark, motto, device, or implement that a manufacturer stamps, prints, or affixes to the goods it produces to identify them in the marketplace and to communicate their origin. Following registration, the owner is entitled to exclusive use.

Trade name. A term used to describe all or part of a business' name; it is closely linked to the reputation and goodwill of the company. Trade names are protected under common law, as well as under trademark law, provided the firm's name is the same as the firm's trademarked property; such as Coca-Cola.

Transnational company. Firm that exports and imports and also conducts business in several countries simultaneously but is not viewed as a multinational corporation.

Treasury shares. Shares of stock authorized by a corporation but not issued.

Treaty. A formal agreement entered into by two or more independent nations.

Trust. A formal business arrangement entered into by two or more corporations in the same industry in which they agree to accept shares of interest in the trust in return for the rights of their corporations; illegal under U.S. antitrust law as a restraint of trade.

Underwriting. Process used by securities firms to prepare an initial public offering (IPO) of stock and to handle the initial transactions.

Vacate. Decision by an appeals court to reverse a lower court's ruling.

Valuation. Process of evaluating the monetary value of a company, typically by a securities firm, in preparation for a corporation's initial public offering (IPO) or for its merger or acquisition.

Vendor. One who sells goods or services to another; a supplier.

Verdict. A formal decision by a jury.

Vertical integration. The result of a vertical merger or acquisition, either backward or forward in the supply chain.

Vertically integrated company. A firm that performs two or more functional phases of a product, such as raw material production, manufacturing, distribution, retailing.

Vertical merger. The acquisition by a company of a company below it (backward) or above it (forward) in its supply chain, such as a vendor or customer, respectively.

Warrant. A stock option. Also a modern derivative product.

Warranty. A commitment that certain facts are true as they are represented to be; a guarantee of quality of a good usually for a specified time period.

Whistle-blowing. Disclosure in an allegation by an employee to a government agency that his or her employer is engaged in unsafe, illegal, or unethical activities.

White-collar workers. A company's salaried workers.

Yugen-Kaisha. Japanese term for corporation, abbreviated Y.K.

Selected Bibliography

Aglietta, Michael, and Antoine Reberioux. *Corporate Governance Adrift: A Critique of Shareholder Value*. Northampton, MA: Elgar Publishing, 2005.

Alsop, Ronald. "Corporate Scandals Hit Home." *Wall Street Journal*, February 19, 2004.

———. "Ranking Corporate Reputations," *Wall Street Journal*, December 6, 2005.

Anderson, John E. *Politics and the Economy*. Boston: Little, Brown, 1966.

August, Ray. *International Business Law*. 2nd ed. Upper Saddle River, NJ: Prentice Hall, 1997.

Bakan, Joel. *The Corporation: The Pathological Pursuit of Profit and Power*. New York: Free Press, 2004.

Baker, George P., and George David Smith. *The New Financial Capitalists: Kohlberg Kravis Roberts & Co. and the Creation of Corporate Value*. New York: Cambridge University Press, 1998.

Balmer, John M. T., and Edmund R. Gray. "Corporate Identity and Corporate Communications: Creating a Competitive Advantage." In John M. T. Balmer and Stephen A. Greyser, *Revealing the Corporation: Perspectives on Identity, Image, Reputation, Corporate Branding, and Corporate-Level Marketing*. London: Routledge, 2003.

Balmer, John M. T., and Stephen A. Greyser. *Revealing the Corporation: Perspectives on Identity, Image, Reputation, Corporate Branding, and Corporate-Level Marketing*. London: Routledge, 2003.

Barone, Michael. "Big Labor, RIP." *Wall Street Journal*, July 28, 2005.

Bartlett, Christopher, and Sumantra Ghoshal. *Transnational Management*. Homewood, IL: Irwin, 1992.

Bartlett, Hale C. *Cases in Strategic Management for Business*. New York: Dryden Press, 1988.

Beatty, Jack, ed. *Colossus: How the Corporation Changed America*. New York: Broadway Books, 2001.

————. "Organize or Perish!" In Jack Beatty, ed., *Colossus: How the Corporation Changed America*. New York: Broadway Books, 2001.

Benoit, Emile. "Interdependence on a Small Planet." *Columbia Journal of World Business*, spring 1966.

Berle, Adolph A., Jr., and Gardiner C. Means. *The Modern Corporation and Private Property*. New York: Macmillan, 1948.

Bianco, Anthony, and Wendy Zellner. "Is Wal-Mart Too Powerful?" *Business Week*, October 6, 2003.

Brenner, Melvin A. "Is U.S. Deregulation a Failure? Here's How to Find Out." *Airline Executive*, September 1980.

Business Week, May 9, 2005; September 26, 2005, February 13, 2006.

Carroll, A. B. "A Three-Dimensional Conceptual Model of Corporate Performance." *Academy of Management Review*, October 1979.

Chandler, Alfred D., Jr. *Strategy and Structure: Chapters in the History of Industrial Enterprise*. Cambridge, MA: MIT Press, 1962.

————, ed. *The Railroads: The Nation's First Big Business*. New York: Harcourt, Brace and World, 1965.

————. *The Visible Hand: The Managerial Revolution in American Business*. Cambridge, MA: Harvard University Press, 1977.

————. "Government vs. Business: An American Phenomenon." *Harvard Business Review*, March 1982.

————. *Scale and Scope: The Dynamics of Industrial Capitalism*. Cambridge, MA: Harvard University Press, 1990.

Charan, Ram. "Boardroom Supports." *Strategy + Business*, winter 2003.

Cheeseman, Henry R. *The Legal and Regulatory Environment*. 2nd ed. Upper Saddle River, NJ: Prentice Hall, 2000.

Conger, Jay A., and Edward E. Lawler III. "Corporate Governance." *Strategy + Business*, fourth quarter, 2001.

Cool, Karel. "Häagen-Dazs and the European Ice-Cream Industry in 1992." In José de la Torre, Yves Doz, and Timothy Devinney, *Managing the Global Corporation: Case Studies in Strategy and Management*. 2nd ed. New York: Irwin/McGraw-Hill, 2001.

Council of Economic Advisors. *Economic Report of the President, 2003*. Washington, D.C.: U.S. Government Printing Office, 2003.

————. *Economic Report of the President, 2005*. Washington, D.C.: U.S. Government Printing Office, 2005.

Cross, Frank B., and Roger Leroy Miller. *West's Legal Environment of Business*. 5th ed. Mason, OH: Thomson South-Western, 2004.

De la Torre, José, Yves Doz, and Timothy Devinney. *Managing the Global Corporation: Case Studies in Strategy and Management*. 2nd ed. New York: Irwin/McGraw-Hill, 2001.

De Meyer, Arnoud. "Nestlé, S.A." In José de la Torre, Yves Doz, and Timothy Devinney, *Managing the Global Corporation: Case Studies in Strategy and Management*. 2nd ed. New York: Irwin/McGraw-Hill, 2001.

Denis, Diane K., and John J. McConnell. *Governance: An International Perspective.* Northampton, MA: Elgar Publishing, 2005.

Diener, Mark. "Seeking Counsel." *Entrepreneur,* January 2003.

DiMaggio, Paul, ed. *The Twenty-first Century Firm: Changing Economic Organization in International Perspective.* Princeton, NJ: Princeton University Press, 2001.

Dimatteo, Larry A. *The Law of International Business Transactions.* Mason, OH: Thomson South-Western, 2003.

Doremus, Paul, et al. *The Myth of the Global Corporation.* Princeton, NJ: Princeton University Press, 1998.

Drucker, Peter F. "The American CEO," *Wall Street Journal,* December 30, 2004.

———. *Management: Tasks, Responsibilities, Practices.* New York: Harper & Row, 1974.

———. *The Concept of the Corporation.* New Brunswick, NJ: Transaction Publishers, 1993.

———. "The Hostile Takeover and Its Discontents." In Jack Beatty, ed., *Colossus: How the Corporation Changed America.* New York: Broadway Books, 2001.

Dunning, John H. *Multinational Enterprises and the Global Economy.* Wokingham, England: Addison-Wesley, 1993.

The Economist, January 11, 2003; April 16, 2005.

Eisenberg, Melvin Aron. *Corporations and Other Business Organizations: Cases and Materials.* 9th ed. New York: Foundation Press, 2005.

Epstein, Marc, and Kirk Hanson, eds. *The Accountable Corporation,* 3 vols. Westport, CT: Praeger, 2005.

Farber, David R. *Sloan Rules: Alfred P. Sloan and the Triumph of General Motors.* Chicago: University of Chicago Press, 2002.

Federal Trade Commission. *Changes in Manufacturing 1935 to 1947 and 1950.* Washington, D.C.: U.S. Government Printing Office, 1954.

Fortune, February 21, 2005; March 7, 2005; April 18, 2005; May 2, 2005; June 27, 2005; July 11, 25, 2005; August 22, 2005; September 5, 2005.

Friedman, Milton. *Capitalism and Freedom.* Chicago: University of Chicago Press, 1963.

———. "The Social Responsibility of Business Is to Increase Its Profits." *New York Times Magazine,* September 30, 1970.

Gabel, Medard, and Henry Bruner. *Global, Inc.: An Atlas of the Multinational Corporation.* New York: New Press, 2003.

Galbraith, John Kenneth. *The Great Crash, 1929.* Boston: Houghton Mifflin, 1979.

General Electric Company. *Proxy Statement for 2005.*

General Motors Corporation 2004 Annual Report.

Grunig, J. E., ed. *Excellence in Public Relations and Communications Management.* Hillsdale, NJ: Erlbaum, 1992.

Gunther, Marc. "Disney's Board Game." *Fortune,* March 22, 2004.

Hamilton, Alexander. "No. 36." In Alexander Hamilton, James Madison, and John Jay, *The Federalist Papers.* New York: New American Library, 1961.

Hammer, Michael, and James Champy. *Reengineering the Corporation: A Manifesto for Business Revolution.* Rev. ed. New York: Collins, 2003,

Heer, Jean. *Nestlé: 125 Years, 1866–1991.* Vevey, Switzerland: Published by Nestlé S.A., 1992.

Heilbroner, Robert S. *The Making of Economic Society.* Englewood Cliffs, NJ: Prentice-Hall, 1962.

Hilsenrath, Jon E. "Look Who Else Is Buying American." *Los Angeles Times,* August 15, 2005.

"Hottest Car Guy on Earth." *Wall Street Journal,* January 14, 2006.

Hunger, David J., and Thomas L. Wheelen. *Essentials of Strategic Management.* 3rd ed. Upper Saddle River, NJ: Prentice Hall, 2003.

Hymowitz, Carol. "More American Chiefs Are Taking Top Posts At Overseas Concerns." *Wall Street Journal,* October 17, 2005.

———. "Globalizing the Boardroom." *Wall Street Journal,* November 14, 2005.

Iacocca, Lee. *Iacocca: An Autobiography.* New York: Bantam Books, 1984.

Innes, Stephen. "From Corporation to Commonwealth." In Jack Beatty, ed., *Colossus: How the Corporation Changed America.* New York: Broadway Books, 2001.

Jobs, Steve. "Stay Hungry. Stay Foolish." *Fortune,* September 5, 2005.

Johnson, Paul. *Modern Times.* New York: Harper & Row, 1983.

JP Morgan Chase Annual Report 2005.

Kaynak, Erdener, ed. *The Global Business.* New York: International Business Press, 1993.

Kaysen, Carl, ed. *The American Corporation Today.* New York: Oxford University Press, 1996.

Kindleberger, Charles. *A Financial History of Western Europe.* Oxford, England: Oxford University Press, 1993.

Kocourek, Paul F., Christian Burger, and Bill Birchard. "Corporate Governance: Hard Facts about Soft Behaviors." *Strategy + Business,* spring 2003.

Kuznets, Simon. *Economic Growth of Nations: Total Output and Production Structure.* Cambridge, MA: Harvard University Press, 1971.

Labich, Kenneth. "Nike vs. Reebok, a Battle for Hearts, Minds & Feet." *Fortune,* September 18, 1965.

Lavelle, Louis, and Amy Borrus. "Ethics 101 for CEOs." *Business Week,* January 26, 2004.

Lechem, Brian. *Chairman of the Board.* Hoboken, NJ: Wiley, 2002.

Lilienthal, David E. "The Multinational Corporation." In M. H. Anshen and G. L. Bach, eds., *Management and Corporations 1985.* New York: McGraw-Hill, 1990.

Los Angeles Times, January 2, 1999; June 11, 28, 2003; November 21, 2003; March 4, 8, 29, 2004; April 7, 2004; December 15, 2004; January 12, 2005; February 10, 20, 2005; April 7, 2005; May 9, 2005; July 20, 21, 27, 2005; August 8, 10, 14, 23, 2005; September 18, 20, 2005; November 4, 5, 2005; February 2, 2006.

MacMurray, Worth D. "Applied Governance: Beyond Compliance." *Strategy + Business,* winter 2003.

Magretta, Joan. *What Management Is*. New York: Free Press, 2002.

Malone, Thomas W., Robert Laubacher, and Michael S. Scott Morton, eds. *Inventing the Organizations of the 21st Century*. Cambridge, MA: MIT Press, 2003.

Marchand, Roland. *Creating the Corporate Soul: The Rise of Public Relations and Corporate Imagery in American Big Business*. Berkeley, CA: University of California Press, 1998.

Margulies, Walter. "Make the Most of Your Corporate Identity." In John M. T. Balmer and Stephen A. Greyser, *Revealing the Corporation: Perspectives on Identity, Image, Reputation, Corporate Branding, and Corporate-Level Marketing*. London: Routledge, 2003.

Mason, Edward S., ed. *The Corporation in Modern Society*. Cambridge, MA: Harvard University Press, 1960.

McCraw, Thomas. *American Business 1920–2000: How It Worked*. Wheeling, IL: Harlan Davidson, 2000.

McLean, Bethany. "Why Enron Went Bust." *Fortune*, December 24, 2001.

Means, Howard. *Money and Power: The History of Business*. New York: Wiley, 2001.

Melloan, George. "Global View." *Wall Street Journal*, January 6, 2004.

Micklethwait, John, and Adrian Wooldridge. *The Company: A Short History of a Revolutionary Idea*. New York: Modern Library, 2003.

Millstein, Ira M., and Paul W. MacAvoy. "The Active Board of Directors and Improved Performance of the Large Publicly Traded Corporation." *Columbia Law Review*, Vol. 98, 1998.

Morison, Samuel Eliot, and Henry Steele Commager. *The Growth of the American Republic*. 4th ed. New York: Oxford University Press, 1958, Vol. II.

Murphy, Cait. "A No-Fly Zone." *Fortune*, April 14, 2003.

Neilson, Gary L., and Bruce A. Pasternack. "The Cat That Came Back." *Strategy + Business*, fall 2005.

New York Times, January 13, 1993; February 10, 2005; September 15, 2005; November 2, 2005.

Nohria, Nitin, Davis Dyer, and Frederick Dalzell. *Changing Fortunes: Remaking the Industrial Corporation*. New York: Wiley, 2002.

Novak, Michael. *The Future of the Corporation*. Washington, D.C.: American Enterprise Institute Press, 1996.

Ohmae, Kenichi. "Putting Global Logic First." *Harvard Business Review*, January–February 1995.

Oksenberg, Michel C., Michael D. Swaine, and Daniel C. Lynch. *The Chinese Future*. Los Angeles: Pacific Council on International Policy, University of Southern California, and the Center for Asia-Pacific Policy, RAND Corporation, 1999.

Palmiter, Alan R., and Louis D. Solomon. *Corporations: Examples and Explanations*. 4th ed. New York: Aspen Publishers, 2003.

Perrow, Charles. *Organizing America: Wealth, Power and the Origins of Corporate Capitalism*. Princeton, NJ: Princeton University Press, 2002.

Porter, Michael E. *The Competitive Advantage of Nations*. New York: Free Press, 1990.

Post, James E., Lee E. Preston, and Sybille Sachs. *Redefining the Corporation: Stakeholder Management and Organizational Wealth*. Stanford, CA: Stanford Business Books, 2002.

President's Committee on Administrative Management (Brownlow Commission). *Report with Special Studies*. Washington, D.C.: U.S. Government Printing Office, 1937.

Puri, Shaifali. "Deals of the Year." *Fortune*, February 17, 1997.

Reich, Leonard S. *The Making of American Industrial Research: Science and Business at GE and Bell, 1876–1926*. New York: Cambridge University Press, 1985.

Rostow, Walt W. *The Stages of Economic Growth*. London: Cambridge University Press, 1960.

Roy, William. *Socializing Capital: The Rise of the Large Industrial Corporation in America*. Princeton, NJ: Princeton University Press, 1997.

Rumelt, Richard P. *Strategy, Structure and Economic Performance*. Boston: Harvard University Press, 1974.

Servan-Schreiber, Jean Jacques. *The American Challenge*. London: Hamilton, 1968.

Sloan, Alfred P. *My Years with General Motors*. Garden City, NY: Doubleday, 1963.

Smith, George David, and Davis Dyer. "The Rise and Transformation of the American Corporation." In Carl Kaysen, ed., *The American Corporation Today*. New York: Oxford University Press, 1966.

Solomon, Deborah. "At What Price?" *Wall Street Journal*, October 17, 2005.

Stewart, James B. *Disney War*. New York: Simon & Schuster, 2005.

Tedlow, Richard S. "Ford vs. GM." In Jack Beatty, ed., *Colossus: How the Corporation Changed America*. New York: Broadway Books, 2001.

Truitt, Wesley B. *Business Planning: A Comprehensive Framework and Process*. Westport, CT: Quorum Books, 2002.

———. *What Entrepreneurs Need to Know about Government: A Guide to Rules and Regulations*. Westport, CT: Praeger, 2004.

U.S. Department of Commerce. *Statistical Abstract of the United States, 1964*. Washington, D.C.: U.S. Government Printing Office, 1965.

———. *Statistical Abstract of the United States, 2002*. Washington, D.C.: U.S. Government Printing Office, 2002.

U.S. Pension Benefit Guaranty Corporation. *2002 Annual Report*. Washington, D.C.: U.S. Government Printing Office, 2003.

U.S. Small Business Administration. "The Changing Burden of Regulation, Paperwork, and Tax Compliance on Small Business: A Report to Congress." October 1995.

Useem, Michael. "Corporate Education and Training." In Carl Kaysen, ed., *The American Corporation Today*. New York: Oxford University Press, 1996.

Van Riel, C. B. M. *Principles of Corporate Communication*. London: Prentice Hall, 1995.

Wall Street Journal, October 26, 2000; December 21, 2000; April 3, 2003; June 10, 11, 26, 2003; July 22, 2003; August 28, 2003; October 3, 27, 2003; January 6, 7,

2004; November 2, 2004; January 19, 20, 28, 2005; February 3, 4, 10, 2005; March 2, 3, 14, 24, 2005; April 7, 15, 29, 2005; May 11, 12, 2005; June 6, 15, 26, 29, 2005; July 6, 8, 13, 14, 15, 21, 25, 27, 29, 2005; August 3, 4, 8, 10, 22, 23, 26, 28, 2005; September 1, 7, 19, 21, 2005; October 24, 31, 2005; November 8, 14, 2005; December 16, 28, 2005; January 6, 12, 14, 21, 24, 30, 2006; February 4, 6, 8, 9, 13, 2006.

Ward, Ralph D. *Improving Corporate Boards.* New York: Wiley, 2000.

———. *Saving the Corporate Board: Why Boards Fail and How to Fix Them.* New York: Wiley, 2003.

"The Way We Govern." *The Economist,* January 11, 2003.

Weidenbaum, Murray L. *Business and Government in the Global Marketplace.* 7th ed. Upper Saddle River, NJ: Pearson Prentice Hall, 2004.

Welch, Jack. *Jack: Straight from the Gut.* New York: Warner Books, 2001.

Wessel, David. "The Politics of Pension Promises." *Wall Street Journal,* July 17, 2003.

"Why GM's Plan Won't Work." *Business Week,* May 9, 2005.

Wikins, Mira. *The Emergence of Multinational Enterprise: American Business Abroad from the Colonial Era to 1914.* Cambridge, MA: Harvard University Press, 1970.

Williams, Walter E. "The Entrepreneur as American Hero." Address at Hillsdale College, February 6, 2005, reprint.

Wines, Michael. "Verdict Still Out on Deregulation's Impact on U.S. Air Travel System." *National Journal,* March 6, 1982.

Womack, James P., Daniel T. Jones, and Daniel Roos. *The Machine That Changed the World.* New York: Rawson Associates, 1990.

Yergin, Daniel, and Joseph Stanislaw. *The Commanding Heights: The Battle between Government and the Marketplace That Is Remaking the Modern World.* New York: Simon & Schuster, 1998.

Yip, George S. *Total Global Strategy.* Englewood Cliffs, NJ: Prentice Hall, 1995.

Young, Jeffrey S., and William L. Simon. *iCon Steve Jobs: The Greatest Second Act in the History of Business.* New York: Wiley, 2005.

Zadek, Simon. "The Path to Corporate Responsibility." *Harvard Business Review,* December 2004.

WEB SITES

www.Fortune.com/500/archive.

www.Wal-Mart.com/facts.

www.bea.gov/bea/newsarchive/2005/gdp.

www.cia.gov/cia/publications/factbook.

www.ita.doc.gov/td/industry/otea/state_reports.

www.nestle.com.

www.oecd/org/document/54/0,2340,en.

www.ss.ca.gov/business.
www.ss.ca.gov/business/corp/corp_formsfees.htm.
www.ss.ca.gov/business/corp/corp_precexp.htm.
www.treas.gov/press/releases/po3643.
www.usdoj.gov/criminal/fraud/fcpa.
www.uspto.gov/web/menu/tmebc/index.html.
www.whitehouse.gov/cea/erpcover2005.

Index

ABOUT THE AUTHOR

WESLEY B. TRUITT is Adjunct Professor at the Anderson Graduate School of Management, UCLA, and former Executive-in-Residence at the College of Business Administration, Loyola Marymount University, Los Angeles, specializing in business planning, business-government relations, and international business management. He is also a member of the Persius Consulting Group and serves as an independent management consultant and as advisor to the RAND Corporation. For over 25 years he served in a variety of management positions at the Northrop Grumman Corporation. He speaks to industry groups, business schools, think tanks, and government agencies, and has testified for the U.S. Senate Foreign Relations Committee and the U.S. House Foreign Affairs Committee. He is the author of *Business Planning* (Quorum, 2001) and *What Entrepreneurs Need to Know about Government* (Praeger, 2004).

Recent Titles in
Greenwood Guides to Business and Economics

The National Economy
Bradley A. Hansen